Steinbeck and Covici

L.G.

Dear Pat—

In haste— The books came yesterday. They are very nice indeed. And the really large advance sale is gratifying. Many thanks.

I am rushing in work because so many things are happening and I do want to get this book through.

Did you like the title, or did Miss McIntosh tell it to you? It is The Grapes of Wrath from the battle hymn of the republic. Read the hymn and you will see how apt the title is. Carol's again. And take the soft with the hard and the marching content and the American revolutionary content. Let me know how you like it. [illegible] I simply have to go to work.

love to Dorothy & Paco.

John

Courtesy of the Humanities Research Center, The University of Texas, Austin

One of the classic Steinbeck letters to his editor, Pascal Covici, explaining that the title of his forthcoming book, *The Grapes of Wrath,* comes from the "Battle Hymn of the Republic." Read the hymn, Steinbeck tells Covici, "and you will see how apt the title is." (Dated September 16, 1938).

Steinbeck and Covici

The Story of a Friendship

Thomas Fensch

PAUL S. ERIKSSON
Middlebury, Vermont

Printed in the United States of America.
9 8 7 6 5 4 3 2 1

Library of Congress Cataloguing in Publication Data

Fensch, Thomas C.
    Steinbeck and Covici.

    Bibliography: p.
    Includes index.
    1. Steinbeck, John, 1902-1968—Editors.   2. Steinbeck, John, 1902-1968—Correspondence.   3. Covici, Pascal, 1885-1964.   4. Authors and publishers—United States.   5. Novelists, American—20th century—Biography.
I. Title.
PS3537.T3234Z633   1979   813'.5'2   [B]   78-26594
ISBN 0-8397-7888-0

For my father—
Edwin A. Fensch,
and for
Roland E. Wolseley,
—with gratitude.

ACKNOWLEDGMENTS

Grateful acknowledgment is made to the following for permission to print or reprint copyrighted material:

Ms. Ellen Dunlap and the staff of the Humanities Research Center, The University of Texas at Austin, for permission to use letters from the Steinbeck-Covici archives and photographs of Steinbeck and Covici;

Pascal Covici, Jr. for permission to use letters of his Father;

The firm of McIntosh & Otis, New York, for permission to reprint additional published letters of John Steinbeck;

Alfred A. Knopf, Inc., New York, for permission to cite selected passages from *The Mechanical Angel* by Donald Friede.

The author is also grateful to the following, who offered guidance and criticism during the completion of this work:

Roland E. Wolseley, Dwight Teeter Jr., Burton Marvin, William Ehling, Lee Becker, Robert Laubach, William Wasserstrom, Pascal Covici, Jr. and Thomas Bonn; to Mrs. Jane Frost, who typed and retyped versions of this work and to Jean, who was always at my side.

CONTENTS

Page

I. Introduction
THE BEST OF TIMES, THE WORST OF TIMES
The Author-Editor Relationship 3

II.
"YOU ARE MY RAREST EXPERIENCE . . ."
The Careers of John Steinbeck and Pascal Covici to May, 1945 .. 9

III.
"HE HELD THEIR LOYALTY OVER THE YEARS
BECAUSE HE GAVE THEM LOYALTY."
May, 1945 to September, 1947 49

IV.
". . . THE GREATEST MAN I HAVE KNOWN AND THE
BEST TEACHER."
September, 1947 to October, 1948 67

V.
". . . I'M FREE. SHE'S GONE. SHE'S OUT OF ME. OH.
CHRIST ALMIGHTY, I'M FREE."
October, 1948 to January, 1949 83

VI.
"IT'S YOUR OWN HOME GROUND, SOMETHING YOU
KNOW ABOUT AND HAS BEEN IN YOUR BLOOD ALL
YOUR LIFE."
January, 1949 to June, 1949 103

VII.
"THE CRITICS MURDERED US."
June, 1949 to January, 1951 123

VIII.
"AND STILL THE BOX IS NOT FULL."
January, 1951 to January, 1952 143

IX.
"I AM STILL DAZED AND INARTICULATE SINCE READ-
ING YOUR DEDICATION . . ."
January, 1952 to June, 1952 171

X.
A BRINGER TO LIGHT . . .
June, 1952 and Afterwards 191-231

Appendix 233

Bibliography 235

Notes 239

Index 245

Steinbeck and Covici

July 2, 1941

Mr. John Steinbeck
Pacific Biological Laboratories
Pacific Grove, California

Dear John,

By all means save three weeks and just give me the corrected second draft.
You can make additional changes on the galleys. In fact, I believe that you
will find that procedure far more convenient. It should help tremendously and
save considerable time if you would mail me chapters as ready. In the interval
we would carefully prepare the manuscript for the printer and shoot galleys back
to you, and thus give you plenty of time to answer queries and make corrections.
Please don't let anything hold this book up any longer than it is absolutely
necessary. Here we are all keyed up about it, giving it a major part in our
sales and advertising preparations for this year. If there is any doubt in your
mind whether we will have it for this Fall, please don't wait until September to
tell me - it will be too, too disappointing.

I am sure you will get quite a variant of reviews, and I am definitely
certain that "Sea of Cortez" will prove exciting, provocative and interesting to
intelligent readers. This book will prove a faster seller than you think.

I am sending you a dummy with the old title page. It will be changed
for the book. I am not sending you a jacket now as some corrections are being
made and will be reprinted.

As to yourself, my worrying about you won't help I know. But I, too,
see what you can give and I am jealous for it. In my little life, which is
about three-fourths done, you are my rarest experience. Take that with all its
implications, cynically as well if you want to. The soul of man is not too
simple; certainly not for me. What I do positively know is that I want you to
go on. I believe most of us, as we grow older, begin to realize that somewhere,
somehow things have gone wrong for us. And when one has touched life very
intimately, sensitively and in humbleness, one has many fears. What surprises
me is that in spite of our fears we have the courage to go on.

I was hoping that your present relationship would give you the exuberance
and zest for life you always wanted. I believe it has, at least to some extent,
otherwise you could not go on writing. Well, as you say, we shall see.

Affectionately,

PC/rw   PASCAL COVICI

"You are my rarest experience . . ." Carbon copy of letter from Covici to Steinbeck
(July 2, 1941).

I. INTRODUCTION

THE BEST OF TIMES, THE WORST OF TIMES

The Author-Editor Relationship

For an author, the act of writing a book-length manuscript and watching it progress through the publishing processes may be, to paraphrase Charles Dickens, the best of times, and the worst of times. It is the best of times, of course, because a creative intellect brought forth the book; the project; the germ of individuality. It may be the worst of times because any number of actual or imagined tragedies may befall the project during the editing and design and publishing stages; the book, even after being completed in manuscript, may not ever reach the book-buying public at all. The author may feel that he is at the whim of a merciless editor and publisher. Even if the manuscript is accepted for publication by a reputable company, the manuscript may be edited by a reputable editor away from the direction the author wished it to take.

The author too, may think that the design of the book itself, the printing, publication, distribution and attendant advertising and promotion may cause the book to fail rather than to succeed; he may believe that the editor and publisher are conspiring to hinder, rather than help him. For some authors, the act of publishing, whether in fiction or non-fiction, may be the worst of times, either in actual fact or in their imagination.

Publishing never has been a process which can be calculated precisely, either in terms of sales of various titles, or in terms of successful author-publisher-public relationships.

Yet one of the indefinable relationships most crucial to the success of the work and the success of the author is the author-editor bond. This bond—acceptance by the editor of the author's work and acceptance by the author of the editor's judgment—is an ethereal one at best. The author-editor relationship has existed in a variety of successful and unsuccessful forms and styles during the course of recent American publishing. One need only suggest some of the major American writers and novelists, to indicate "the best of times" and "the worst of times."

Edna St. Vincent Millay worked successfully with editor Cass Canfield of Harper & Brothers; Millay and Canfield reached an understanding of mutual admiration. Canfield was especially impressed with Millay's professionalism during her career with Harper's.

Max Perkins, legendary editor at Charles Scribner's Sons worked most closely with Tom Wolfe; their relationship has been documented. Many critics suggest that without Perkins's help, Wolfe may never have been able to hack his novels out of the enormous manuscripts he brought to Scribner's. For several years, their relationship was one of mutual admiration, understanding and affection, yet eventually Wolfe grew disenchanted and distrustful of Perkins; Wolfe took his last manuscripts to the firm of Harper and to different editors, yet Maxwell Perkins was named in Wolfe's will as his literary executor.

Similarly, Perkins's relationship with F. Scott Fitzgerald was very nearly as intimate at Perkins's relationship with Wolfe. Fitzgerald was originally discovered by Perkins and published by Scribner's; Perkins and Fitzgerald remained steadfastly loyal to each other until Fitzgerald's death. Perkins once told Fitzgerald that Scribner's was "backing you for a long race." Perkins edited Fitzgerald's novels, acted as arbiter between Fitzgerald and Ernest Hemingway, created a revolving fund with the Scribners' financial office to allow Fitzgerald to draw against future royalties and unfailingly sustained enthusiasm in Fitzgerald's worth.

Even when Fitzgerald's career had fallen into disarray, Perkins never lost his belief in Fitzgerald's talent. Perkins once said that working with Fitzgerald and editing *The Great Gatsby* was very nearly the most perfect thing he ever did.

Perkins also worked closely with Ernest Hemingway, although not to the extent that he had worked with Fitzgerald and Wolfe. Hemingway seemed not to need Perkins quite so drastically as did Wolfe or Fitzgerald, but Hemingway did hold Perkins in high regard. Perkins, a New England Yankee, seldom took vacations from his work, but he did vacation with Ernest Hemingway in Florida and, as Hemingway's career gained prominence (at approximately the same time Fitzgerald's declined), Hemingway placed greater value in his editor, Perkins.

While Cass Canfield was establishing his career at Harper's, and Perkins at Scribner's, Harold S. Latham was beginning his career at

Macmillan. The authors in his coterie eventually included Vachel Lindsay, Richard Llewellyn, H. G. Wells, Edward Arlington Robinson and a Georgian, Mrs. Peggy Marsh.

As Perkins drew the core of material from Tom Wolfe's massive manuscripts, so too did Latham draw the heart from a disjointed manuscript given to him rather reluctantly by Mrs. Marsh. The novel was eventually titled *Gone With the Wind* and Latham published it under Mrs. Marsh's maiden name, Margaret Mitchell; As *Gone With the Wind* made her reputation, it also made Latham's reputation in publishing. Latham later deprecated his work by suggesting that any editor worth his salt would have accepted the manuscript. But Latham did; he impressed Mrs. Marsh with his manners and sophistication; he worked the manuscript into publishable form and he engineered the contract. *Gone With the Wind* is still in print with Macmillan.

And while Latham believed in Margaret Mitchell's success, he also believed in the success of Edward Arlington Robinson, and published book after book of Robinson's poetry, which seldom turned a profit; Latham was as convinced of Robinson's success as Perkins was of Fitzgerald's; Robinson's reputation was eventually confirmed, largely the vision of Harold Latham.

Hiram Haydn's career, as editor, took him from Crown Publishers, to Bobbs-Merrill and finally to Random House, where he spent most of his career. (He eventually helped found the firm of Atheneum Publishers with Simon Michael Bessie and Alfred Knopf, Jr.) He writes that editorial work on a manuscript which an author has completed includes an attempt to grasp what the author has intended in the project; where he might have fallen short of that goal or goals and the "give and take," in Haydn's words, of the revisions necessary for the book.

Haydn believes that editorial judgment and the intent of the author often make the author-editor relationship a strained one;

> It is true that an editor can, and sometimes does, meddle with a writer's work. The attempt to grasp another's intent, and help him fulfill it, is often bumbling and presumptuous. How, in such a task, to disentangle the editor's subjective preoccupations and emotional prejudices from his inquiry into the nature of the work at hand?[1]

That answer, Haydn suggests, lies in the nature of reading; the editor must read to explore and understand the writer's meaning; of what the book *does* and how it does it.

What kind of personality should an editor be possessed of, to insure success in editorial work? Haydn suggests that his first love is that of exploration—in literary terms—and discovery of the "human experience" in manuscripts which cross his desk:

> . . . day in and year out, his richest excitement and his surest pleasure will be instead to read a script that he finds good: strong in wisdom, illuminating of the human experience, possessed of the gift of style—that sureness with words that dazzles or satisfies through the unusual juxtaposition of the usual. I find the true editor a votary of sorts—his creed that of the word and the book.[2]

At least in principle "the best of times" occur when author and editor work together for mutual benefit and common purpose. The worst of times, in contemporary publishing history, occurred to two novelists, each published by the same firm and almost at the same time.

Indiana-born Ross Lockridge, Jr. began writing when he was in graduate school in English at Harvard. Lockridge, a compulsive overachiever, ultimately completed a manuscript which was sent to, and accepted by, Houghton Mifflin. Lockridge's work, *Raintree County*, was based loosely on the experiences and observations of distant relatives in early Indiana.

Published in 1947, it did phenomenally well for a first novel. It was accepted by the Book-of-the-Month Club; the film rights were sold to M.G.M. with a film planned immediately, and "escalator clauses" in Lockridge's contract with M.G.M., which promised larger profit margins for him as sales went up, would reap great checks as the Book-of-the-Month Club and the film spurred sales of the hardcover edition.

Lockridge had been asked to cut 50,000 words from the manuscript before publication, often a normal editing procedure, and it had hurt him terribly. He began a bitter dispute with the Houghton Mifflin editors on the division of profits from the motion picture rights and he began to feel, as the popularity of *Raintree County* grew and grew, that no one at Houghton Mifflin cared for him; that all they wanted was great sales figures for his work. Plans for a second novel lay incomplete and unappealing to him. Disagreements with Houghton Mifflin remained unsolved; they became an obsession which hindered all other work for him and further attempts at negotiations with Houghton Mifflin.

Lockridge could not escape the view that his publisher had not been fair with him on the division of spoils of his work, specifically the division of profits from M.G.M. He became increasingly ill; unbalanced and neurotic.

Raintree County was officially published on January 5, 1948, and Lockridge celebrated by signing copies in a hometown department store. On the evening of March 6, 1948, he got into a new Kaiser automobile he had bought from profits of his masterwork, turned on the engine, but left the automobile in his closed garage. His wife, Vernice, discovered him later, a suicide.

Like Ross Lockridge, Tom Heggen was, by birth, a mid-westerner. Born in Iowa, Heggen attended college first at Oklahoma City University, then at Oklahoma A. & M.; he transferred to the University of Minnesota, where he worked for the student newspaper. After graduation he worked for *The Reader's Digest*, which he found boring. When the Japanese attacked Pearl Harbor, Heggen volunteered for the Navy. He served on a variety of ships in non-battle duty; his views of the war through the eyes of his fictional junior grade officer, Doug Roberts, eventually became the novel and play, *Mister Roberts*.

Heggen was unable to turn his novel into a play; he met Joshua Logan, the producer-director, who could and did turn Heggen's book into a first-rate hit. In February, 1948, when the novel, fashioned by Heggen (and in no small part by Logan) was first produced, it was a monumental success. Yet Heggen felt the production was a creation crafted by someone else. When he learned that Logan was to move to a different project—the stage version of *Tales of the South Pacific*—Heggen felt betrayed by Logan and by Houghton Mifflin. He journeyed to Cuba, shipped out on the merchant seaman, the *S.S. Topa Topa*, but he could not begin any other projects.

By April, 1948, friends noticed he appeared calmer and more relaxed. Perhaps by then he might have thought of taking his own life. On May 19, 1948, he did so, but not the way Ross Lockridge did. Late in the evening he drew a bath and took pills which he had been taking for months previously. A maid found him the next day and a medical examiner decided the cause was an overdose of barbiturates. Heggen was twenty-nine years old.

The profiles of Ross Lockridge and Thomas Heggen have been included here briefly because they constitute the most tragic examples in contemporary American publishing of promising careers which ultimately ended in "the worst of times."

The relationship between John Steinbeck and Pascal Covici was however, one of "the best of times." Their relationship, begun in the middle 1930s, was broken only by the death of Covici in 1964; this relationship between Steinbeck and Covici must stand as one of contemporary American literature's most faithful and strongest author-editor combinations, at times most poignant and evocative, and continually fascinating.

Note: Unless otherwise cited, the letters of John Steinbeck and Pascal Covici are published as originally written.

II

"YOU ARE MY RAREST EXPERIENCE . . ."

The Careers of John Steinbeck and Pascal Covici to May, 1945

By 1945, John Steinbeck had published eleven books of fiction and non-fiction; the last eight of these were published with Pascal Covici as editor. The first three, which were commercial failures, were published by firms which ultimately went bankrupt. Steinbeck's first novel, *Cup of Gold,* a fictionalized biography of the pirate, Henry Morgan, was published by the firm of Robert M. McBride & Co., in New York, in 1929.* Lewis Gannett, the critic, wrote that his first book sold only 1,533 total copies, because few critics bothered to review it when it was published, two months after the beginning of the Great Depression.[1]

His second book, *The Pastures of Heaven,* did little better. Published during the Depression year of 1932 by the firm of Brewer, Warren and Putnam, it earned Steinbeck $400. Neither his first nor his third book earned more than the publisher's advance of $250.[2]

Although Steinbeck probably did not realize it at the time, 1933 marked the beginning of his sustained success as a professional, saleable writer. He published two short stories, which would later become parts of *The Red Pony,* and his third book, *To a God Unknown,* found a publisher, this time the firm of Robert O. Ballou, in New York.

Before the publication of *The Pastures of Heaven,* Steinbeck had married his first wife, Carol Henning. He began the nomadic moving and settling and moving which he would continue throughout his life. Between 1930 and 1933, the Steinbecks lived in Pacific Grove, California, moved to Los Angeles and then moved again to the Monterey area, scene of his later successful novels, *Tortilla Flat,* and *The Long Valley* and near the Salinas Valley, locale of *East of Eden.*[3] For many

* The Appendix contains a summary of the important dates in Steinbeck's career, and the Bibliography contains publication dates of all of Steinbeck's major works.

of Steinbeck's major works, he figuratively never left the California coast, and the images of people, and places in Del Monte, Pacific Grove, Pebble Beach, Monterey, Carmel, the Corral De Terra (which became the fictional *The Pastures of Heaven*) and Salinas. Only in his later works, notably his two books written during the Second World War, *The Moon is Down* and *Bombs Away,* and his subsequent books, *A Russian Journal, The Short Reign of Pippin IV, Once There Was a War, The Winter of Our Discontent, Travels With Charley in Search of America* and *America and Americans,* did he depart from his fictional home in the California fruit lands and small towns of his youth.

With the film scripts for *The Forgotten Village* and *Viva Zapata!* and in *The Pearl, Sea of Cortez* and *The Log from The Sea of Cortez* he ventured across the border into Mexico, but still figuratively stayed close to the land of his childhood.

California not only furnished the locale for the best of Steinbeck's novels and short stories, but also it was in New Monterey, in 1930, that he met Ed Ricketts, a marine biologist. Ricketts and Steinbeck had heard of each other, and they immediately became great friends, a friendship which would endure until Ricketts's death in an automobile-train accident in May, 1948.

Ricketts was in many ways as important to Steinbeck as was Pascal Covici, or Steinbeck's literary agent, Elizabeth Otis. It is generally believed that Ricketts furnished the character for the fictional "Doc" in Steinbeck's short story, "The Snake," and the fictional character of "Doc" in *Cannery Row* and *Sweet Thursday.* Part of his personality can be seen in the character of "Doc" in *In Dubious Battle.*

Ricketts also helped Steinbeck crystalize his "non-teleological" thinking; their philosophical friendship is analyzed in Richard Astro's book *John Steinbeck and Edward F. Ricketts: the Shaping of a Novelist.*

Steinbeck and Ricketts were co-authors of *Sea of Cortez* in 1941 and after Ricketts's untimely death, Steinbeck's lengthy and intimate portrait of Ricketts, "About Ed Ricketts," appeared in a new edition, *The Log from The Sea of Cortez,* ten years later.

Warren French, in his biography, *John Steinbeck,* writes, "Since little attention had been paid Steinbeck's first two novels, his third, *To a God Unknown* (1933), did not impress the public of the early thirties as the surprise that it is to one who today reads the novels in the order of publication. It marked another of the 'changes of pace' for which Steinbeck was to become famous; but these changes are largely superficial, signifying not a change in the author's ideas but experiments in communicating them to a not very perceptive public."

While Steinbeck's first three books were largely languishing on the bookstore shelves of mid-Depression America, he was already at work on his fourth book, *Tortilla Flat.* As he was producing that manuscript, a chance meeting in Chicago between two old friends helped change Steinbeck's career. The meeting was between a Chicago bookstore owner, Ben Abramson, and Pascal Covici, who had previously owned his own bookstore in Chicago, and later his own publishing company, Pascal Covici, Inc., Publisher. He had moved to New York to overcome the cultural disadvantages of publishing in Chicago, away from the rest of the literary world.

Covici was later described by his partner, Donald Friede in his autobiography, *The Mechanical Angel,* as:

This flamboyant Roumanian with the shock of white hair on a poet's head, which in turn was set on a football player's . . . body, was, is, and always will be one of the most unusual men I have ever known. We were to be associated in business for . . . ten years, and almost as closely in many other ways after that, and in all that time we never once fought or had any real basic disagreement. Very probably the reason for this could be found in one of Covici's many quotations from his Roumanian grandfather. 'When two people tell you you're drunk,' Covici would quote him as saying, 'go to bed.' It was applied by him to any and all differences of opinion. And he followed his own advice and expected the people who worked with him to follow it too. The result was an effectively harmonious relationship that made life enjoyable and exciting.[4]

The results of that chance meeting between the bookstore owner and the publisher have been cited in several authoritative studies, including those by Warren French, Pascal Covici, Jr. and by Peter Lisca. Charles A. Madison's analysis of the Steinbeck-Covici friendship is the most detailed record hitherto extant; it appeared in Madison's *Book Publishing in America* and, in different form, in his *Irving to Irving: Author-Publisher Relationships in the U.S.*

Abramson urged Covici to read *The Pastures of Heaven,* which Abramson had been remaindering; Covici did so and decided that Steinbeck was an author worth publishing. Upon returning to his New York office, Covici communicated with Steinbeck's agents, McIntosh and Otis, and received Steinbeck's next manuscript, *Tortilla Flat*. It was published in 1935, a year and one-half after Steinbeck sent it to his literary agents for submission.

Because of the novel's thinly-disguised Arthurian-myth theme, or because the nation was gradually recovering from the Depression, or perhaps because of Pascal Covici's enthusiastic promotion, or a combination of all these factors, *Tortilla Flat* did well; Peter Lisca wrote in his *The Wide World of John Steinbeck,* "It appeared on the best-seller lists for several months, received the California Commonwealth Club's annual gold medal for the best novel by a California writer, was produced as a stage play, obtained for Steinbeck a Hollywood contract, and was sold to Paramount Studios."

For the first time in his career, John Steinbeck had money enough to relax and escape poverty. With the publication, by Covici-Friede, of *Tortilla Flat,* Steinbeck's literary foundations were set—and remained so until his death. Steinbeck continued steadfastly loyal to two people who befriended him early in his career, his literary agent, Elizabeth Otis, and Covici. Despite occasional quarrels, he remained with both Otis and Covici.

Steinbeck's first mention of Covici occurred in a letter to a friend, George Albee, after Steinbeck had finished the manuscript of *Tortilla Flat* and while he was working on his next novel, *In Dubious Battle*. He wrote, "I had a letter from Covici which sounded far from over-enthusiastic. I liked it. It gave me some confidence in the man. I like restraint. Covici says, 'I am interested in your work and would like to arrive at an agreement with Miss McIntosh.' My estimation of him went up immediately. It is nice to know that he is more enthusiastic than that, of course."[5]

After Covici acquired Steinbeck's *Tortilla Flat* for his publishing house, he bought the rights to Steinbeck's earlier works and began to reissue them under the Covici-Friede imprint. It was with Steinbeck's *In Dubious Battle,* however, that Covici almost lost his newly acquired author: when Steinbeck's manuscript arrived at the Covici-Friede offices, it was evaluated by an editorial reader, while Covici was out of the office on business. The reader rejected Steinbeck's manuscript because of what the reader analyzed as ignorance of communist labor tactics, ignoring the fact that Steinbeck's novel was *fiction*. Steinbeck was ready to turn to other publishers if Covici rejected *In Dubious Battle*. He told his agent, Mavis McIntosh, who first handled his work, to consider submitting the manuscript elsewhere if it came back from the Covici offices: "You will find a well-aroused interest in my work both at Houghton, Mifflin and at Random House." Only by frantic telegrams from Covici, who discovered what had happened when he returned to his office, was he able to convince Steinbeck and his agents that, the reader's evaluation notwithstanding, Covici *did* wish to publish *In Dubious Battle* under the Covici-Friede imprint.

After the publication of *In Dubious Battle,* Steinbeck and his wife moved to Los Gatos, California. He turned to newspaper journalism and under the title, "The Harvest Gypsies," wrote a series of eight articles on migrant workers and their plight in California which were published by *The San Francisco News.* The plight of farm workers, migrant laborers and the dispossessed would remain lodged in Steinbeck's mind for four years, appearing in print in a variety of forms and styles, from *In Dubious Battle,* through "The Harvest Gypsies," and *Of Mice and Men* to *The Grapes of Wrath,* published in 1939. Selection of *Of Mice and Men* by the Book-of-the-Month Club gave Steinbeck his first taste of real financial success and allowed him to do things which he previously had only dreamed of; travel and time to pursue his novels for as long as he needed.

The earliest letter from Steinbeck to Covici extant is dated February 28 (1937) and was written from Steinbeck's home in Los Gatos:

Dear Mr. Covici;

You do such nice things. The Rivera book came and I am very grateful for it. It is a valuable thing and a beautiful job. Thank you.

You know, we've been married seven years or going on seven and one of the dreams of our marriage was that the moment we could, we would do some traveling. Well we're going to do it. My wife has never been on a ship. We're taking booking on a freighter sailing for New York about the first of April. We plan to go on to Europe from there. I'll give you the ship's name before we start. We haven't closed the booking yet. The boat is very slow, 31 days to N.Y.

Joe Jackson told me that you had sold 117,000 copies of Mice. That's a hell of a lot of books.

Anyway I'll hope to see you before very long. You couldn't
arrange to sail with us, could you, train here and freighter
back. That would be fine.
Anyway thank you again for everything.

John Steinbeck *

In *Book Publishing in America,* Madison writes that total sales for
Of Mice and Men immediately after its release was "around 150,000
copies."

The publishing house of Covici-Friede, during its ten-year existence,
published a wide variety of genteel authors; Covici had begun publishing art books with Billy McGee out of their bookstore in 1922-1923.
After McGee had to go to Michigan because of his tuberculosis, Covici
went on alone in Chicago until 1928 when he left for New York City.
Covici-Friede continued this operation. In his autobiography, Donald
Friede remembered:

We had started our house at the apex of the limited edition
craze, and the selling of limited editions by a publisher, with
good taste in content, typography, and illustrations, plus a good
mailing list, was not the most difficult of problems in the summer and fall of 1928. By sacrificing taste in content, and often
in illustrations as well, even better results could be obtained.
Polite erotica, in editions of five to fifteen hundred copies, never
stayed on the booksellers' shelves very long. They were the
twentieth-century version of the library set, except that they
were usually sold by means of very elaborate circulars, rather
than by house-to-house canvassers. Covici had brought the art
of limited-edition publishing to a high state in Chicago. Together
we proceeded to improve it still further.[6]

During the existence of the Covici-Friede firm, notable publishing
successes were Ben Hecht's and Charles MacArthur's *The Front Page,*
Theodore Dreiser's *An American Tragedy,* Radcliffe Hall's early fictional
work about lesbianism, *The Well of Loneliness,* books by e. e. cum-

---

* Covici had sent Steinbeck a copy of a recently published book by the artist,
Diego Rivera. Joe Jackson was Joseph Henry Jackson, book reviewer for *The
San Francisco Chronicle,* who had previously reviewed *In Dubious Battle.*

mings, and a modern version of *The Canterbury Tales* with illustrations by Rockwell Kent. Even before Steinbeck's *In Dubious Battle* and *The Grapes of Wrath,* Covici-Friede had been interested in books in the same genre. It had published successfully *Revolt Among the Sharecroppers, Revolt on the Campus, The Decline of American Capitalism* and *America Faces the Barricades.*[7]

Shortly after the publication of *Tortilla Flat,* Donald Friede, disenchanted with the publishing business, sold his shares in Covici-Friede, sublet his apartment and journeyed west, to begin a new career as a Hollywood literary and film agent. He continued, however, to follow the progress of Covici-Friede and its continuing battle with creditors, notably J. J. Little and Ives, Inc., a printing and binding company, which held notes on Covici-Friede indebtedness. As Friede remembered in his memoirs:

> I was filled with happiness when Covici wired me that *Of Mice and Men* had been chosen by the Book-of-the-Month Club, our first book-club selection. I proudly watched it climb up on the best-seller list. I was excited by the beauty that Elmer Adler got into the limited edition of *The Red Pony,* a throwback to the day when you could still make a profit out of honestly produced books. And, in mid-1938, I felt that we safely passed the dangerous shoals, when our tenth-anniversary list announced such books at Walter Pach's *Memories,* Irving Fineman's *Doctor Adams,* new novels by Ben Hecht and Ludwig Lewisohn, a collection of short stories by John Steinbeck —and promised for the spring of the following year a new novel by Steinbeck tentatively entitled *L'Affaire Lettuceburg.*[8]

But the firm of Little & Ives called its notes due: the indebtedness which had burdened Covici-Friede could not be repaid. Colonel Arthur W. Little, owner of J. J. Little & Ives, met with Covici and discussed the financial prospects of every manuscript in the hands of Covici-Friede. It was by accident that Covici had a rough proof of Steinbeck's *The Long Valley* when Colonel Little was examining the assets of Covici-Friede. As Friede remembered it:

> It was at this point that the Colonel had exploded. He produced the manuscript we had sent to Little & Ives to be set

up (in type), and shook it under Covici's nose. 'Look at it!'
he said, pointing to the sheaf of bedraggled papers he held
in his hand. 'Look at those filthy pages! It is obvious that this
book has been turned down by every publisher in the country.
And you dare to tell me that it will sell more than ten thousand
copies!' In vain Covici tried to interrupt him, to explain that
when it had been decided to publish this collection, Steinbeck
had not bothered to have the manuscript retyped but had
merely collected, from all the magazines that had published
these stories, the original manuscripts from which they
had been set. Of course they were dirty and bedraggled:
compositors are not in the habit of washing their hands between pages. But the Colonel would have none of it. He had
had enough, he announced. We were through. He called the
creditors' meeting then and there.[9]

The firm of Covici-Friede was quickly liquidated. Friede reports that
no one except himself and Pascal Covici really lost anything: every
author was paid the royalties due him; creditors received full payment on
past-due bills; and all office employees were able to get jobs at other
publishing houses immediately after leaving the debacle of Covici-Friede.
As publisher Cass Canfield noted in his book, *Up and Down and
Around*, with sympathy:

We all know of conventional publishers who have failed and
whose passing evoked little regret; it is for the business failures
of pioneers like Thomas Seltzer, Ben Huebsch, Pat Covici and
Robert Haas that we have sympathy, for they first published
writers of the stature of D. H. Lawrence, James Joyce, Thorstein Veblen, Sherwood Anderson, John Steinbeck, William
Faulkner, Robert Graves and André Malraux.[10]

Covici joined Harold Guinzburg's The Viking Press and Steinbeck's
first book under the Viking imprint was *The Long Valley,* which Colonel
Little had deprecated.

It was the sudden and violent demise of Covici-Friede, however,
which led to the loss of early Steinbeck-Covici papers. Only thirty-one
letters and notes from Steinbeck to Covici written prior to 1944 are
extant; one of these was cited earlier. That letter and nine others writ-

ten before 1945 appear in the Steinbeck-Wallsten collection, *Steinbeck: A Life in Letters*. Only two letters from Covici to Steinbeck exist; neither appears in that collection. Much more material from the Covici-Friede years should exist. In *The Mechanical Angel,* Donald Friede explains why it has disappeared:

> Obviously there was little we could do to stop him (Colonel Little). We none of us had any more money to put into the firm, and besides the very calling of the meeting had given us a black eye from which it was doubtful if we could ever recover. The vultures were already swooping around, picking the titles they would like to have for their lists as soon as our corporate body was cold. But we could make sure of one thing: that no manuscript that was not already in work would fall into Little & Ives' clutching hands. We did a good job of it too. I personally drove up to Vermont to give Fineman back the manuscript of his novel and to explain the situation to him. And Covici had a closetful of manuscripts in his apartment— safe from Colonel Little's inquiring eye.[11]

Covici's son, Professor Pascal Covici, Jr., believes that early Steinbeck-Covici correspondence may have been stored in a warehouse by his father following the foreclosure of Covici-Friede—and then was lost or forgotten, or destroyed after the firm's liquidation. The correspondence which exists was sold to the University of Texas Humanities Research Center, and no other Steinbeck-Covici material is extant.

Despite the unhappiness of the closing of Covici-Friede, Pascal Covici was now able to do what he did best—be an editor, and not a publisher. Friede notes that when Covici joined the staff of Harold Guinzburg's Viking Press he could "finally function as the editor he is without waking up in the morning in a cold sweat, wondering if he is going to be able to get the paper he needs without paying for the paper he has already used."

Covici's son, in an interview, amplified Friede's comments:

> My father was probably the world's worst businessman. It was not just Friede who gave away money (during the Covici-Friede years); my father did too. Both of them gave out vast royalties in advance hoping for excellent manuscripts in return.

They were often disappointed, but often delighted. I think
he was secretly glad to go to Viking, where he didn't have to
concern himself with such matters.[12]

Covici took a calculated risk when he joined Viking; he must have
realized that his success with Viking was dependent upon Steinbeck's
next work. *The Long Valley* did moderately well—it sold 30,000 copies
—and when Covici joined Viking, Steinbeck was well enough along with
The Grapes of Wrath for the manuscript to be passed through the editorial department, after he had withdrawn the title, *L'Affaire Lettuceburg.*

Elaine Steinbeck and Robert Wallsten in their book described the
reaction at The Viking Press after the management had read *The Grapes
of Wrath* in manuscript:

On January 9, 1939, Pascal Covici wrote Steinbeck that he,
Harold Guinzburg, President of The Viking Press, and Marshall
Best, Managing Editor, had been 'emotionally exhausted after
reading *The Grapes of Wrath.*' Harold Guinzburg has said 'I
would not change a single comma in the whole book,' and Marshall Best had called it 'the most important piece of fiction on
our list' as he announced that the initial advertising appropria-
tion would be $10,000. 'It seemed like a kind of sacrilege to
suggest revisions in so grand a book,' Covici went on, but:
'We felt that we would not be good publishers if we failed to
point out to you any weaknesses or faults that struck us. One
of these is the ending.
'Your idea is to end the book on a great symbolic note, that
life must go on and will go on with a greater love and sympathy and understanding for our fellowman. Nobody could fail
to be moved by the incident of Rose of Sharon giving her
breast to the starving man, yet, taken as the finale of such a
book with all its vastness and surge, it struck us on reflection
as being all too abrupt. It seems to us that the last few pages
need building up. The incident needs leading up to, so that
the meeting with the starving man is not so much an accident
or chance encounter, but more an integral part of the saga.'

In a postscript, Covici added:

'Marshall has just called my attention to the fact that de Maupassant in one of his short stories 'Mid Summer Idyll' has a woman give her breast to a starving man in a railway station. Is it important?'[13]

Steinbeck's conviction about the book he had just completed is revealed in the answer he sent Covici, from his home in Los Gatos:

Los Gatos
January 16, 1939

Dear Pat;

I have your letter today. And I am sorry but I cannot change that ending. It is casual—there is no fruity climax, it is not more important than any other part of the book—if there is a symbol, it is a survival symbol not a love symbol, it must be an accident, it must be a stranger, and it must be quick. To build this stranger onto the structure of the book would be to warp the whole meaning of the book. The fact that the Joads don't know him, don't care about him, have no ties with him—that is the emphasis. The giving of the breast has no more sentiment than the giving of a piece of bread. I'm sorry if that doesn't get over. It will maybe. I've been on this design and balance for a long time and I think I know how I want it. And if I'm wrong, I'm alone in my wrongness. As for the Maupassant story, I've never read it but I can't see that it makes much difference. There are no new stories and I wouldn't like them if there were. The incident of the earth mother feeding by the breast is older than literature. You know that I have never been touchy about changes, but I have too many thousands of hours on this book, every incident has been too carefully chosen and its weight judged and fitted. The balance is there. One other thing—I am not writing a satisfying story. I've done my damndest to rip a reader's nerves to rags, I don't want him satisfied.

And still one more thing—I tried to write this book the way lives are being lived not the way books are written.

This letter sounds angry. I don't mean it to be. I know

that books lead to a strong deep climax. This one doesn't except by implication and the reader must bring the implication to it. If he doesn't, it wasn't a book for him to read. Throughout I've tried to make the reader participate in the actuality, what he takes from it will be scaled entirely on his own depth or hollowness. There are five layers in this book, a reader will find as many as he can and he won't find more than he has in himself.

I seem to be getting well slowly. The pain is going away. Nerves still pretty tattered but rest will stop that before too long. I fret pretty much at having to stay in bed. Guess I was pretty close to a collapse when I finally went to bed. I feel the result of it now.

> Love to you all,
> John

Steinbeck did, eventually, change the last scene as the editors at Viking wished him to. Marshall Best said, thirty-six years after *The Grapes of Wrath* was published, that "everyone was terribly excited about it," when the manuscript reached the Viking offices. "One of our readers noticed that Steinbeck had the girl—Rose of Sharon—offering her breast to the starving man too soon after her baby was born, stillborn and blue. We pointed this out to Steinbeck and he made a change in that last scene—he lengthened it to make the act physiologically possible."

Steinbeck's statement "The pain is going away. Nerves still pretty tattered but rest will stop that before too long . . ." was in reference to a dislodged vertebra and general exhaustion following the completion of *The Grapes of Wrath.*

Steinbeck was overwhelmed with the publicity attendant to publication of *The Grapes of Wrath.* He wrote Elizabeth Otis:

The telegrams and telephones—all day long—speak . . . speak . . . speak, like hungry birds. Why the hell do people insist on speaking? the telephone is a thing of horror. And the demands for money—scholarships, memorial prizes. One man wants 47,000 dollars to buy a newspaper which will be liberal —this is supposed to run with a checkbook. Carol turned down the most absurd offer of all yesterday, to write a script in

Hollywood. Carol over the telephone: 'What the hell would we
do with $5,000. a week? Don't bother us!'[14]

Ultimately, the publicity and the clamor became too much for Stein-
beck and his wife to handle quietly, even though his literary agents and
The Viking Press replied to some. Steinbeck was warned, candidly, that
he had better watch himself while in California, for the Associated
Farmers, upset by the picture Steinbeck painted in *The Grapes of
Wrath,* might attempt to smear him if the opportunity presented itself.
Later, he wrote to Chase Horton, a family friend:

> Let me tell you a story. When *The Grapes of Wrath* got loose,
> a lot of people were pretty mad at me. The undersheriff of
> Santa Clara County was a friend of mine and he told me as
> follows—'Don't you go into any hotel room alone. Keep rec-
> ords of every minute and when you are off the ranch travel
> with one or two friends and particularly, don't stay in a hotel
> alone.' 'Why?' I asked. 'Maybe I'm sticking my neck out but the
> boys got a rape case set up for you. You get alone in a hotel
> and a dame will come in, tear off her clothes, scratch her face
> and scream and you try to talk yourself out of that one. They
> won't touch your book but there's easier ways.'[15]

That, and other similar incidents, convinced Steinbeck to place records regarding inhumane treatment of migrants in locked safety deposit
boxes. He also informed the FBI about the situation, and he did remain
cautious when away from his home.

To protect himself and his family from continued veiled threats
generated by the publication of *The Grapes of Wrath,* and to begin a
new project, Steinbeck planned a trip into Mexico with Ed Ricketts.
They would make a leisurely expedition through the Gulf of California,
which they preferred to call by the older name, The Sea of Cortez. Although their collaboration was not published until December 5, 1941,
Steinbeck was planning the book as early as December 15, 1939, as
seen in this letter to Elizabeth Otis:

> Now—the collecting. I got a truck and we are equipping it.
> We don't go to Mexico until March, but we have the hand-
> book to do first and we'll go north in about a week I guess

for the solstice tides. It will be a tough job and I'm not at all sure we can get it done by March. And I have a terrific job of reading to do. Ricketts is all right but I am a *popular* writer and I have to build some trust in the minds of biologists. This handbook will help do that. The Mexican book will be interesting to a much larger audience, and there is no question that Viking can have it.

Yesterday we went to Berkeley with a design for our traveling refrigeration plant and it is being built. Also ordered a Bausch and Lomb SKW microscope. This is a beauty with a side bar and drum nose piece. Primarily a dissecting microscope. My dream for some time in the future is a research scope with an oil immersion lens, but that costs about 600 dollars and I'm not getting it right now. The SKW will be fine for the trip. But that research model. Oh boy! Oh boy! Sometime I'll have one. It may interest you to know that business at the lab is picking up. I can't tell you what all this means to me, in happiness and energy. I was washed up and now I'm alive again, with work to be done and worth doing.[16]

In the spring of 1940, Steinbeck won the Pulitzer Prize for fiction for *The Grapes of Wrath.* Other winners that year were Carl Sandburg, in history, for *Abraham Lincoln: The War Years,* and William Saroyan, in drama, for *The Time of Your Life.* Steinbeck's statement about the Prize was short and succinct: "While in the past I have sometimes been dubious about Pulitzer choices I am pleased and flattered to be chosen in a year when Sandburg and Saroyan were chosen. It is good company." He later told his friend Joseph Henry Jackson that it was one of the few times "when tact and truth seem to be side by side."[17]

Still later that spring, the Steinbecks returned to Mexico where he was to write a screenplay on the life of a backward Mexican family. He was part owner of the Mexican corporation which would produce the film, "The Forgotten Village." This marked the first time Steinbeck would write for the medium of film. He later wrote the script for "Lifeboat" (1944), was co-author of the script for "A Medal for Benny" (1945), and wrote "Viva Zapata!" (1950).

Late in 1940, through friends in Hollywood, Steinbeck met a singer, Gwendolyn Conger, and they became infatuated with each other. His marriage to Carol Henning was breaking up and he and Gwendolyn met secretly when the occasion permitted.[18] Steinbeck's marriage to Carol ended in divorce in early 1943.

The relationship between John Steinbeck and Pascal Covici, which previously had been cordial and mutually appreciative, began to be extremely warm and intimate. Covici worried about Steinbeck's productivity and pace, with a concern not just for a widely read and profitable author but for Steinbeck as a friend. Steinbeck, too, worked closely with Covici; he kept Covici well informed with the progress of his manuscripts, as well as his thoughts on a variety of subjects. On March 29, 1941, he wrote and asked for an advance on *Sea of Cortez,* and hoped that illustrations he and Ricketts wished to use wouldn't be prohibitively expensive:

Monterey
March 29, '41

Dear Pat;

I got your letter from the plane. Hope you were not too shocked by the request for money. But these . . . illustrations are expensive and I have quite a lot in this book already. I hope you like the color plate of the shells. I think it is beautiful. Thought perhaps you might like to print it in your prospectus. Only a suggestion. I have nearly 55,000 words of my trip narrative done and nowhere near finished. It may go as much as 80, or 90,000 thousand words and I don't care. It is a timeless job—one of the few being done in the world today— a world that is concerned with immediacies. For that reason it might have some interest if only relief to a people too raddled (*sic*) with explosives. And I think it is going to be a good job. I hope so. It will be about the only true and complete account of an expedition that I know of.

I suppose you have every reason to worry about me but when things happen by the day, sometimes they can be weathered. And that's the way they go. The word rate every day and meals and sleep. That's the way to get through.

Carol is getting back next Wednesday. She says she feels fine and healthy. I hope so. She hasn't had an easy time of it in health, as you know. I have many plans but I don't know whether any of them are feasible. This London matter becomes a little ridiculous. So many correspondents are going over that they must be cluttering up the country. Maybe I should chose some other place. Maybe Chungking or Vichy or something. One might get tromped to death by reporters in London. But if it is even reasonably possible I shall not move until this book is done. It is the last stand of sanity; and there's too damned little of it left. It seems to me a better and more important book than I had thought. But in some places it is throughly disreputable. But if it is part of the book, it goes in. And it is fun.

Mavis is not here yet. I'm anxious to see her. She will probably arrive the same time as Carol.

I guess that will be all now. Just wanted to tell you how the book was going.

John *

Later, Covici queried Steinbeck on the progress of the work. Steinbeck felt compelled to clarify the progress of the book and reiterate to Covici what the book *was* and what it was *not,* as Steinbeck could foresee problems with the book's merchandising. This letter was written on stationery of Ed Ricketts' Pacific Biological Laboratories, in Pacific Grove:

Pacific Grove, California
April 18

Dear Pat;

I had your letter and Ed answered most of the questions through Mavis: The main answer is to keep your shirt on. You know I won't send out second draft mss ever. [and] this less than any. Don't rush us. We're trying to do a good job and hurry [won't] help us at all. So don't sell this book until you

---

* Steinbeck had long-range plans to be accredited as a war correspondent in the European Theater, which, at that time, was a favorite locale for the adventuresome. He feared too many reporters might already be covering the war from England. Mavis McIntosh, of his literary agency, McIntosh & Otis, was planning a visit, about the same time his wife, Carol, was returning from a vacation.

have it. It is a huge undertaking. Another thing—this is no adventure story except as an adventure of the mind, so don't try
to build up that end to your booksellers or they will just be
let down. Some pictures went off to Elizabeth and she will
turn them over to you for experimentation. Mostly I want you
to remember that this is a scientific book. It has some general
interest quite a bit in fact, but it is truly a work of science or
philosophical science. What ever you wish. I'm sure you understand this and I don't want any prospective reader to be
misled about it.

   I hope you are well. I do about the same. My work is
slowed up, I hope temporarily. But it has to come as it comes
and there aren't any happy short cuts—any.

Love to you all
John.[19]

Steinbeck later wrote Bo Beskow, a friend in Sweden, about how he
worked on his part of *Sea of Cortez:*

When I wrote the text of Sea of Cortez, Gwen and I were
hiding in the pine woods in a cabin and she would sleep late
and I would get up and build a big fire and work until noon when
she woke up and that would be the end of work for the day
and we would go walking in the sand dunes and eat thousands
of doughnuts and coffee. I worked very hard.[20]

The problems of his collapsing marriage to Carol, his relationship to
Gwen and the completion of his book with Ed Ricketts led him to a
lengthy self-analysis in a letter to Elizabeth Otis:

(Pacific Grove)
May 19, 1941
Monday

Dear Elizabeth;

   I had your letter with the check in it a few days ago. Many
thanks. I've been very [raddled] and torn out by the roots.
Nightmared, etc. In many ways I have more of a sense of
peace than I have ever had and am working hard but I get the

horrors pretty often. It's an awful thing to me to be cruel. I don't
do it well. Meanwhile, as you know, I am having my assets
gone over very carefully and will give Carol half and her
interest in my contracts will probably make it more. Terrific
income tax this year and heavier next will cut it down of
course.

I'm putting an awful burden on you. Came very close to
cracking up and I guess did but not finally. Getting stronger
now though. The work saves me a lot. If only Carol can be
happy and whole, it will work. I don't know. I had arrived at
your advice independently, not to try and think but to let the
work go on and time get in some licks. Seems to be the only
thing. I don't know that it is true but from her letters Carol
seems more perturbed about people finding out about the
separation than about the separation itself. Her terrific pride,
I guess. But she is being very fine. I hope she is finding some
content.

We got off a lot of ms. to you which you probably have by
now. It is more than Pat asked for. A brutally peremptory
letter from him to Ed this morning demanded it.

Don't expect any sense from me for a while or maybe
never. If I can get a little work in that's all I can expect.

Meanwhile my love to all of you and don't think too badly
of me—or do if it is necessary.

John [21]

A month later, he replied to a letter from Covici; Covici had referred to Steinbeck's sub-title for *Sea of Cortez* (A Leisurely Journal of
Travel and Research), and Steinbeck discussed the philosophical content
of the book. Steinbeck's wariness of critics remained high, as seen in
this letter, written on stationery of Ed Ricketts's Pacific Biological Laboratories:

Pacific Grove, California
June 19.

Dear Pat:

Good letter from you this morning which I will answer at
once. I'm glad you like that subtitle. It seems with every word

to define some part of the book. Personally I think there are some very funny parts in my part of it. Yesterday there was a dissertation on cannibalism and Ed today said, "Well, you have outraged every other kind of people in the world, now I think this closes the circle and everybody will be outraged at you." It isn't bad of course, just an addenda to Swifts suggestion about a use for Irish babies and drawn out by the myth that the Seri Indians of Tiburon are cannibals.

We are anxious to see the jacket and the dummy. Could you send us one? We will send you as many more of the illustrations as we have right away.

Now you want to know when we think we can get the material in. I seem to see an end to my part at last. I think with two or three more good weeks I will have the first draft, barring accidents. Then the matter of second draft, another month. If you would wish to have very carefully corrected second draft rather than clear and perfect copy in a final, I could save about three weeks for you but that is for you to say. It would seem that by the first of september, we should have it in, but there are many things which might make that impossible. I think my part should be in in august sometime. That's the best and nearest information I can give you. I think the book holds up. I'll be interested to see what response the salesmen find on the road, whether any interest or a lack of it. I'm pretty sure the book will be good but that doesn't mean it won't flop completely. But I do think if it gets a slow start, it will gradually pick up because there is much more than just collection in it. Gradually it will be discovered that it is a whole new approach to thinking and only very gradually will the philosophic basis emerge. Of course people like Fadiman will never know but he has kept his position not knowing things for a long time so that is not a matter to worry about. Scientific men, the good ones will know what we are talking about. In fact some of them out here already do. It will only outrage the second rate scientists, who are ready to yell mysticism the moment anything gets dangerously near to careful thinking and a little bit out of their range.

As for myself, and you say you are worrying about me.— I would give up worrying. I am working as hard and as well as I can and I don't dare do anything else. I've been pretty near to a number of edges and am not away from them yet by any means but I find safety in work and that is the only safety I do find. There is no ego in my work and consequently there is no danger for me in it. All of it is extension. If I once became introverted I wouldn't last twenty-four hours. But I know that and thus am able to take care of myself. When this work is done I will have finished a cycle of work that has been biting me for many years and it is simply the carefull statement of the thesis of work to be done in the future if I survive. There will be found in it hints of everything I have been driving toward and it will not be pleasant to the members of any party at all. Some one has to sit out these crises in the world and try to see them in perspective. Perhaps this book does that and perhaps it doesn't. But it does say by implication that the world will go on and that this isn't the first time.

My personal life is a curious thing which I won't permit myself to think about yet. I don't want it to get important until I have finished this work. And don't worry about my cracking up. I won't. You'll get the book and you won't be ashamed of it I don't think although you will probably be pretty much scorned and excoriated for having printed it. Because it does attack some very sacred things, but not at all viciously. Rather with good humour which may be much more devastating.

You say that you hope all will be well with me. That is a nice thing to hope although you know it won't and can't be. I haven't a hell of a lot more time but I have some. I make messes every where but I guess everyone does only with some people they don't show. So don't worry about me. I can see myself pretty objectively and the picture is a little silly.

love to you all

John

In a letter typical of his understanding, sympathy, and editorial support, Covici mailed Steinbeck his reply, citing Steinbeck as his "rarest experience":

July 2, 1941

Mr. John Steinbeck
Pacific Biological Laboratories
Pacific Grove, California

Dear John,

By all means save three weeks and just give me the corrected second draft. You can make additional changes on the galleys. In fact, I believe that you will find that procedure far more convenient. It should help tremendously and save considerable time if you would mail me chapters as ready. In the interval we would carefully prepare the manuscript for the printer and shoot galleys back to you, and thus give you plenty of time to answer queries and make corrections. Please don't let anything hold this book up any longer than it is absolutely necessary. Here we are all keyed up about it, giving it a major part in our sales and advertising preparations for this year. If there is any doubt in your mind whether we will have it for this Fall, please don't wait until September to tell me—it will be too, too disappointing.

I am sure you will get quite a variant of reviews, and I am definitely certain that "Sea of Cortez" will prove exciting, provocative and interesting to intelligent readers. This book will prove a faster seller than you think.

I am sending you a dummy with the old title page. It will be changed for the book. I am not sending you a jacket now as some corrections are being made and will be reprinted.

As to yourself, my worrying about you won't help I know. But I, too, see what you can give and am jealous for it. In my little life, which is about three-fourths done, you are my rarest experience. Take that with all its implications, cynically as well if you want to. The soul of man is not too simple; certainly not for me. What I do positively know is that I want you to go on. I believe most of us, as we grow older, begin to realize that somewhere, somehow things have gone wrong for us. And when one has touched life very intimately, sensitively and in humbleness, one has many fears. What surprises me is that in spite of our fears we have the courage to go on.

I was hoping that your present relationship would give you the exuberance and zest for life you always wanted. I believe it has, at least to some extent, otherwise you could not go on writing. Well, as you say, we shall see.

Affectionately,

PASCAL COVICI *

Steinbeck replied to this letter with unusual thoughtfulness. The following letter and his previous letter dated June 19 offer a rare understanding of how and why Steinbeck was writing his share of *Sea of Cortez*. It was to continue his philosophy as previously stated ever since the publication of his first book, *Cup of Gold*:

Pacific Grove, California
July 4

Dear Pat—

I had your good letter this morning. I cannot see, Pat, any reason why this should not be there by September. I have finished my first draft and we are now doing a second like mad. I haven't talked to Ed but I think he will agree to send it as it is corrected. I'll be glad to see the dummy. I hope this is good. I (*sic*) still shaky from finishing it. It might be all right. We'll have a hundred pages, triple space typed by tomorrow and perhaps will get right to the corrections. We should be able to get out a hundred and fifty pages of this a week.

Thanks for the good thoughts. Certainly there is fulfillment here but the haunting is here too and I don't know when

---

* All Covici's letters to Steinbeck were written from Covici's New York Viking Press offices, and signed "Pat." For convenience and to save space, Covici's office address has been omitted from the top of all his letters, as has his typed name at the bottom.

I will lose that. Maybe never. There are great changes in me some for the better and some, socially at least, for the worse. Word comes to me from Hollywood that I am drinking myself to death and indulging in all kinds of vices. As a matter of fact I am drinking very very little and if that other is a vice then I'm vicious. And I'm doing more work than I ever did. I love the things people say. See if the manuscript sounds like drinking. This book is very carefully planned and designed, Pat, but I don't think its plan will be immediately apparent. And again there are four levels of statement in it and I think very few will follow it down to the fourth. I even think it is a new kind of writing. I told you once that I found a great poetry in scientific writing. Perhaps I haven't done it but I've tried and it is there to be done.

I'm going to take another try at the Pipes as soon as I get a little rested—in a week or so that is. I put a hell of a lot into this ending and it pooped me a little.

Well anyway I hope you like the book. There is almost everything in it and it steps on a lot of toes. Also it is very good natured.

I guess that is all. Aren't the color pictures beautiful?

love to you all

John * [22]

The key section of Steinbeck's June 19 letter is, of course:

When this work is done I will have finished a cycle of work that has been biting me for many years and it is simply the carefull (*sic*) statement of the thesis of work to be done in the future if I survive. There will be found in it hints of everything I have been driving toward and it will not be pleasant to the members of any party at all.

The key section in his letter to Covici of July 4 is: "And again there

---

* Steinbeck's reference to "and if that other is a vice then I'm vicious" apparently refers to Hollywood gossip about his extramarital affair with Gwen Conger. Reference to "the Pipes" was to a piece of fiction he never completed.

are four levels of statement in it and I think very few will follow it down to the fourth."

Steinbeck never stated explicitly what his "four levels of statement" were. Peter Lisca suggests that Steinbeck has in mind "non-teleological thinking, ecology, the possible individuality of a group-animal, 'survival of the fittest,' group psyche-memory, and the mystic unity of all life. These are germinal concepts in Steinbeck . . ."[23]

Lisca also suggests that *Sea of Cortez* is as crucial to an understanding of Steinbeck as *Death in the Afternoon* and *Green Hills of Africa* are to an understanding of Hemingway's philosophy.

Whether Covici understood Steinbeck's "four levels of statement" in *Sea of Cortez* is not certain, for there are no known letters of Covici's in existence which comment on Steinbeck's philosophy on that book.

Steinbeck finished his work on *Sea of Cortez* in August, 1941, and he and Gwen moved to the east coast. He devoted the rest of that year to beginning *The Moon Is Down*, participating in plans for the release of his film, "The Forgotten Village," and negotiating for his divorce from his first wife, Carol. *Sea of Cortez* was published December 5, 1941, with an initial first printing of 7,500 copies.

In one short letter to Covici, late in October, Steinbeck writes, "Started my play and it went wrong and I had to tear it down and start again. But that is normal." His "play" was *The Moon Is Down*, which he conceived as both a novel and a play. It was published March 6, 1942, with a first printing of 55,000 copies. The Dramatist Guild published it in play form August 11, 1942 and The Viking Press also published a play form September 25, 1942, with a first edition of 250.

Steinbeck later wrote to a friend how surprised he was at the acceptance of *The Moon Is Down*, after a slow sales record for *Sea of Cortez*:

> The new book is doing frighteningly well. Pre-publication it is outselling Grapes two to one. In trade edition there will be a pre-publication sale of 85,000 and Book of the Month Club is ordering 200,000. It is kind of crazy. The hysteria of the bookshops in ordering is very wild. The play is being cast now and should go into rehearsal about the 15th of February and will open about a month later.[24]

Steinbeck's next project was suggested to him by General "Hap"

Arnold of the Army Air Force. General Arnold suggested that Steinbeck write a book about how bomber crews are selected, trained and sent into combat. Steinbeck liked the idea despite some bottlenecks, which he wrote about to Covici at the end of June, 1942:

> Dear Pat—
>
> Here are some introductory pages. Look at them and see if you like them at all. The material I was promised, hasn't come from Washington and I am almost at a standstill. I suppose I'll have to learn the army game of doing nothing and passing the buck. And I don't like that game. But the Air Force set the deadline not I. If they can't get the stuff to me, there's nothing I can do about it.
>
> Let me have that copy back. It can't even be copied until the censors are done with it.
>
> John

The Viking Press published *Bombs Away: The Story of a Bomber Team* on November 27, 1942, with a first printing of 20,000. As Lisca writes:

> The Air Force could not have chosen a better man for the job. Steinbeck's prose is straightforward, simple, but retains some of the effectiveness of the intercalary chapters in *The Grapes of Wrath*. *Bombs Away* had a wide sale and bought by Hollywood for $250,000, but Steinbeck turned over all royalties to the Air Forces Aid Society Trust Fund. Even in such a piece of journalism as this, Steinbeck refused to compromise his integrity. The book's last chapter was to depict the climax of that rigorous training which the book describes by giving an account of an actual bombing run. Steinbeck refused to write such a chapter because he had never been on a real bombing run and was afraid his description might be false. Instead, he ended the book very effectively with the bombers taking off for a raid . . .[25]

Steinbeck's divorce from Carol Henning was granted March 19, 1943; on March 29, he and Gwyndolyn Conger (she had recently changed the spelling from Gwendolyn) were married in New Orleans. In early April, he became accredited as a war correspondent, working in the European Theater for *The New York Herald Tribune*. Steinbeck published articles in *The Herald Tribune* from the European Theater from late June, 1943, through early December. Many of the pieces were collected later and published as *Once There Was a War*.

To get over the unpleasant memories of the war, the Steinbecks vacationed in Mexico, where Steinbeck learned how to sketch. He also complained about the changes in the film "Lifeboat," which had premiered, and for which he had written the script. Covici, in New York received his complaints with a greater perspective:

And so you are learning how to draw. And like Browning's Fra Lippo Lippi

You dream men's faces on your copy-book,
Find eyes and nose and chin for A's and B's,
And make a string of pictures of the world,
Betwixt ins and outs of verb and noun.

Lippi so began and why not you. And no doubt like Fra Lippo you will emerge the artist who "gives us no more of body than shows soul" and then takes breath and adds life's flash of hope, fear, sorrow or joy. I hope in your color work you prefer the most brilliant hues—the magentas, cerises, the peacock blues and Moorish yellows. What fun!

I for one don't appreciate all this fuss about "Lifeboat." The photograph work was extremely good and very tricky, and the acting intelligent. The story never moved me nor convinced me. I was glad when it was over—it made me a little seasick.

Right now in New York there is Spring in the air. I can almost feel the buds swell and see the purple tinge the tree trunks. Primavera is hovering over our skyline. Better come home and turn the pages with me of tomorrow.

Harold Guinzburg, as you probably know, is now in London for the O.W.I. and will shortly, perhaps, land in Italy. We shall miss him. My love to you both.

As ever

By the summer of 1944, Steinbeck was well at work on *Cannery Row,* and he and Gwyn had moved to New York City because Gwyn was pregnant. She gave birth to their first son, Thomas, on August 2, 1944. By September, they were planning to move to the Monterey area, and then Steinbeck would travel to Mexico, from October 15 to Christmas, to write a script, to be made into the film "The Pearl," which had been a local Mexican fable, which Steinbeck mentioned briefly in *Sea of Cortez.* But his plans changed. He bought a house in Monterey, and stayed there until after the first of 1945. In letters to Covici, Steinbeck had described his new home, "Soto House," and detailed plans for repairing and remodeling it. Covici, who was not as handy with tools as Steinbeck was, nonetheless wanted to help. With Steinbeck back in the country, and settled, at least temporarily, and with *Cannery Row* about to be published, their correspondence became more frequent. During this period, Covici's letters to Steinbeck were written more often than Steinbeck could reply. In the following, Covici rejects a charge made by Carlton A. Sheffield, a long-time Steinbeck friend, that Steinbeck, with *Cannery Row,* was beginning to repeat himself:

November 15, 1944

Mr. John Steinbeck
460 Pierce Street
Monterey, Calif.

Dear John,

I should love to paint the house with you. You know how mechanically inclined I am, especially changing tires with a no good jack.

Yes, I ordered the encyclopedia and the dictionary from John Newbegin before I left. So far I haven't heard from him. I wired him today.

Here is Virginia Kirkus's comment to the trade—the booksellers throughout the country. I don't agree with your friend Sheffield. Intelligent literary critics won't say you have repeated yourself, for that doesn't mean anything. Shakespeare's "Hamlet" as well as a great many of his other characters, under different names, appear in a great many of his plays. And that doesn't make the plays less great. During

the Renaissance the great painters painted the same themes over
and over again and they still remain the great masterpieces
of all time. I, for one, am very grateful to the spirit of
your genius that when you write you never worry what the
little critic will have to say.

The orders on "Cannery Row" are still coming in 60%
higher than the "Moon is Down," and the advance on the
"Moon" was 65,000 copies. We have ordered paper for
250,000 copies now and I have a feeling we will have to order
more.

I am very anxious to have pictures of your house, trees,
your son, Gwyn and Willie. Regards.

Yours ever,

Covici's reference to "I ordered the encyclopedia and the dictionary . . ." were part of a long-standing custom with the two. If Steinbeck found a book in a catalogue which he needed, Covici would order
it, and usually get it at a discount, at The Viking Press. Covici would
then mail it on to Steinbeck and charge the cost of the book or books
against Steinbeck's earned royalties. Covici's feelings were that this type
of errand was the least that he could do for his busy friend—there is
no evidence that he ever passed the jobs off to secretaries or other staff
members. (Willie was the current Steinbeck dog).

A week after his letter of November 15, Covici explained why
the finished copies of *Cannery Row* contained no illustrations. He was
also concerned that Steinbeck relax before tackling his next project,
The Pearl:

22 November, 1944

Artzybasheff could not possibly undertake to do the drawings
for "Cannery Row." It would have been good but would not
have sold additional copies. There wasn't time to experiment with other artists. I hope you don't mind too much.

Yesterday I mailed you a copy of the paper edition, one of
the 500 going out to the booksellers. The orders are still
coming in and I am quietly excited.

Now that you have baptized your new home in the name of
the Father, Son and Holy Ghost—what a rambunctious ghost

Gwyn would make—I hope you will take a few days off and relax completely before you start working on Pearl. Quietly soak in some ocean breezes and let your mind dwell in the depths measureless to man, then cover yourself with the hills and, the dreams will come. The Pearl should be pure fantasy and imagination, grounded on reality.

Kindest regards.

Yours ever,

Publication of *Cannery Row* marked the public identification of the character "Doc" as Steinbeck's friend, Ed Ricketts. Although the character of "Doc," or Ed, had been seen earlier in Steinbeck's short story, "The Snake," *Cannery Row* brought Ricketts unwanted publicity and Monterey international fame. Quoting Lisca:

The extent to which Doc is modeled on Steinbeck's good friend, Ed Ricketts, is clear from the biographical sketch which Steinbeck published in *The Log From the Sea of Cortez,* after Ricketts' death. Almost every detail about Doc has its parallel in the actual life and personality of Ed Ricketts. *Cannery Row* is itself dedicated to Ed Ricketts—'For Ed Ricketts who knows why or should.' After reading the novel in manuscript, Ricketts expressed concern that it would make him a popular figure; and it did. *Life* wanted to print photographs and a story about him and his laboratory, which Ricketts did not allow. Tourists began to drive slowly by the Pacific Biological Laboratories at 800 Oceanview Avenue. Frequently they would stop and ask if they could come in and look around.[26]

On November 30, Steinbeck wrote to Covici:

Dear Pat;

I got a running start at this Pearl thing. Too fast. Had to throw the first days work away. But then it settled down. Don't know that it is any good but it moves so far and sticks together and that's all I can expect of it. But at first I got off on the wrong foot entirely. Anyway, it is moving along and will probably pick up momentum.

Long distance phone call last night. Many from Christian
Science Monitor. Wants to come down [sunday] to discuss
Cannery Row. Seems they have heard that I said half the
whores were Christian Scientists. On the phone I said—"would
you be upset if it were so? There were only two chief woman
characters in the life of Jesus and one was Magdalene." "No," he
said, but he wanted to discuss it. So he's coming over
on Sunday and the discussion should be fun. Maybe if I work
it right we can get banned not only by Boston but by the
Christian Scientists as well. The ideal is to be banned by
everybody—then everybody would have to read it.

After the meeting with the man from *The Christian Science Monitor,*
Steinbeck wrote to Mildred Lyman, of the staff of McIntosh and Otis:

Well, the [Xtian] Science man came and he seems very nice
and cagey and clever. He wondered if people wouldn't get
the wrong impression. I said that some people always got the
wrong impression. There wasn't much he could say without
giving the impression of snobbishness. When he left, he said,
'I just leave this thought with you. If they practiced prostitution *and* Christian Science, they were not good Christian
Scientists.' And I said, 'Well, that's all right, because they
weren't very good prostitutes either.' So he laughed and we
parted on a friendly basis. He said they would have to make
a statement and I said I would be upset if they didn't.[27]

The dialogue between Steinbeck and representatives of the Christian Science Church went on throughout the month of December. Representatives of the Christian Science Church visited Pascal Covici in his
Viking Press offices, but *Cannery Row* was not changed in any way.
Steinbeck viewed their concern as needless meddling in his novel; Covici,
who viewed the dialogue at a great distance and with less involvement,
cherished the whole matter as an amusing anecdote.

Meanwhile, Steinbeck had written Covici that he no longer felt at
ease in his own home town—his successes had alienated him with the
local leaders. Steinbeck felt they believed that *Cannery Row* had thrown
their community in disrepute:

Dec. 3

Dear Pat;

The first reviews seem to bear out Sheffield's thesis exactly. But there was something he forgot. There is a time in every writer's career when the critics are gunning for him to whittle him down. This is my stage for that. It has been since the Grapes of Wrath. I see it all the time. The criticism is good but what saddens me is the active hatred of most of the writers and the pseudowriters around here. It will not be terribly long before we will be associating only with fishermen which is the best thing of all. There is a deep and active jealousy out here that makes me very sad. I haven't mentioned it before. It is a natural reaction of course but I don't like it any the better for that.

In the same letter, he added, referring to the filming planned for *The Pearl:* "I'm still in a slump with the Pearl. This has been a long slump. But I have a feeling that it will never be made anyway."

Covici's son has said, "My father was usually subtle with his authors. He never said 'Do this . . .'; he usually said 'This doesn't persuade me . . .' I think that this subtle approach worked very well for him."[28]

From his offices, Covici worried that Steinbeck might sell his idea too quickly; that *The Pearl* might be made into a mediocre film before Steinbeck had a chance to capture all the potential which was inherent in his fable:

December 12, 1944

Mr. John Steinbeck
460 Pierce Street
Monterey, California

Dear John,

Thanks for the two snapshots of your house. What I see of it looks like an old Spanish mansion with the dust of the ages over it. The tree in the front looks magnificent. I wish I could be with you to work in the garden. Judging from the

pictures I think it needs a tremendous amount of work. I
know you will have fun there.

I hope you don't yield to RKO and the other movie stooges
in selling your story now for a movie. At least wait until
you have written your story as you really feel it should
be done. You conceived your story beautifully with poetry and
a universal philosophy—all of which I am sure no movie
enterprise, certainly no Hollywood studio, would even dream
of reproducing on the screen. They will maim, torture and
destroy what is most precious about it. I know of no reason why
you should rush the story or sell it as a movie.

Harold just returned from London. He looks much better
than the last time. He will stay here now and only be with
the OWI part of the time. He asked about you and Gwyn
and your son. He is very happy with the wonderful advance
of CANNERY ROW.

The slow recovery of Gwyn doesn't sound very good
to me. What does the doctor say? I know your contempt
for doctors.

Love,*

The next week, with the official publication date of *Cannery Row*
approaching, Covici sent Steinbeck further details of the book's publication. This letter also suggests the intimacy which Covici wished with
his favorite author. With Steinbeck living on the west coast and Covici
in New York, they could breakfast together only in Covici's imagination:

December 19, 1944

Mr. John Steinbeck
460 Pierce Street
Monterey, Calif.

Dear John,

No, I haven't received your report of the Christian

---

* The Viking Press only held the rights to publish Steinbeck's work in book
form in the U.S.; film rights, magazine rights and overseas publication rights were
held by Steinbeck's agents, thus the right to sell *The Pearl* to a Hollywood film
company could be negotiated by McIntosh and Otis, with Steinbeck's approval,
without the approval of Covici or The Viking Press.

Science interview. Please let me have it. I am sure it's
too good to miss.

"Cannery Row" will be published on January 2nd. Judging
from the orders already in I would say that the advance will
be between 90,000 and 95,000. If you remember the advance
on "The Moon is Down" was 65,000 in spite of the
book club selection. Our total sales of the "Moon" was
about 165,000 copies. I am still willing to stick my neck
out and say that "Cannery Row" will sell not less than
250,000 copies. We shall see.

You are surely beginning to enjoy your son. It wasn't
until he was about nine months old when I really began to
notice Pascal. From then on he was fun.

I should be there when you start out for your office,
meet you casually and go for breakfast. What will you have?
Yes, let's have coffee first, lots of it. Orange juice? No. Let's
have some Persian melon this morning, ham and eggs, please,
for two, rye toast, and please have it well done, almost
burned. We like it burned. Do you think they will give it to
us burned? Probably not. The coffee is good here, is it not?
Very good.

Well, now that we have had breakfast you can start to work.

Love,

Cannery Row was officially published on January 2, 1945, with a
first printing of 78,000.

On December 29, Steinbeck wrote a typical letter to Covici; however,
in this letter he discusses the problems of sustained creativity:

I've gone into a slump on the Pearl and that bothers me
even remembering that I always go into two or three slumps
on every book. But it always worries me. . . . You know
I can inspect my slumps pretty well. I go grey in the head
and then I begin to worry about not working. Then I get
disgusted with myself and when this disgust grows big
enough the whole thing turns over like an iceberg and I go

to work again. It's always the same and it's always new.
I never get used to it.

After the first of the year, Covici encouraged Steinbeck to forget
the criticism of *Cannery Row,* forget the pre-Christmas problems with
the Christian Scientists, and stop worrying about his writer's slumps:

January 8, 1945

Mr. John Steinbeck
460 Pierce Street
Monterey, California

Dear John,

Reorders are already coming in. The American News Co.
received 20,000 copies last week, the initial order, and they
called up today for 2500 more. Smaller shops who originally
ordered 25 and 50 are wiring in for duplications.

The small fry of writers and some of the academic ones
will always be gunning for you. Were you to be merely
a successful writer, like Fannie Hurst, Temple Bailey or
Dr. Cronin, you would be occasionally patronized in an oily
way but mostly ignored. But to be successful and command
serious critical attention—that's too much. They can't stomach
it and so they will take it out on you no matter what you
write. Better start building a tougher protective skin around
you. Poisonous javelins will be constantly coming your way.
Make good use of your philosophic calm and demeanor,
even against your friends. They, too, are human and
frailty, thy name is human.

Why don't you leave Pearl rest a while and to hell
with deadlines? You shouldn't whip yourself into work.
It just isn't any good. San Francisco should give you some
respite. I should be with you now drinking wine and
listening to some old Roumanian songs, grow sad and mellow
and warm inside. That's a very good feeling to have.

Love,*

* Most of Covici's letters to Steinbeck were signed "Pat," omitted throughout
to save space; thus his signature is omitted on all of them.

A generation later, editor William Targ has noted:

It is essential that an editor and publishing executive remember
his *humanness.* . . .
  The author and his manuscript are the most important
elements in your professional life. Let the author know
this. Everything you do, every action you undertake should
be with this in mind. . . .
  Treat the author with every possible courtesy;
remember he's palpitating from blood-drain, from the efforts
expended on his book, and needs encouragement and
friendship. . . .
  Your author must know in his heart that you are always
leveling with him. If you don't like something, tell
him/her; if you are pleased, speak up. Your author must
trust you. . .[29]

Covici's letters to Steinbeck exhibit the qualities of humanness which
Targ later suggested were so important in the professional life of the
publisher. Covici had, at his best, a perceptive understanding for treatment of his authors. In Steinbeck's case, his relationship was far beyond
that of author and publisher, to that of a spirited, caring intimacy, concerned with Steinbeck's physical and emotional health, as well as his
professional career.
  In the middle of January, 1945, Steinbeck wrote to Covici, again
saying he didn't believe that the critics had discovered the structure
of *Cannery Row:*

. . . It is interesting to me, Pat, that no critic has discovered
the reason for these little chapters in C. R. You would have
known. Nearly all lay readers know. Only critics don't. Are
they somehow the lowest common denominator. If in
pictures, the thing must be slanted for the 9 year old mind, in
books they must be slanted for critics and it seems to amount
to the same thing. Far from being the sharpest readers,
they are the dullest. You say I am taking it philosophically.
I'm not and I feel wonderful. Don't you remember the years
when these same critics were sneering at every book—the
same books incidentally that they now remember with awe.

No I feel all of the old contempt for them and it is a
good feeling. I *know* C. R. is a good book.

On January 18, 1945, Covici wrote, "If the reviews make you feel
full of hell and arouse your energy they have done a remarkable deed. . . .
It is a good mood to begin anything in—I mean full of hell."
He also noted, in that same letter, "I have just been informed that
the Book-of-the-Month Club selected your *Red Pony Illustrated* for a
dividend book this year. In shiny dollars that means a minimum of
$16,000. for you."

The next week, (January 25) he felt compelled to write:

I read "Cannery Row" over again. It's a good book, John.
You poured a great deal of poetry into it. You give a
good many reasons for living and for dying. And I am glad
you were born and happy that you are alive. Certainly
life is an accident. Man is no more important to the Universe
than an ant on the Sahara Desert. But we are important
to each other—we are born in each other's image.

Later that spring, Steinbeck wrote to Covici of his ever-increasing
belief that he could not live in Monterey, where all his former friends
had turned against him:

Dear Pat;

This is a private letter really. We're going to Mexico
in a few days. And I'm glad to go. You remember how happy I
was to come back here. It really was a home coming.
Well there is no home coming nor any welcome. What
there is is jealousy and hatred and the knife in the back.
I'm beginning to think I made a mistake. I don't mind
that but I'm not going to let a mistake ride me on through.
This is no new thing. I've tried to conceal it and explain
it and analyze it and make a joke of it and to ignore it. It's
much more than a feeling.
    Our old friends won't have us back—always except Ed.
Mostly with them it is what they consider success that gets
in between. And the town and the region—that is the people

of it—just pure poison. I laughed about being refused an
office. But the local gas board cut off my gas in spite of the fact
that I had a job with the War Food Administration. Ours is
the first request to repair a house that has been rejected. 60
homes are being built for rent but we can't get a plank to
replace a rotten board in the kitchen. These are just two
of many things. I hate a feeling of persecution but I am just
not welcome here.

But I'm not going to jump any guns. We're going to be
in Mexico four or five months and then we'll give it
another try and if it doesn't work we'll clear out.

Maybe you can figure something, but this I can tell you,
I was happier in New York. Living is people, not places.
I have no peers here—in notoriety and so called success—
and the people who are coming up are ferocious. There's
no one to talk to except Ed. You see, Pat—I would and
can forget all the publicity etc. but these people can't
and won't.

This isn't my country anymore. And it won't be until
I am dead. It makes me very sad.

John

Before Covici could reply, Steinbeck moved to Mexico. Covici's
answer was mailed to him there, in care of the company which was
producing the film, "The Pearl."

April 10, 1945

Mr. John Steinbeck
Aquila Films
Ejida 43
Mexico, D. F., Mexico

Dear John,

Your letter made me very sad. I expected a different
homecoming. When you bought your house, the home you
really wanted, I was glad and very hopeful for your happiness.
This small town stuff never occurred to me. Thinking it
over, as I have done for the last few days, I believe I

understand quite clearly why you feel that way. New York is a big metropolis of many races and nationalities where big reputations are made and lost almost daily, where poverty and riches change hands almost hourly. One more reputation, one more success is quickly swallowed. You lived in New York long enough to hate the provincialism of a small town, their jealousies and hatreds. You are a real success, one of their boys who tops them all; tops them too much for their comfort. You have a national reputation and came home to enjoy it and I am afraid they won't let you. There are plenty of the same calibre in New York but you don't have to see them nor be with them. You can choose your friends here and plenty to choose from. One can live in an apartment here for years and not know one's next door neighbor. Not so in a small town. Either they take you in or you are forever an outsider.

The combined provincial hostilities of the town pitted against you is tragic to contemplate. There is a certain voiceless, lacerating malice in small town inhabitants that can be deadly poisonous. They have no loyalties except for their own of equal stature. Of course, try it again when you return. But as you say, living is people not places and New York has both. You have a great many friends here, and I am afraid that destiny has something else in store for you.

"There's a divinity that shapes our ends,
    Rough-hew them how we will . . ."
Maybe so.

Affectionately yours,

As the Steinbeck-Covici relationship grew stronger, Covici occasionally had to explain Steinbeck's perceptions, needs and problems in a way Steinbeck himself could understand. This letter above is one of the first in which Covici, as a master psychologist, must explain Steinbeck's own choices and thoughts to him.

Steinbeck, who had first written about the fable of the "Pearl of the World" in *Sea of Cortez,* now finished his book-length treatment of that story and had forwarded it to Covici for publication. Covici replied as soon as he could, comparing it to *The Grapes of Wrath* in excellence:

Mr. John Steinbeck   April 26, 1945
Hotel Reforma
Mexico, D. F., Mexico

Dear John,

I just finished "La Perla" and I like it. To me it is as tense
and compelling a story as I have read in years. In this
parable you say there are only black and white things and no
in-between, but what rich blacks and what dazzling whites.
The love of Juana for Kino is quite elemental, but with
the strength and vividness of all things elemental. Kino's
exulting response to the song of the family which runs
through your story like a light motif, a distant and insistent
beat of a tom-tom, is also primitive and elemental but it
is eternal in the heart of man. One could also say about
your parable that, like Juana's song to Coyotito, it has only
three notes—love, hunger and freedom from greed. But again
what infinite longings you put into them.
   This undoubtedly contains some of your best prose.
The scorpion passage and the one where you tell of
the trackers pursuing Kino, his breathless escapes, his final plunge
in the dark and his knifing the man are, to my mind, the most
intense, exciting, compulsive prose you have ever written.
   If this sounds over-bubbling I can't help it. It is what I feel.

                                        Affectionately,

   Later Covici wrote again, sketching in possibilities of combining
The Pearl with other Steinbeck works to make a larger volume. Eventually, *The Pearl* was published separately, but this letter indicates how
a good editor evaluates possibilities for an in-coming manuscript:

Mr. John Steinbeck   May 7, 1945
Hotel Marik
Cuernavaca, Morelos
Mexico

Dear John,

   After I talked to Elizabeth Otis I was convinced more

than ever that the Pearl should be published either in a
limited edition similar to the first issue of "The Red Pony"
or, and that would delight me most, to wait until you have
two more similar stories and then bring out a volume of
three novelettes of Mexico. So published the book would not
only receive serious critical attention, but I believe it
would have a very good sale. What's far more interesting,
a volume of short novels would be so completely different
than anything you have published. What do you think?
Couldn't the new Mexican story you now have in mind be one of
them? Then that Good Neighbor story which you never
finished. Don't you think that you could do something with it?
The first half I thought was superb. Anyway, let me know
how you feel about all this.

I could use a bit of Mexico, and to be there with you
and Gwyn would be a wishful dream fulfilled, but there
isn't a ghost of a chance of my coming now. By the time this
letter reaches you the war with Germany will undoubtedly
be over and then what? Chaos for the next hundred years
or a new dawn? Your guess is as good as mine.

The years 1945 to 1952 offered a panoramic view of Steinbeck;
his career and his relationship to Covici. This period reveals Steinbeck
at his best; from *The Pearl* and *The Wayward Bus,* through the book
which critics generally agree was his worst, *Burning Bright,* and then on
to the work he considered his magnum opus, *East of Eden.* These years
reveal Steinbeck happily married to Gwyn Conger, then sadness during
their divorce, then happiness again when he meets and marries Elaine
Scott.

Throughout these years, the support of Pascal Covici, his editorial
and personal friendship and guidance continues, culminating in the
dedication of Steinbeck's *East of Eden* to Covici, and the collection
and eventual publication of *Journal of a Novel: The East of Eden Letters,*
which were all written to Covici during the progress of *East of Eden.*

III

"HE HELD THEIR LOYALTY OVER THE YEARS BECAUSE HE GAVE THEM LOYALTY"

May, 1945 to September, 1947

Toward the end of May, 1945, Steinbeck had told Covici about his next work, the novel *The Wayward Bus*. Covici was thinking about how *Tortilla Flat* could be illustrated:

May 23, 1945

Mr. John Steinbeck
Hotel Marik
Cuernavaca, Morelos
Mexico

Dear John,

The cataclysmic roar of battle in Europe seems to be over. The bickerings and fight for position in power politics are rumbling on and anything may happen. The world hasn't changed much and neither has human nature. But what's 25,000 years in the life of our solar system.

I like your title "The Wayward Bus" for your Mexican story. I was never in Mexico, but if they have buses there I am sure they are vacilador. That and the "Pearl" will make a goodly book. Of course, I still prefer three, that's such a lucky magic number. Maybe next year you will have a third one.

The other day I was shown some proof sheets of the four-colored illustrations for "The Red Pony," and I think

they are beautiful. The colors are fresh and clean and warm.
I know that you will be pleased. That set me thinking of
another illustrated book for next year. I would love to see
"Tortilla Flat" illustrated in color, done either by Henry V.
Poor or Miguel Covarrubias. Either one of them, because of
their reputation, would expect a split in the royalties. The
usual division is 60% for the author and 40% for the
illustrator, but the sale of the book is so certain that I am
confident either would accept 33%. What one of the
artists would you prefer?

The sulfa drugs have all left me, and what a relief. I
hope I never have to take them again. Life doesn't seem
worth while with sulfa in your system. I never felt so washed
up. I am all right now with a few pains and aches here and
there but, then, who hasn't? It is good to hear that you are
feeling fine now and eager to work. Thank God for Gwyn
and Mexico. Please give her my love.

Adios,

A week later in a letter to Covici, Steinbeck described an occur-
rence which fascinated him:

Last night a very strange thing happened—Anciently it
would have had a very definite effect on a person. The moon
came up red and sullen through a black haze. We sat on the
porch watching it because of its very threatening color.
Then black clouds like mare's tails moved up from the
horizon, big black streaks. Jack Wagner yelled suddenly—
"look!" It was a very strange thing. The clouds spelled in
huge black letters John right across the moon. It was very
definite and lasted five minutes before it drifted away. We
called Gwyn to look at it. I have seen letters in clouds
before but never four definite letters. The form was almost
exactly as I have drawn it. Isn't that a strange thing? In
an age of portents it would be effective. Such a thing might
have caused the Magna Carta not to be signed.*

---

* Jack Wagner was a friend of Steinbeck's; working on the film-making of "The
Pearl." As far as is known, Steinbeck never used this as an incident in any subsequent novel.

Covici also found it fascinating. On June 14, he replied:

What a mystic, breathless experience seeing one's name
in the clouds. There are at least 90% of the world's
population who would see a sign and a portent in your
name written in the sky. There are more things in heaven
and earth than are dreamt of in our philosophy. I pride
myself in having a scientific approach to things, but with so
vast a universe surrounding me I often feel as if I were
floating in some infinite vacuum when I so long at times for
some safer anchorage. And this is not a sign of old age or
infirmity of intelligence, though I could easily lay claim to
both. Both my Greek orthodox and early Hebraic teachings
bereft me of any belief in a personal God. Their potent,
penetrating fingers, nevertheless, still are on my plastic soul.

On July 12, weary of the film-making, Steinbeck wrote:

Cuernavaca

July 12

Dear Pat:

I am heartily sick of this picture now and there are stirrings
in me for new work. This is like beating a down dog. I've
never liked rehashing but I'll do it this time and it is once
for all. There's too much new work to do—to go over one's
old.

The people down here are very kind to us. And I hope
out of this stay to write a book that may be something for
them to have. For the Wayward Bus could be something
like the Don Quixote of Mexico. The more I think of it the
better I like it and the better I like it the longer its plan and
the wider its scope until it seems to contain the whole world.
From the funny little story it is growing to the most ambitious
thing I have ever attempted. Not that it still won't be funny
but funny as Tom Jones and Tristram Shandy and Don
Quixote are funny. And it isn't going to take a little time to
write but a long time and I don't care, for my bus is
something large in my mind. It is a cosmic bus holding

sparks and back firing into the Milky Way and turning the corner of Betelgeuse without a hand signal. And Juan Chicoy the driver is all the god the fathers you ever saw driving a six cylinder broken down, battered world through time and space. If I can do it well the Wayward Bus will be a pleasant thing.

So long—we'll have fun.

John

Steinbeck later described to a friend, Charles Brackett, the origin of his title, *The Wayward Bus:*

> I don't think I ever told you the origin of this story. It was first projected in Mexico, and its first synopsis was written in Spanish for Mexico. At that time it had a wonderful title, I think. It was called El Camion Vacilador. The word vacilador, or the verb vacilar, is not translatable unfortunately, and it's a word we need in English because to be 'vacilando' means that you're aiming at some place, but you don't care much whether you get there. We don't have such a word in English. Wayward has an overtone of illicitness or illegality, based of course on medieval lore where wayward men were vagabonds. But vacilador is not a vagabond at all. Wayward was the nearest English word that I could find.[1]

Through the end of July, Covici was busy at work with Steinbeck material; a new edition of *The Portable Steinbeck* and the continuing problems of finding an illustrator for a new edition of *Tortilla Flat:* (Written before he received Steinbeck's letter of July 12.)

July 19, 1945

Mr. John Steinbeck
Hotel Marik
Cuernavaca, Mor.
Mexico

Dear John:

Miguel Covarrubias's agent tells me he is not interested

in illustrating TORTILLA FLAT. He'd rather do GRAPES
OF WRATH. Why—because GRAPES OF WRATH has
social significance and TORTILLA FLAT is one of these
candle-for-the-church stories and he doesn't like the church.
Well, of course he never read the book; he just saw the
movie and, as you well know, ninety-five percent of the
book's pagan poetry and joy of living and charm of
camaraderie simply isn't there. Maybe if I convince him to
read the book he might change his mind. I don't know.
He'll be here for another two weeks.

We are just about ready to print another edition of
your Portable. We want to include your Stevenson story,
"The Frog Hunt," and maybe several more connecting
essays from GRAPES OF WRATH. The book also needs a
long biographical and critical introduction, with notes on
the different selections. Am lunching with Lewis Gannett
tomorrow and will ask him to do it. I think he will, at least
I hope so.

With this in mind last night, I dipped into the GRAPES
OF WRATH, paying special attention to the overture essays,
in fact reading them consecutively—and what organ music
they are. And I was thinking—please forgive me—when
will you put your clarinet away (not that I don't enjoy
greatly its lovely lyric music) and take up the organ again.
There is a time for each, I suppose.

It would be good to see you again and just talk.

Affectionately,

Playwright Arthur Miller said, of Covici: "Pat stood rather alone,
superbly himself, eager to be moved by something true. . . . He was
the slave of an appetite for excellence, and, while he could set forth
all the right reasons for his judgments, his real calculus was that of
the heart. He loved best whatever lifted up the human possibility;
what really made him slap the table and roar out his laugh was the out-
break of light over the passionate dark."[2]

Steinbeck's "cosmic bus holding sparks and back firing into the
Milky Way . . . And Juan Chicoy . . . all the god the fathers you ever
saw driving a six cylinder broken down, battered world through time

and space" aroused Covici's imagination and he urged—almost pleaded
—with Steinbeck to complete it:

July 26, 1945

Mr. John Steinbeck
Hotel Marik
Cuernavaca, Mor.
Mexico

Dear John:

I wish you would leave Mexico right now. You had
enough of it. "The Bus Story" is growing into epic
proportion and it is not going to give you any rest until
you buckle down to it. My imagination leapt into infinity
when I read your last letter telling me how the story is
evolving. If I had a plane, I would fly myself there and bring
you back pronto. I don't mean that you should rush the
story; this cannot be done. You will take as much time as
you need, of course, but I do want to see you begin and be
immersed in it. It sounds like a natural for you, something
that is struggling to come out of your guts and your whole
being is vibrating in the process.

As you probably know by this time, Churchill is out
and the Labor Party is in. The world is moving fast, faster
perhaps than we believe. Some of our Senators still think
in terms of the middle ages; the economic and political world
is changing nevertheless and our Democracy will change
with it.

I gave up the idea of Covarrubias doing TORTILLA
FLAT. Too bad, he would have done a beautiful job.
Now I have to look around; the idea is still good.

Gannett hasn't said yes to writing an introduction to your
Portable, but I'm confident he will. He suggested including
two or three stories from the European front. I think I
know the stories I want.

I do hope you decide to come East sooner than October.

Adios,

On August 22, Covici wrote to Steinbeck about what was happening at Viking, and what the end of the war might mean. He also asked Steinbeck if he could invest in the film "The Pearl," even though he had previously lost money investing in "The Forgotten Village":

> There is some excitement here. We have a possible best
> seller in THREE O'CLOCK DINNER by Josephine Pinckney.
> It is not a great story nor a very important one, but the
> writing is good, good characterization and understanding, and
> a discriminating poetic feeling. The book has all the lucky
> breaks. First the Literary Guild took it and are printing
> 650,000 copies, then Metro-Goldwyn-Mayer got excited and
> are paying $125,000. When I signed her up I was lucky enough
> to get 25% of the movie rights and so Viking isn't doing
> so badly either.
> What the end of the war will do to the publishing business
> is anybody's guess, and what shape the world will take,
> well I'm on the optimistic side. I can't imagine Homo sapiens
> toying with atomic energy.
> Now I have an inspiration. You seem to have a lot of fun
> with that movie you are doing. It seems to me very good
> and I would like to join in the fun. How about investing a little
> of my savings? I'd love to do a little gambling, or am I
> too late? See what you can do—say $1000, yes?

Steinbeck tactfully answered:

Aguila Films
Ejido 43
Mexico D. F.
Aug. 29

Dear Pat;

Moved up here a few days ago to help with casting, etc. We should go into production in three weeks. I'm a little under the weather but not badly. Lonesome for Gwyn mostly. I'll be talking to her tomorrow. I asked whether any money could be invested in this film and was told no. Could only be done by buying stock in RKO or Aguila Films and there is none for sale. I'm glad in a way because I would hate to have you lose more money as you did in Forgotten Village.

If all goes well I might try to get up there in a few weeks and then come back. But can't tell yet. Right now we are looking at actors. Not a job I admire. I'm pretty homesick.

This is just a note. And not a very good one. I hope to see you soon.

So long

John

Steinbeck remained in Mexico until late in the year. Gwyn sold their home in Monterey, and in mid-December they moved to New York City. But in November, Covici wrote Steinbeck:

November 20, 1945

Mr. John Steinbeck
Hotel Marik
Cuernavaca, Mor.
Mexico

Dear John,

Well, you didn't get the Nobel Prize this year, but I am willing to make a bet that you will in the next three years. It is inevitable.

Your outline of the "Wizard of Maine" has grand possibilities, only I wish that you had worked on it a little more and then you would have had a delightful short novelette. There is enough of the "Arabian Nights" in it—and I don't mean because of the magic wand—to have something quite different in fiction. Maybe you will some time.

See if you can work that wand of yours and bring me to Mexico so that I can drive back with you. I don't know who your traveling companion will be but I bet he won't have the fun that I would. In the first place I would see that Willy wouldn't get sick again and I would, of course, tell you exactly how you should change a tire. And then you are accustomed to my snoring.

I have been reading so many dull manuscripts lately,

and from authors who should know better, that I am beginning
to think atomic bombs or no, certainly the literary field
seems completely sterile, and unless some vigorous, lusty
authors impregnate the earth again we might just as well
call it a day, crawl back into caves and scribble on the
walls. You better hurry some and begin writing.

My best to you both.

As ever,

"The Wizard of Maine" was a project Steinbeck never finished. And
as to the Nobel Prize, Covici was wrong about it—but only about the
year. It was awarded to Steinbeck seventeen years later.

Malcolm Cowley, the critic, later said of Covici:

Pat had what was less an acquired taste than an instinct for
good writing; that was why he became a publisher in the
beginning. He would never be one of the editors who
prescribe minutely what an author should do. Instead he simply
encouraged an author to do his best, then grandly
appreciated what he had done. If there happened to be some
weakness in the finished production, his instinct picked
it out infallibly but hearteningly.

From the Chicago days of the robin's-egg renaissance,
through the booming twenties in New York and the era of
social rebels, to this later time when novels deal with a search
for identity, his career might serve as a history of
American publishing. He made friends in each of these periods
and kept them to the end. But let us not say that he exhibited
a universal and undistributed benevolence. There is no
opportunity for that in the publishing world, or rather there
is too much opportunity, so that such kindness becomes
thin and mechanical. Pat was truly kind and devoted to the
many authors in whom he believed, whether or not they had a
wide public. He was their friend, their first audience, their
protector, almost their father, and he held their loyalty
over the years because he gave them loyalty.[3]

Cowley's statement that "he held their loyalty over the years
because he gave them loyalty" is illustrated over and over throughout

the Steinbeck-Covici correspondence. Steinbeck appreciated, and needed the encouragement.

Work on his next novel, *The Wayward Bus,* kept Steinbeck busy throughout the spring of 1946. He wrote to his friend, Jack Wagner, on May 2: "For two months I've been fighting the Bus and only now have I got a start which seems good. I've thrown away thousands of words. But I think it is good now. At least it is moving."[4]

On June 12, Steinbeck's second son, John, was born in New York. Throughout 1946 and 1947, Steinbeck's correspondence with Covici and his other old friends was sparse, as Steinbeck was traveling and meeting new friends and working slowly on *The Wayward Bus* and other projects. The Steinbecks visited Denmark and Sweden in the fall of 1946 and returned to New York in time for Christmas of 1946. *The Wayward Bus* was published in February, 1947. He wrote John Wagner:

I hope you like it although 'like' is not the word to use.
You nor anyone can't *like* it. But at least I think it is effective.
It is interesting to me—the following—This book depends
on mood, on detail and on all the little factors of writing
for its effectiveness. It has practically no story. Yet the picture
companies seriously read synopses of it and think that is the
book. The Bus, incidentally, has 600,000 Book of the Month
and 150,000 trade first edition before publication. And with
all that I had to borrow money to pay my income tax.[5]

Lisca's analysis of *The Wayward Bus* is perhaps the most succinct and clearest:

The frame story of the wayward bus taking its assorted
passengers cross-country from one main highway to another,
coming to washed-out bridges, traveling the forgotten
back road, and finally arriving at San Juan de la Cruz, becomes
itself part of the novel's meaning. There are two main
'plots': the gathering of the characters and their actual
interaction with each other; the actual journey of the
allegorical bus.

Lisca also writes that:

None of (the) characters actually changes during the trip, but in a chain reaction of events culminating during Juan Chicoy's temporary desertion of his six-cylinder world, each of these characters bound for San Juan de la Cruz undergoes some dark night of the soul in which he achieves a measure of self-knowledge.

Finally, Steinbeck's use of a portion of *Everyman* adds emphasis to the allegorical nature of the book. Lisca writes:

> Although the journey from Rebel Corners to San Juan de la Cruz is described in realistic terms, most of the book's geography and toponymy is fictitious, and there is an underlying suggestiveness in almost every detail. That *The Wayward Bus* is intended as more than a realistic narrative is also pointed out by its epigraph.

> > I pray you all gyve audyence,
> > And here this mater with reverence,
> > By fygure a morall playe;
> > The somonynge of Everyman called it is,
> > That of our lyves and endynge showes
> > How transytory we be all daye.[6]

Later in 1947, *The New York Herald Tribune* hired Steinbeck to visit the Soviet Union, with photographer Robert Capa. Steinbeck's material from this visit was to be the source for his next book, *A Russian Journal,* published the following year.

On July 10, 1947, Covici wrote to Steinbeck, who was staying at the Hotel Lancaster, in Paris:

> Are you going to Russia and is Capa going with you? I hope that you are. If nothing else it would bring you back to earth again, face to face with fundamental human values. There is a giant dormant in your soul and I want to see it stir with the compassion and generous understanding that is yours, yours above any other writer in America.

On July 13, Steinbeck discovered that birthday presents, sent to his son Tom, at summer camp, had not arrived. It is an example of the closeness of Steinbeck and Covici that he asked Covici to make sure sufficient presents were sent, although late, for his son's birthday. He also asked Covici to send presents for his son John's birthday,* which was forthcoming. (John's family nickname was "Catbird" or "Cat.") Both boys were attending the same camp. There is more than a little sarcasm in the following letter, written on stationery of the Hotel Lancaster, Paris, directed at Steinbeck's wife. They were divorced the next year, and this period may have been the first of their marital difficulties:

Dear Pat:

We just got in a little while ago. Four days of pretty hard and pretty hot driving but interesting at that. I must admit that I will not be unglad to sit for a few days without fighting traffic which in Italy at least is awful. But I managed to get an European rythm (*sic*) so that I can handle traffic very well, I think.

We are kind of tired but will go out tonight to see the dancing in the streets.

July 14,

We did go out but not for so very late. The main celebration is for tonight.

I have just learned a sad thing which bothers me very much. The presents for Catbird's birthday did not arrive, indeed have never arrived. They are in New York finally. Of course Gwyn never let me know about it. She is a lovely girl. I had written him that they would surely arrive, and then they didn't. I'm going to have them sent to camp but it isn't like having them on your birthday, especially if they have been promised. Nobodies fault. I got them off a month early and every thing misfired. . . . Now Tom's birthday is on the second and I don't want the same thing to happen there. It is August second. The boys are at Maranacook, Readfield, Maine. Gwyn never told me. I had to get the information from Elizabeth Otis. Will you please buy for him some things and get

---

* Because of Steinbeck's travels and because of his marital situation, his son John was well below grade-school age when he first began to attend summer camp.

them off so that they will surely be there for his birthday?
It would be awful if I missed both of them. I want as his
main present a simple little box camera which is very easy to
operate and a dozen rolls of film. Then I want about ten
dollars worth of the things you have for birthdays, poppers,
baloons (*sic*), horns, celebration things. I will reimburse you as
soon as you get back. The camp Counseller is named Mr.
Stainback which is odd. I am going to write him and tell
him to expect the things for Catbird and also since I am sure
that you will do this I think I will tell him to hold the
package from you until Tom's birthday. Maybe since it is so
hard to make any contact this would be better. I have not
heard one word about nor from the boys. Gwyn will burn in
some hell for this I hope. I can imagine no greater crueltys (*sic*)
than the ones she practices so casually.

I want very much to get this off today. I will write you
further in a day or so. Will you please let me know that you will
be able to get the things for Tom? I'll be here about a week
and then I think I am going to England. Write me there
care of Heinemann and Sons or better call Elizabeth and she
will tell you the most recent address. Love and I'll probably
get another letter off to you tomorrow.

John

Charles A. Madison, former editor at the Henry Holt Company
(now part of Holt, Rinehart and Winston), said:

I have known about Covici since 1922, when he ran his
own bookstore in Chicago. I did not know him then, but
knew about him. I also knew about Covici and Friede. Covici
didn't have the money to start that firm, but (Donald)
Friede did. I knew Covici fairly well from the time he
joined Viking Press and brought Steinbeck with him. In
connection with Viking Steinbeck was his author and chief
author. Covici once invited me to his home, during the work on
East of Eden, and showed me his correspondence with
Steinbeck and the box which Steinbeck made for him, for the
manuscript of the book. Covici then spoke very freely about

East of Eden and about Steinbeck. Covici told me that he had to hold Steinbeck's hand during Steinbeck's marital troubles—with Steinbeck's first wife and then with his second, and later, even during his successful third marriage. Covici said that Steinbeck seemed unable to do anything by himself.[7]

In his next letter, Covici mentioned for the first time the project which Steinbeck had in the back of his mind—"your novel on Salinas." The novel, which was five years away from publication, was Steinbeck's *East of Eden,* the work he later considered his ultimate achievement. Steinbeck's early working title was *The Salinas Valley.*

July 17, 1947

Mr. John Steinbeck
Hotel Lancaster
7, Rue de Berri
Paris, France

Dear John,

And Baroness Maxwell lured you to her party for Lords and Ladies. Paris can do anything. Well, at least she's intelligent —she recognized Gwyn's sense of humor and reported that you are the most popular American writer in France. That was good.

The other day when I went to your house I found, in the yard, John Jr. and the Benchley youngster in a crib together and on the best of terms. Tom was in the swimming pool under the shower having a wonderful time. He couldn't be bothered with me at all. He was a very very busy young man.

Of course I was happy to hear that Capa and you will go to Russia. Whatever the outcome it will sharpen your pencil for your novel on Salina.

I just received a cable from Gwyn asking me to meet her at the airport on July 19th. It will be good to see her.

Affectionately,*

* The "Benchley youngster" was Peter Benchley, the son of novelist Nathaniel Benchley. Peter Benchley grew to become the author of the popular success, *Jaws.*

On July 26, Steinbeck wrote Covici from Stockholm and expressed the idea that he believed all his letters from Russia would be read by censors. He wrote:

> We leave on Monday for Moscow by plane. I imagine
> this is the last unlooked at letter you will get before
> I get home. For I haven't any doubt that our friends will read
> my mail to try to fortell (*sic*) attitudes. And because I
> want to do the work, I shall write vaguely from there.

During Steinbeck's stay in Russia, he was able to send only three letters to Covici. His longest and most informative, was written from Kiev, August 11, 1947:

Dear Pat;

A short note anyway. We've been down here for a week and will stay until next Friday. It is a beautiful country and a beautiful city but it was brutally, insanely destroyed by the Germans. The rebuilding goes on everywhere but under the great difficulty of no machinery yet. My note book is getting very full and Capa is taking very many pictures, many of them fine I think. We are getting very fine material but I'm afraid the Hearst papers are not going to like it. These Ukranians are fine hospitable people with a beautiful sense of humor. I am getting down whole conversations with farmers and working people for fear I might forget them. We are very lucky to be able to come here. We have seen so many things.

Aug. 13—Just came in from a farm. Very good time and lots of information. Again my note book took a great jump. We are the first foreigners who have been in the country here in many years. They look at us in wonder for they have only heard of Americans and sometimes not too favorably. Fisher— now of Harpers came to Kiev . . . sat in the hotel, didn't go about the country nor talk to the people and then went home and wrote an authoritative book. These people resent that very much. I am keeping notes on many conversations. They are highly illuminating. The farmers and working people are a pleasure to talk to and even the necessity of talking through interpreters does not eliminate the salt of their speech. Also I am learning much about their farming and my own knowledge of agriculture at least allows me to ask intelligent questions. So far the trip is turning out very nicely. And if it continues at this rate we will have mountains of material.

Thank you so much for meeting Gwyn. She was really dead tired. Sea flights are exhausting. I've only had one letter but there will probably be others waiting in Moscow. I try to cable now and then to relieve her mind.

Day after tomorrow we go back to Moscow. Then to Stalingrad and probably on the river . . . to Georgia. Then back to Moscow for the celebration of the 800th anniversary of the founding of the city. We will come out through Prague. The Czech government has invited us. And we will be home as planned about the 1st of October.

I have no news of America. I don't know anything that is happening and it is rather nice. I couldn't change anything and it is good to be away from the turmoil for a while.

Here in Kiev we have a nice room in a very pleasant hotel and the people are very kind to us. I've met a number of Ukranian writers, dramatists and novelists and have seen some plays and a circus. I write to Gwyn every day but only send the letters about once a week. I hope she is getting them by now. It takes about 12 days by airmail. Why don't you drop me a note and let me know how things are going. Address c/o Joe Newman, Hotel Metropol, Moscow.

Evening is coming now. We are going to a symphony concert in the park on the cliff above the Dnieper. It should be very good. Playing Brahms and Prokofiev. I have a dreadful time with the spelling of Russian names and my language is limited to about 10 words, most of which have to do with drinking. Also some Ukranian words with the same basic values. I guess that is about all I have to say. I'm keeping all that happens in notes.

Please call Gwyn when you get this. I like her to hear from me as often as possible.

The time won't be very long until we will get home.

Only about six weeks. I'll be glad for a few days in Prague.
I have always wanted to see that city, which I have
heard is very beautiful.
     That's all Pat. Do drop me a line

love

John

By the end of the month, the strain of constant travel, strange food
and daily interviewing was beginning to show in Steinbeck's letters. On
August 25, he wrote Covici:

> We are surely getting what we came for but I am not quite
> sure what it is. I have many pages of notes which will have
> to be decifered. And Capa has hundreds of pictures. We'll
> just have to see what it amounts to. We are sticking to our first
> idea—people not politics.

And in the same letter, he added:

> We have been bumming around so much that anything
> larger than a suitcase seems like a duplex to me.

Covici finally answered (on 9 September, 1947):

> I needn't tell you how anxious I am to see what you are
> really getting out of your Russian observations. From
> your letters I can't quite make up my mind. It will be good to
> see you soon.

Thus Steinbeck returned from his Russian trip, as far removed
geographically and symbolically from his normal sphere of interest as
he ever traveled. From 1947 to 1952, he began a slow return to the
country and the subjects he loved and wrote about best, from the
publication of *Log from the Sea of Cortez* in 1951, to *East of Eden,*
in 1952.

IV

". . . THE GREATEST MAN I HAVE KNOWN AND THE BEST TEACHER"

September, 1947 to October, 1948

By late 1947 and early 1948, Steinbeck was becoming more and more preoccupied with *The Salinas Valley,* the early working title for *East of Eden.* From late 1947, through the publication of *East of Eden* in 1952, Steinbeck worked at it doggedly, and usually with great concentration. Although interrupted with death, divorce, other misfortunes and other writing projects, his novel, whether it was called *The Salinas Valley* or later *East of Eden,* weighed heavily upon him. On November 17, 1947, he wrote to his old college friend, Webster F. Street:

I have a great deal of work to do this year and I would like to get it all done by this summer because then I would like to stop everything to do a long novel that I have been working on the notes of for a long time. It seems to me that for the last few years I have been working on bits and pieces of things without much continuity and I want to get back to a long slow piece of work. I need to go out there for a lot of research so I may be out in California this summer. I'd be glad if I could for a little while. I'm living too hectic a life then so are you and so is everyone.[1]

He was, of course, referring to 1948, and shortly before moving to California, he wrote to the publisher of the *Salinas-Californian,* Paul Caswell:

New York
January 2, 1948
Dear Mr. Caswell;

I am gathering material for a novel, the setting of which is to be the region between San Luis Obispo and Santa Cruz, particularly the Salinas Valley; the time, between 1900 and the present.

An exceedingly important part of the research necessary will involve the files of the Salinas papers; will it be possible for me to consult those files? Do you know what has happened to the files of the Index-Journal and would it be possible for you to arrange my access to them?

I expect to be in Monterey soon after January 20th; could you let me know as soon as possible (by collect wire if necessary) if those files can be thrown open to me.

I will very much appreciate your help in this project.

Very truly yours,
John Steinbeck

Later, Caswell wired Steinbeck:

YOU ARE WELCOME TO SALINAS NEWSPAPER FILES.[2]

In late January, Steinbeck moved to California, to begin background research in the Salinas Valley, staying first at the Casa Munras, a hotel-cottage complex in Monterey. On February 4, 1948, Covici wrote to him there, with news on the on-going publication of *A Russian Journal:*

Mr. John Steinbeck
Casa Munras
Monterey, California

Dear John,

This Casa Munras sounds new to me. That isn't where I stayed, is it? It is good that you are there now; we have been having cold weather again and more snow. The weather man is promising snow and sleet and cold. I don't mind occasional cold weather but neither do I want to be a part of the North Pole.

So far I have seen nothing from Pravda. I imagine that they are waiting to see the complete book. I have had many calls from editors, publishers, etc., all keenly interested in your Tribune articles and anxious to get copies of the book. I think that it will be a good book. I saw the dummy with pictures in it and it is a beautiful job. The salesmen are now on the road and I am anxiously waiting to see the advance. It is going to be difficult I imagine to convince the bookseller that this is not just another book on Russia. Heaven knows they have had plenty that haven't sold. I shall keep you informed.

Please remember me to Ed and to your sister. And please let me hear from you.

Love,

A week later, Steinbeck wrote to Covici about his arrangements regarding the newspaper files:

I have been moving about out here not far from the base because of the heavy rains but in this neighborhood. And I've been to look at the Salinas papers and to talk to their owner who turns out to be a fine fellow and is even willing to let me take the files to New York where I can work over them at my leisure. I will photograph them there. This will give me much more time to go about the country here and to get reacquainted with things. Looking at the old papers and the immediacy one gets from reading say the daily dispatches from the Boer war if anything has increased my enthusiasm for this work. I had to give the Salinas paper an interview about the work. After all you cannot borrow these unique files without paying off some how. I haven't seen what they did with it.

Covici was pleased with Steinbeck's return to his native California, encouraging him to stay there, where the story could grow in his mind:

February 13, 1948

Mr. John Steinbeck
Casa Munras
Monterey, Calif.

Dear John,

Your last two letters sound very good, more like your old

self. I am happy that the story is getting hold of you, growing and expanding in your mind. It will be a great story, my spine tells me so and it never lies to me.

I was surprised to learn that THE PEARL sold over 2,000 copies in January. The book didn't move much during the holidays, as you know.

The first orders on THE RUSSIAN JOURNAL are coming in; they look good. It is too early of course, to say what the advance will be. The book stores are stocked to the gills with books on Russia. Yours is different and that will help.

Harold is leaving for southern California on Saturday for a rest. He needs it, for he hasn't been feeling well.

John, I hope that you stay in Monterey as long as possible, soak in all the sunshine and color and talk that you can. You will need it for the book and for your mind and body and soul.

We had dinner with Toni;[6] I enjoy her very much. She has a good mind and a good heart. The Palestinenian (sic) guy is still worrying her; she hasn't made up her mind yet and one can't advise her.*

Pleased with his background research and happy to be back in California, Steinbeck wrote quickly to Covici, on the 13th of February and later, on the 24th:

Dear Pat:

This is in the nature of a note and nothing else. All goes well here. I am getting a superb rest and getting things done too. The rain is over and the hills are turning green. I sleep about twelve hours every night and then go out and look at bushes. Went collecting the other morning and it was very fine. The owner of the Salinas paper is going to send the files

---

* Harold Guinzburg, president of The Viking Press; Toni Ricketts, divorced from Steinbeck's friend, Ed Ricketts, was on her way to Palestine, where she would make a new life.

to me to New York little by little. This is very good of him
inasmuch as the files are unique and there are no copies. I
am having a box made for the volumes now so that they can
go and come by express. Then I will have plenty of leisure
to work on them and it leaves me more time here to run about
the country.

I have been seeing people I haven't seen for years. Things
do not change so much. People erode and there are some
new buildings but on the whole there is not much of a change.
And the hills don't change. This is sea monster time. One
has been reported in the bay again, that same Old Man of the
Sea I wrote about. I would like to see him myself some
time. Lots of people have seen him.

I'm not thinking much about the book, just getting myself
thoroughly exposed to the background for it. I'll get into
it when it comes time to write it. I have been checking one
thing that is very interesting. I look up something in the files
of the paper and then ask an old timer what happened. And it is
as I suspected, the old timer is very inaccurate. Sometimes
his memory doesn't remotely resemble the actual event. My
research motto is Never Trust an Old Timer. I guess that is all
for now. Keep me posted on events.

so long jon

On the 24th, he wrote:

Arrangements have finally been made for the photographing
of the Salinas papers which will give me as fine a reference
library on the daily history of a community as it is possible to
have. The oblique information in these old papers is
enormous in addition to the direct information. I have now
checked the storys of old timers against the reports of the
papers of the time and I find that old timers are almost
invariably wrong not only in their information but in their
attitudes. Time is the most violent changer of people. I've
been into the river beds now and on the mountains and I've
walked through the fields and picked the little plants. In other
words I have done just exactly what I came out here to do. What

will come out of it I don't know but I do know that it will
be long. There is so much, so very much. I've got to make it
good, hell I've got to make it unique. I'm afraid I will have to
build a whole new kind of expression for it. And maybe go
nuts doing it—and pay the price for doing it and climb on it and
tromp on it and get my nose rubbed in it. I hope I have the
energy to do it and without accidents I think I have. The
yellow pads will catch hell for the next few years and nobody better try to rush me because I will not rush this one.
I'll make a living at something else while I am doing it. But
its the whole nasty bloody lovely history of the world, that's
what it is with no boundaries except my own inabilities. So
there.

The country is drying up as badly as the time I wrote
about it to a god unknown. It is the same kind of drouth that
used to keep us broke all the time when I was growing up.

I guess that is all. I just wanted to send you a report.

jn *

Steinbeck returned to New York in April, and from there he described his novel-in-progress to Ed Ricketts:

I am practicing for the novel very hard and I think I am
getting some place. I do not want to start it until I am pretty
sure that I have what I want in style and method but I
am gradually getting through to the light. It is going to be
bitterly resented by critics and the reader starting it may
have some kind of hard going until he gets used to it but I do
think that once he does, most other things might seem a little
pale and bloodless. Anyway I am excited by the experiment.

It will be a hell of a long experiment though, nearly half a
million words and by far the most ambitious book I have
ever attempted. God help us all, we go on trying to climb that

* Steinbeck always wrote his work on yellow legal pads. End papers on the
first edition of *Journal of a Novel: The East of Eden Letters* (New York: The
Viking Press, 1969), show samples of Steinbeck's handwriting on his yellow pads.
That work reveals Steinbeck's fixation with the absolutely right kind of yellow
pads and the perfect pencil to write with.

miserable mountain and it is always higher than the last rise we scrabbled onto. It seems to me that I have more than I can do and its frightens me sometimes until I think how it would be if I had less than I can do.[3]

And, on April 29, he wrote to Bo Beskow, a Swedish friend:

You are right. I am on my marathon book, which is called Salinas Valley. It is what I have been practicing to write all of my life. Everything else has been training. I feel that I am about ready to write it. It will take maybe three years to write and it is going to be the best that I have learned and a lot that I have never even indicated. . . . I wouldn't care if it took all the rest of my life if I got it done. It is going to take enormous energy.[4]

Then, on May 11, 1948, when Steinbeck was least expecting it, Ed Ricketts, a major influence in his life, was killed in an accident. On his way home from work at his lab, he drove his car onto the tracks of the Southern Pacific railroad, just in time to be hit by the on-coming Del Monte Express. Ricketts suffered massive internal injuries and died three days later. Ricketts was, in many ways, as important in Steinbeck's career as was Pascal Covici or Elizabeth Otis.

Later, in *The Log From The Sea of Cortez,* Steinbeck wrote of Ricketts:

Knowing Ed Ricketts was instant. After the first moment I knew him, and for the next eighteen years I knew him better than I knew anyone, and perhaps I did not know him at all. Maybe it was that way with all his friends. He was different from anyone and yet so like that everyone found himself in Ed. and that might be one of the reasons his death had such an impact. It wasn't Ed who had died but a large and important part of oneself.

It took Steinbeck a long time to get over the actual event of the death of his close friend and perhaps he never really got over the loss of his collaborator; Ricketts was his philosophical conscience as well as the basis for a number of characters in his novels. Steinbeck himself admitted to using him as the character of "Doc" in *Cannery Row* (and then subsequently in a sequel, *Sweet Thursday*), and he wrote about it in "About Ed Ricketts," in *The Log From the Sea of Cortez:*

> I used the laboratory and Ed himself in a book called *Cannery Row.* I took it to him in typescript to see whether he would resent it and to offer to make any changes he would suggest. He read it through carefully, smiling, and when he finished he said, "Let it go that way. It is written in kindness. Such a thing can't be bad."

To his Swedish friend, Bo Beskow, Steinbeck wrote:

> You see, Ed Ricketts' car was hit by a train, and after fighting for his life for three days he died, and there died the greatest man I have known and the best teacher. It is going to take a long time to reorganize my thinking and my planning without him. . . .
> Naturally this changes all of my plans about the summer and about nearly everything except my big book. . . . As to the immediate future, I don't know. I may do a picture of the life of Emiliano Zapata if I can find someone to do it honestly.[5]

And to early friends, Ritchie and Natalya Lovejoy, he wrote:

> Impact is not sharp now—all dulled out. It would be interesting if we all flew apart now like an alarm clock when you pry off the mainspring with a screw driver. Wouldn't it be interesting if Ed *was* us and that now there wasn't any such thing or that he created out of his own mind something that went away with him. I've wondered a lot about that. How much was Ed and how much was me and which was which.[6]

In early June, Steinbeck made one trip to Mexico, to research the life of Emiliano Zapata. He had changed course and decided to make the Zapata project his next work, and to delay, at least in part, *The Salinas Valley.* He made a return trip to New York to clear up his life there, then returned again to Mexico. By that time, he had confided to Pat Covici the second major blow in 1948: that his marriage to Gwyndolyn was breaking up.

Covici tried as best he could, at long distance, to explain Steinbeck's emotions to him. Covici had occasion to aid and comfort others of his authors, during marital problems.* It took Steinbeck many months to get over the separation (and eventual divorce) from Gwyn.[8] Covici's urgings for a "quick clean-up . . ." were not possible for Steinbeck.

July 29, 1948

Mr. John Steinbeck
Marik Hotel
Cuernavaca, Mexico

Dear John,

This is just a note to tell you about my friend who has just returned to Mexico. She is an author and a journalist, very intelligent and charming, at least I find her so. What is more important she seems to know a great deal about Zapata and where unknown documents can be had. She mentioned one Pepe Valades who has many unknown documents. It may be worth your while to talk to her. You can telephone her between 7 and 8 P.M. at 12-19-60, or between 9 and 10 A.M. at 13-61-84. Her name and address are Magdalena Mondragon, Edison 84A, Mexico, D.F.

I hope while you are in Mexico that you will do some tall thinking and wake up to yourself and your own peace of mind. It isn't simple, nor is it pleasant to look at the smashed pieces of something that you wanted to build and have. You may live a minute longer and then again you may go on for another 40 years. It seems to me that a quick clean-up is the less painful, and a sober realization of what is sterling and what is not is creating values that one must have.

I shall be in Hollywood from August 1st to August 11th at the Hollywood-Roosevelt Hotel.

Love,

By the fall of the year, Steinbeck had moved into a small (three-

---

* Marshall Best, managing editor of The Viking Press, during the Covici-Steinbeck years, said that Covici let "two major living writers" share a spare bedroom in his New York apartment during periods of their marital problems, presumably Saul Bellow and Arthur Miller, both Covici authors.[7]

room) home in Pacific Grove, California, which his father had built before Steinbeck had been born. Steinbeck and his first wife had lived in the house years before and now he had not only the memories of their life in that house, he also had massive amounts of cleaning and repairing to do, which taxed his energy and yet kept him content. On September 12, he wrote to Covici:

Pacific Grove

September 12 [1948]

Dear Pat:

It is night and the low fog is down and the buoy is bellowing off the reef and it is very fine. I have a good fire going and no one is likely to come over tonight. I'm getting rested and working hard outside too. This whole place is a mess but in two weeks you won't know it. Garden will be cleaned and re-planted and the house will be painted inside and out. And during that time I do not intend to touch a pen to manuscript. My hands are getting calluses already. I don't know many people here any more and that is a good thing. It will be more time for working and reading. Oddly enough I do not feel lonely at all yet. I know I will soon enough. I know it will come like little fingers of ice but not so far except once or twice a kind of blind panic. However, that is perfectly natural and would happen to anyone.

This house is also almost completely without furniture. Various non-rent paying tenants have seen to that. I don't need very much but some I guess I must have. I have a bed (new) my old work chairs and a card table to write on and that is all I actually need. It will cost something to paint this house but that will be all right too. I have to buy everything for it—even pots and pans and knives and forks but Wool-worth still lives, thank god. I remember how Carol used to be afraid I would get loose in Woolworth's with five hot dollars in my pocket. It was a nightmare thought to her. She never got used to it.

This garden needs peat moss and fertilizer and needs it badly and it is going to get it too. It is going to be a very pretty garden if I can make it so. It is getting late now. I've kind of nodded away the evening. And I have to get up early tomorrow because then the work starts. But I wanted to get a note off to you.

bye
John

Covici responded as if he could speak to Steinbeck in person and these letters to and from Covici remained Steinbeck's closest link with the outside world. He did not correspond with anyone else as much during this emotional-recovery period. Covici again explained to Steinbeck:

September 15, 1948

Mr. John Steinbeck
147-11th Street
Pacific Grove, Calif.

Dear John,

It was very good to hear from you for many reasons. What delighted me most is the air of strength and determination not to kid yourself. You have a tall task to perform with yourself, and you are doing it with philosophical cheer and large mindedness. With your feet in the soil and your head in the mist you are conjuring up the stars. Reading between the lines, however, I can also feel the pain and agony that will be yours. Waves of loneliness and depression will also be yours. Nevertheless, there is a feeling of exaltation in you too, a sense of freedom and an aching need to shape things to your own desire.

You make me feel useless when you tell me of things you are doing with the house and garden. Of course I am not much of a painter, nor can I fashion things with lumber, but I could help you with the garden. I would love it. When I come out I shall take charge of the garden.

We had a lovely evening with Beth.* She is so honest and forthright. You are never in doubt about her. She is generous and full of compassion and she loves you very much.

No news here that you don't know, but will write again.

Love,

* Steinbeck's sister.

On September 19, Steinbeck wrote to Covici:

Dear Pat:

You are right—I do get the horrors every now and then.
Comes on like a cold wind. There it is, just a matter of weather-
ing it. Alcohol doesn't help that a bit. I usually go into the
garden and work hard.

At that moment Ritch and Tal Lovejoy came in for a
cup of coffee and then I watered the garden and here it is dusk.
A very quiet Sunday and I've enjoyed it. My hands are
literally tired from moving rocks. And it is a fine feeling.

It has been one of the dark days that I like very well—
overcast and almost cold except that flowers like it and seem
to be on fire in such a light. I think flowers' colors are brighter
here than anyplace on earth and I don't know whether it is
the light that makes them seem so or whether they really are.

I debated strongly about whether to dress and go out to
dinner or whether to cook something and stay home in quiet
and determined on the latter.

So I'll close and I will send you more reports.

Covici again wrote and sketched his feelings about personality, which
Steinbeck would read and think over. Marshall Best has observed:

One type of editor can help an author contribute to what
the author is able to do or wants to do. It can be because the
editor is a good literary man and makes suggestions about
how to word his writing, (or) how to edit his copy. Or the
editor can be such a good person with the author that he
makes the author feel better and gives him the possibilities of
feeling freer to express himself in his writing.

Covici, Best added, was very much the second type of editor.[9]
Covici's empathy toward Steinbeck during Steinbeck's personal crisis
is seen in his letter of September 23, 1948:

Mr. John Steinbeck
147-11th Street
Pacific Grove, Calif.

Dear John,

I am glad Neale * is with you. He is a good man and will
be of great help. You are doing better than I had hoped. In
fact you are doing remarkably. It is difficult to get rid of poison
which has permeated your whole body and mind for so long.
You could never say No to any second-rater who forced himself
upon you. It is not difficult to analyze. By nature shy and
retiring and almost uncommunicative, you never would go out
of your way to meet the people of your choice but the second-
raters, who never wait, forced themselves on you and you,
being also very compassionate and human, made easy com-
panions of them when at heart you really didn't want them and
much preferred to be alone. In other words, you had plenty of
bastards and bitches clinging on to you. Your secretary I
understand is also claiming your soul, the little bitch. Just because you are a writer doesn't mean you have to be milked.
There are two places that have proved poisonous for you—
Hollywood and New York. As far as you are concerned they
are good to visit but not to take to heart.

All last week Dorothy† and I were busy getting Pascal
ready for Harvard. We have just received a letter from him,
very cheerful and he seems satisfied that he will like it there.
So that worry is over.

I had lunch with Arthur Miller yesterday, whose play I
read the night before. It looks like a winner. He has already
started on his novel and hopes to have it ready in the late Fall
of 1949. When I told him that you are back in California on
your own home ground he exclaimed, "Wonderful, the best

---

* Steinbeck's houseboy-valet. Steinbeck has described him as "Neale, my
fine man . . . a good man and will keep me fed and washed and clean. I've
had him quite a long time. Ex-navy, C.P.O., colored and very intelligent, excellent driver, cook, valet and damn good friend. He will stay with me as long
as he wants to."

† Covici's wife.

thing he ever did. Now he'll go back to his writing and that is great." Arthur is a very perspicacious young man. He wants to be remembered to you.

Well, this will do for the day. I'll write again soon. Love, and remember me to Neale.[10]

Steinbeck replied:

You are right, I can't even hire a secretary without getting the bite. I think this jewel was the worst I have ever come across though. She is so obviously on the make. . . . I will write you a sizeable letter just the moment the dust and dirt are out of the house and I haven't a gritty feeling of plaster dust on me.

Later, Steinbeck's sister Beth visited him, which pleased Covici. Covici suggested that Steinbeck's writing would be the best therapy for his emotional unhappiness, during this period:

October 6, 1948

Mr. John Steinbeck
147-11th Street
Pacific Grove, California

Dear John,

I was glad to hear that Beth was with you. Besides being keen in human understanding, sympathetic and compassionate, she has a great deal of common sense and unflinchingly honest. You could do worse than listen to her.

It will be good when you finish putting your house in order and settle down and enjoy it. You won't feel like working until then. When you say that you don't give a darn that you have done no writing, that means that you are worried. You shouldn't. You forget that it takes time to make so drastic a change as you have undertaken. It was a god-send not only that you had a home to go to but that you were kept busy cleaning and fixing it up to your own desire and that you can really call it your own, every inch of it. So don't expect to do any writing until your house completely covers you and you

have plenty of native dust in your eyes. You have a great
deal to shed and you will never shed all of it, and it won't be
pleasant. But between pain and exaltation you will go back to
your writing and find it good.

You remember that convict novelist that woman wrote you
about? I received his manuscript the other day and Bob Ballou
just told me that the first 100 pages are good. Maybe we have
something but I doubt it very much.

I would greatly enjoy seeing a snapshot of your house
and garden or a sketch of it if you can do it. Maybe Neale can.

Love,*

Covici was a remarkable man because he so carefully and deliberately was able to catalogue Steinbeck's personality. When he had to be,
Covici was an excellent counsellor, who was able to explain to Steinbeck the moral and psychological consequences of Steinbeck's own behavior. Thus, Covici's remark to Charles A. Madison, "Steinbeck seemed
unable to do anything by himself." Covici's ability to chart Steinbeck's
personality and guide him through the swamps of Steinbeck's own mind
can be seen again and again, throughout their relationship, when Covici
must write Steinbeck and present Steinbeck with an accurate analysis of
Steinbeck's own behavior—and moral choices.

---

* Bob Ballou was the publisher Robert O. Ballou, who published Steinbeck's *To a God Unknown,* in 1933. When Ballou's publishing house went
under, (before Covici's), he also joined The Viking Press, but he became a consulting editor and reader, instead of a staff editor, as Covici did.

The book by the convict which Ballou was reading and reporting on was
ultimately rejected by Covici and The Viking Press.

V

"... I'M FREE. SHE'S GONE. SHE'S OUT OF ME.
OH. CHRIST ALMIGHTY, I'M FREE."

October, 1948 to January, 1949

Throughout the rest of 1948, Steinbeck worked quietly at his old home in Pacific Grove, slowly mending spiritually from the separation from Gwyn and the death of Ed Ricketts which especially hurt him. On October 18, he wrote to Covici, in part:

The last of the paint is on now and the place is finished except of course for the endless little things that I am always making. But that is a good kind of work and I like it. My vines will be coming up soon and in a short time no one will recognize this place. It is so changed already that people hardly do but its essential character has not changed. In a way I wish I didn't have to go* but I guess it is good. I will be doubly glad to get back. The place has charm and pace. Maybe I am kidding myself but I don't really think so. I think I can spend good times here if it is permitted me. And it costs very little to operate now that the cost of fixing it up is about over.

I can't get the good legal pads here that I got in New York. This paper absorbs a little ink and the others did not. Can you get me a few of the yellow pads? I go through them so fast.

I have not worked on the Salinas Valley. I don't want to now until everything is clear because I think I am about

* He was planning to go to Mexico to do research for *Viva Zapata.*

ready for it and I'm letting it stew. It would be bad if the whole conception turned out no good. But I'll do it anyway. I am really looking forward to the doing of it. Good or bad.

I miss Ed and I don't all at the same time. It is a thing that is closed—that might possibly have been closed anyway. Who can tell? Great changes everywhere and every which way. I still get the panic aloneness but I can work that out by thinking of what it is. And it is simply the breaking of a habit which was painful in itself but we hold onto habits even when we don't like them. A very senseless species. There is no future in us I'm afraid. I can hear the music beginning[1] to turn in my head. And by the time the spring comes I hope I will be turning with it like a slow and sluggish dervish or some mushroom Simon Stylites, a fungus on a stone pillar. I'm taking an uncommonly long time with this letter which isn't a letter at all.

So long

John

Later in 1948 in an undated letter, he wrote Covici:

Dear Pat:

The week I've put in planting—things I'll probably never see flower—either because I won't be here or I won't be looking. I have no sense of permanence. This is a way stopping place, I think, as every other place is. I've made my tries at "places" and they don't work. But this is a good way stopping place and a good one to come back to—often.

I awakened the other night with a great sense of change happening somewhere. Could not sleep any more and all night the sense of change, neither pleasant nor unpleasant but happening. It hung on for several days. Gradually my energy is coming back a little at a time. It is so strange that I could lose it so completely. One never knows what he will do ever.

Just now the rain started, very gentle and good. I hope it rains a long time. There has never been enough.

I'm sorry I was so closed in, in New York. But I realized more than any time in my whole life that there is nothing anyone can do. It's something that has to be done alone. Even with women, and that's good, there is largely no companionship except for a very little while.

This has been a bleak day.

Covici returned Steinbeck's letters, and suggested strongly that Steinbeck accept the consequences of his own behavior and begin again his novel, which was his first priority.

October 25, 1948

Mr. John Steinbeck
147-11th Street
Pacific Grove, Calif.

Dear John,

Your last two letters were full of cheery news. Your little house is almost done and you are satisfied. You want to live in it and also work there. You also note the growing of new cells and tissue. Of course you do. The reason you note them is because you are healthier and more on the normal side. We don't change at bottom. No logic and thinking ever changes our fundamental existence. You will do what you have to do and suffer what you have to suffer. We are neither free nor slaves. We are both. We do make choices of course, but don't they depend partly on our dispositions and partly on our imminent needs?

I hope you won't have to stay in Mexico too long and that you will finish your movie script shortly. You want to go back to your main interest. The novel is taking hold of you and you will have to do it. The shape and form it takes does not matter. Many beginnings you will throw away and start all over again. It will come never fear—it always does with you.

I would very much like to be with you and enjoy your little house. Maybe when you are well along in your work and you want me to listen to your tale or walk the fields with you, I shall want to come.

Love,

But Steinbeck soon received another shock. In late October, 1948, Gwyn journeyed to Reno for her final divorce decree, which Steinbeck did not contest. While there, she met a man in a casino, went with him to his home, and was there when he attempted suicide. The ensuing scandal rocked Steinbeck, and Covici did all he could, from New York, to dispel Steinbeck's black depression about the situation, which neither he nor Steinbeck could control in any way:

October 27, 1948

Mr. John Steinbeck
147-11th Street
Pacific Grove, Calif.

Dear John,

At first the news about Gwyn and gambling and suicide shocked me. Of course I am still disturbed and so are you. Thinking it over calmly and dispassionately it is an unfortunate break for Gwyn. It could have happened to any one of us. To visit a gambling place in Reno isn't anything unusual and to be taken home by a fellow traveller is no crime. That he should have shot himself the very night he took her home is, to say the least, startling and unfortunate but it could have happened, as I said, to anybody. I am not trying, God knows, to exonerate her but you will have to steel yourself to other happenings, heaven knows what. You are not responsible for her and you cannot allow yourself to go to pieces because of what she does or whatever happens to her. Of course it will hurt you and perturb you, but you can't give all your life to her, or anybody else for that matter.

This is unfortunate but you can expect anything at all and there is certainly nothing that you can do about it. The sooner you realize that you have your own life to live the saner you will be.

Love,[2]

After the divorce from Gwyndolyn became final, Steinbeck wrote to Covici:

Nov. 1

Dear Pat:

Well that is over, at least for the time being. It was a rough time and of course there will be other messes. But I'll be rested by then. Thanks for your letters. They helped. I'm leaving for Hollywood tomorrow and for Mexico on Friday. And I plan to be back here not later than the first of December to spend winter and spring and summer if I can. I'm pretty much relaxed. I think things have been about as disgusting and nasty as they can get and they didn't kill me. There is one more bit of terror but I'll face that when it is necessary and for the first time I will call the tune on that. But it won't be for a while I hope. I wish I could thoroughly believe that this is to be a new leaf. I wish I could be sure I have learned something. I am not sure of either. But I can try. At least if I try it again there will be a shudder of apprehension. I guess that is as much as I can expect. There will be more and more messes and finally the last mess. But I feel detached. Gwyn once told me she could do anything and I would come crawling back. At the time I was very much in love with her but even then I told her not to depend on it. A woman holds dreadful powers over a man who is in love with her but she should realize that the quality and force of his love is the index of his potential contempt and hatred. And nearly no women or men realize that. We will not mention this again in a post mortem sense. Only if it becomes active will it be necessary. I think I am getting strength back—perhaps more than I have had in 17 years and perhaps more than I ever had. I don't know. I just feel that it might be so. We shall see. I want the hot words to come out again and hiss on the paper and I think they may. My needs are filled. God help the others! Having seen treachery they will never trust themselves or each other. What a curse to carry. Even if it is not there they will be looking for it always. There is a species chuckle in this. The cells are laughing and the cortex and the inevitable flow of the veins and vessles that ceaselessly feed the impulses toward the unchangeable future. And I do not feel like laughing.

In Mexico City I will be at the Hotel Prince and a little later I will be at the Hotel Marik in Cuernavaca. I hope you will write to me there. I thank you for the fine bale of yellow pads. I shall make good use of them I hope. And on your next trip out here I will get you drunk on red wine and music and the old ghosts we have neglected will walk again and wail on the wet rocks. This is a time of change and maybe destruction but the waves and the tide will not change no matter how much we blast or are blasted. The black roots of the little species may put out new leaves. It is about time. There has been nothing created for a long time. Matter is creative, that we have known and studied but we have forgotten that the grey lobes in the head are creative too—the only and unique creative thing in the whole world of our seeing and hearing and touching.

A lot of high flown language but let it flow. Never again does it have to stoop to critics, or friends or lovers. It can be good or as silly as it can be, not wise and smart and little.

And that's all for now. I will write to you from Mexico. I'm working on the life of a very great man but primarily a man. It would be good to study him closely. His life had a rare series—beginning, middle and end and most lives dribble away like piss in the dust.

I'll be talking to you soon.

affectionately

John[3]

Covici's next letter reveals how well he had read Steinbeck's personality. Covici's uncharacteristic ". . . when you paint your house or weed a garden with *some Mexican or other lowly person* at your side . . ." is perhaps more indicative of Steinbeck's view than Covici's. Steinbeck had written of Mexicans in *Tortilla Flat*, while Covici had no immediate experience with Mexicans; Covici traveled west infrequently and spent little time in California. Thus he appears to be speaking Steinbeck's prejudices, not any of his own. Covici exhibits a substantial amount of cynicism in this letter: "Kiss them and kick them out . . ." and exhibits strong loyalty to Steinbeck in his comments about Gwyn.

November 15, 1948

Mr. John Steinbeck
Hotel Marik
Cuernavaca, Mor., Mexico

Dear John,

Your last letter from P.G. was the first real indication of your returning strength and stirring dormant power. Whatever was ill-tempered about it was welcome to me. You are best when you do the things you know best. You often stray in alien places. You can't always help that because of your restless and creative spirit. When done with one thing you must immediately tangle up with something else, whether it's writing or other things. I only know that when you paint your house or weed a garden with some Mexican or other lowly person at your side and you talk of many things, something passes through you, something deep and human is communicated to your soul and becomes part of your book and it is great. Nothing in the movie medium will give you that satisfaction. No matter how much you love your Zapata, when you see it on the screen I doubt whether you will be satisfied. The same is true about the stage or Broadway. Nevertheless, I don't suppose that you can keep on writing books all of the time, but neither can you rest between times.

There wouldn't be any reason for any new messes if you weren't such a Puritan at heart and you wouldn't take your love affairs so seriously. Why not play around for two or three years? Kiss them and kick them out—you could do it more gently, of course—but don't make the promise everlasting in sickness or in health, or whatever they call it. Whether you will ever find one with whom you will want to mate for life is doubtful but ever hopeful—I hope you choose just to be hopeful for some time.

Gwyn called me a few days ago telling me that she is back and well and that the children are also well. She just wanted to know how I am and would like to see me some time and that she would call me. Frankly, I hope she doesn't as I have nothing to say to her and I am sure she has nothing to say to me that I care to know. She will try, I am sure, to gather around her all your friends and hers, too. She will find out sooner or later that she can't do it, with few exceptions.

Love,

But Steinbeck couldn't handle Mexico at that period in his life; he wrote to Covici briefly, "The bloom is off Mexico for me right now. All the people I knew are gone and in every way it is a sad place." Covici had to write to Steinbeck again, in Pacific Grove, in a futile attempt to discover what Steinbeck wanted to do:

November 17, 1948

Mr. John Steinbeck
147-11th Street
Pacific Grove, Calif.

Dear John,

Right after I airmailed my letter to you to Mexico I had lunch with Mildred* who told me of your sudden flight back to Pacific Grove. This lunch was in celebration of your emancipation, or at least we call it so—you probably wouldn't. At any rate, we drank to your health and well being, and most of all to your peace of mind, since you have very little of that.

Mildred is very hopeful about you. You have done remarkably well she said, considering the tight squeezes and heartaches you have experienced. She is right, of course, but she doesn't realize that we all are a bit masochistic and in a sort of subversive way we enjoy the pain we often inflict

---

* Mildred Lyman—a staff member of McIntosh and Otis.

on ourselves. You are not indulging I know and you have
work to do which, too, is painful, but the after effects are
almost pure exaltation.

I am anxious for you to tell me what your program is,
even if it still is somewhat nebulous.

A week later, in an uncharacteristic letter, it was Covici who expressed thoughts of depression and worldweariness:

The holidays are nearing and the idea depresses me. As
I grow older to be with people scares me, drives me into a
shell and I long to be alone. I don't think I love people less
but I am more easily irritated. It is possible also that I am
less satisfied with myself and subconsciously wish to hide. I
don't know. If it weren't for Pascal's coming home for
Christmas I'd fly to the coast and spend a couple of days
with you. I know that you will be lonesome for your family
and that you will have plenty of heartaches.

Did you ever get the letter I sent you to Mexico?

Commenting on Covici, Thomas Guinzburg, who succeeded his
father as president of The Viking Press, has said: "He was an extraordinary guy—he was some part psychiatrist, some part lawyer, some
part priest. . . . Covici didn't work on books, he worked on people.
He fought for his people, inside and outside the publishing house."[4]

Whether Covici was seriously depressed by the forthcoming holidays (he had not mentioned such depression in other years) or whether
he was attempting to distract Steinbeck, it worked. In his next letter,
29 November 1948, Steinbeck wrote:

Your letter sounded sad. And I hope you are not sad.
I wish you could come out for a while and you might before
too long. I did Thanksgiving very well but Xmas I will not
try: I will get a gallon of wine and the prettiest girl I can
find and I will forget Christmas this year. I don't see any
reason for ritual nonsense if it is painful and no good can
be accomplished by it.

The next week Steinbeck was informed that he had been elected to The American Academy of Arts and Letters. He replied:

I am extremely sensible of the honor paid me by the Academy in making me a member. Having been blackballed from everything from the Boy Scouts to the United States Army, this election is not only a great experience but for me a unique one. My most profound thanks.

Yours sincerely,
John Steinbeck[5]

Steinbeck's long, self-analytic letters to Covici continued throughout December:

Dec. 6 (1948)

Dear Pat:

Very quiet week and even a quiet weekend. I don't go out very much. Maybe not enough. Anyway I finished the introduction to my script today and I can start the dramatic action tomorrow if it comes and I will try to make it. Sometimes the evenings are very long but I go out less and less. I am living almost as I did at Lake Tahoe,* seeing nearly no one. It is a kind of laziness, I guess. And it can grow to be bad. But there is no one I want to see. I have not established a bed relationship with any one girl as yet. There are several and at irregular intervals. I would like to keep it that way. There are several nice things about this way of living—I can sleep or not, eat or not, read or not exactly when I want to. And if it is a lonely life, it is not nearly as lonely as the one I have been living for the past three years. That was real loneliness. I hope I never have that kind again.

Starting the script sequence, I have all of the old terrors. Perhaps the very length of the introduction was an unconscious attempt to put off the dramatic action until later.

* Steinbeck spent from 1926-1928 at or near Lake Tahoe, when he began his writing career, including the first drafts of his *Cup of Gold.*

But the introduction was really necessary. They had to know what I was talking about. I hope I have made it clear. And tomorrow I flog myself into the opening scene. And if I do it well it can be quite a scene. I hope I can do it well.

I had dinner a little while ago and afterwards a hot bath and it is still only 8:30. There is good music playing and I should want for nothing. And I don't want much. I weeded part of my garden today and put in a few bushes. I will fill the garden with fushias *(sic)* and make them grow into trees. They do so well here and they are in many varieties— all colors and shapes. I will fill the garden with them and let the other things go. There can be every color combination imaginable in that one flower and they go on year after year.

It is rather odd that I have not run into Carol, not even in the street. Of course I do not go out very much but even then it is odd. I am not avoiding nor otherwise. I have no feeling about it. Of course if there were a party and I knew she would be there I would not go because Carol drunk is formidable and there is no reason to take it. One day while drinking she decided to come over and I was warned but she lost her nerve I guess. She is supposed to be going to France to do nursing at which I am told she became proficient during the war. I think it would satisfy her lusting for power to have sick men dependent on her. I am told that when she washed them, they bled.

I hear from people who have seen them that my children are fine and growing like weeds. I look forward so to seeing them this summer.[6]

I didn't really have anything to write about. Duke Sheffield* was down last weekend. He has not changed. His is a very little mind. I had forgotten how small. He is still picking at pronounciations and grammatical excellences. In many ways he has the qualities of a mediaeval schoolman. And he does not change only it seems to me that his horizons have narrowed. I find that I don't like him. Perhaps I never did. So many people I thought I liked when I was only sorry

---

* An undergraduate friend at Stanford University.

for them. And that is enough of this wandering.

affectionately,

John

Covici again encouraged Steinbeck to turn to *The Salinas Valley*. Steinbeck went through periods of depression, and he had to be encouraged by Covici. In *Irving to Irving* Charles Madison writes: "Aware of Steinbeck's tendency to depression, Covici wrote him strongly encouraging letters and telegrams in an effort to bolster his fluctuating self-confidence. Steinbeck deeply appreciated these warm and reassuring missives." This period of late 1948 to early 1949, was one of Steinbeck's darkest:

December 9, 1948

Mr. John Steinbeck
147-11th Street
Pacific Grove, Calif.

Dear John,

I read your last letter over and over again. I think that you have gone a long way in adjusting yourself, not that the heartaches and mental perturbations have left you— they never will—but you can, to some extent, philosophize about them and almost half regretfully pigeon-hole them, even if you never forget them. Environment does modify man and, happily, you are on native ground and the changes are not foreign to you and surely most welcome.

It is good that you are working again and with a great deal less disturbance than heretofore. I know of your keen interest in ZAPATA and I hope with all my heart that the result will be as great as your enthusiasm. I have every reason to believe that it will be so. I can't, however, help but wish it speed so that you can begin on your Salinas Valley. I think of it as your major work. I haven't mentioned the book to you since you left New York, but lately I have been scrutinizing your letters in the hope of seeing some mention of it. Your last letter made me at least feel that you are

turning toward it. Sometimes we fear to do what we
ultimately best do.

Gene Fowler is coming to New York right after Christmas
to do some cutting and editing on his manuscript, BEAU
JAMES. The portrait of Jimmy Walker is done with a certain
flamboyancy, but the story makes interesting reading and
the writing is lively.

Where are my pictures of the house and the rock
garden? Has Neale broken his camera?

Affectionately,

Just before Christmas, Steinbeck again wrote to Covici, this time
apologizing for the lack of Christmas presents; Steinbeck had already
received holiday presents from the Covici family:

I'm sorry though because I am sending no Xmas
(presents) except to the kids. I can't. I am absolutely broke
and probably will be for some time to come. I may have to
get a woman to support me. That would be a change.[7]

Covici never used any sort of profanity in his letters to Steinbeck
and he almost never "lectured" to him in any paternal sense. But the
following letter is as close as Covici ever got to being disturbed at his
friend's personal and financial behavior:

December 21, 1948

Mr. John Steinbeck
147-11th Street
Pacific Grove, Calif.

Dear John,

We have had more than 19 inches of snow, but the City
seems to have done a very good job and traffic is moving.
It is warmer today and the snow is beginning to melt and
it is bound to be most unpleasant.

Indeed, I know you are broke. I checked up your
February statement and I couldn't believe it. You will have

to start all over again and you will, and I am sure there is nothing to worry about. Only it is a shame to have pissed away two fortunes in so short a time. That's the stuff that life is made of I suppose and with a few other ingredients, good or bad.

I have been wondering whether you haven't too much time on your hands. Why don't you take your jeep and go on some long expedition, through the mountains or over the hills and explore the countryside or circle the shores of your ocean and seek new animal life—something to divert and use up your extra energy? To my mind it would be perfect if you would, for instance, supervise some ranch and breed ponies or anything else that you like. All this may seem empty talk but I am groping for something I am convinced you need, but I am not so sure that what I am suggesting is at all practicable. Even if you were to spend six or seven hours working on your book you would still have plenty of time on your hands, and I know that you are restless and unhappy looking for something to do.

I have a package for Tom and John Jr. which Pascal will take over some time on Thursday. In Tom's package there are the Blue and Green fairy books edited by Andrew Lang. I want him to have the complete set one of these days.

Here's to better and happier days.

Love,[8]

Steinbeck celebrated Christmas of 1948 in Pacific Grove, visited by "a few people, old friends." He wrote to Covici on the 24th and 27th:

Dec. 24, '48

Dear Pat:

I have your letter today. Don't worry about me. I'll be all right as soon as this beastly year is over. Then I will get to work and all the nonsense will be over. Of course I am broke, maybe bankrupt but that doesn't make any difference. I don't need much myself and I don't have to worry about it. Or at least I shall refuse to worry about it. I have no sympathy if Gwyn's income drops because mine does. She not only killed the Goose but sold the feathers. And I am not a bit sorry if she cannot go to the Colony every night. As for the children, they do not need the things they are getting their Private schools and new shoes every four weeks and three dollar hair cuts. As a matter of fact they would be healthier in all ways in overalls and public schools. I am not being alone too much. I need to be alone quite a lot. That is the only way I can get some kind of confidence back. And for energy there is the traditional way and one I am not ignoring by any means. That would be better if there were some love involved with it but love or not it is a fine institution.

Meanwhile I have a scunner on this year and I will be much better when it is over.

Your very nice presents came and I thank you for them very much. I didn't want you to send anything. I didn't send anything to anyone except the children. But it is nice of you to remember.

The things you suggest for me to do are not practical. They would be forced and untrue. I will do only things that are natural. I saw a beautiful place down the coast and thought I would buy it when I could but almost at once decided that that was not natural and was just a repetition of what I have been doing for the last nearly twenty years, substituting things for feelings and I won't do it again. This little house is really all that I want.

Today, of course is the bitterest day of all. But it will be over soon. You can take anything if you are reasonably sure that there is an exit.

Thank you for everything Pat and please do not worry about it. Even if nothing worked out of it, it is just one thing among very many. Far from being unique, it is getting to be the commonest and corniest story in the world. And in a very little while it will not be bad.

love to you and Dorothy and Pascal and a good christmas

and a good year to follow to you all.*

Dec. 27

Dear Pat:

Well that's over and I'm glad. Now I will try to get to work again. And it is about time too. I feel pretty good today. The rain is over and the sun is out. I am getting my correspondence up to date and I will try to plunge into work tomorrow. I hope that this time it goes. I really think that Christmas was the main hazard. I just stayed home and quite a few people, old friends came by and that was all. I didn't feel like drinking and celebrating.

I have no details of my kids christmas. Marge Benchley† called and said that they had had a good time but that is all I have heard so far. Gwyn of course would not and will not write. Funny girl.

Lord we are really getting rain this year and the land is practically gurgling with joy. It will be beautiful.

You and Dorothy sent so much to me for Christmas that I am ashamed. But I must say the things were very welcome. I can now bathe myself and my mind.

I don't seem to have much anything to say today except that I hope you have a very fine year and that I will be seeing you amongst it.

love to you both

jn

Early in January of 1949, Steinbeck's thoughts were still concerned with his financial state, caused by the divorce from Gwyn. On January 5, he wrote to Covici, in part:

So it's going to be a thin year financially for me and maybe this is permanent but I don't much care. There will

---

* Steinbeck wrote this letter and his subsequent letter of 27 December, on a typewriter which was, for him, unusual.

† Wife of Nathaniel Benchley, the novelist.

be others who do. Once my taxes for this year are paid I'll know how I must live and it will be lean.

He added, "My book should be starting and pretty soon." On that slender blade, Covici honed his encouragement. On January 12, he wrote:

> The most exciting news in your last letter is that you will soon be working on your novel. I wouldn't care how long it took you to finish it as long as it held your interest and you kept at it. Of course, I realize that writing the novel will probably keep you broke, but then I also know that you would be financed if you found it necessary, and so you need not worry. This almost parallels THE GRAPES OF WRATH period when you didn't have money enough to take a trip to Oklahoma, and you graciously turned down my offer of $250. Frankly, I think we were both happier then.

Steinbeck continued to write Covici almost every day. This was an unofficial prelude to his diary which later was published as *Journal of a Novel: The East of Eden Letters.*

On the 13th, he wrote:

Dear Pat:

> The copies of The Red Pony came today. Many thanks. In a few days (or weeks) I shall bring the safe up from the lab.[9] It is fire proof and I will put all such things in it. And I will lock it when I go away so the few things I value will be safe. . . .
> I'm having my eyes tested tomorrow. I suspect they are badly strained. But we shall see. I have been fighting this script unsuccessfully so far but then that is alright I think. It will come out in the end. I'm pretty sure I am much better than I was. My energy comes and goes but I think it is with me more than not.
> I hardly go out at all in the evenings. It is very pleasant at home. I have good music and a good fire. It has been

colder than any time known in this state. Maybe I brought
in a new ice age with me. Who knows.

He failed to mail that letter and simply began adding to it. On the
15th, he wrote:

About then some influenza cut me down. I went to bed and
knocked it off. Today weak but I think (I) have killed the
bug. Am going down to have my eyes tested today. While in
bed your letter came. . . . And I hope I can clean out this
emotional dust bin and do something else besides. It is a
great mess inside of me. Recently I saw Carol. She hasn't
changed a bit—the old resentments, nerves, angers. It took
me back and dumped me in that old mess. What a child but
an angry destructive child. It gave me a very sad feeling.

Jan. 16

This letter is beginning to look like a diary. I get interrupted.
I went to the eye doctor (we have an excellent one here)
and he says I very definitely need glasses for reading and
have needed them for a long time. So I will have them next
week. Also I came down with a beautiful beginning of
influenza yesterday. So went to bed, took large physic and
a load of army cold tablets, was dingy all night and today I
think I have beaten it. I feel fine and the pressure has gone
off. I really don't want a cold and I think many people do
because it excuses them. Seeing Carol threw me into sadness
and promptly I got the symptoms of flu. A real psycho
cold I guess. But I haven't it now. These periods of weakness
and despondency haven't the power if you know what they
are.
　　No, I wouldn't call Gwyn if I were you. If she calls you,
fine. . . . I think she is still in a state of shock. But she will
be coming out of it pretty soon. No one stays in it indefinitely
unless it is of some psychic value. Sickness was a creative
thing while I was there. But it will have no value if there is
no one to control by it. If she gets sick now it will be real
sickness.

Steinbeck described again the chance meeting with his first wife Carol. This next paragraph of his letter of January 16 was used later in a scene in *East of Eden:*

> The cold weather has broken and it is a most beautiful day.
> It has never been so cold as it has been the last two weeks. But
> it is broken now. And I'll tell you something else that is
> curious—seeing Carol broke something else free that has been
> bothering (me) for years—maybe a submerged sense of
> guilt I was not even conscious of. But even that is out now. Her
> complaints, and untruths and malice tore it all free. And what
> I suspected is now true. If after six years she hasn't changed,
> then nothing I could have done would have helped. But there
> are several levels of knowing.

> So long and love

> John

In *East of Eden,* Adam Trask visits his wife, whom he hasn't seen for years. She had left him and become a prostitute-madam. After a traumatic visit in her house of prostitution, Adam returned to his ranch. Steinbeck wrote:

> On his drive back to the ranch, Adam found that he was
> noticing things he has not seen for years. He saw the wild-
> flowers in the heavy grass, and he saw the red cows against the
> hillsides, moving up the easy ascending paths and eating as
> they went. When he came to his own land Adam felt a quick
> pleasure so sharp that he began to examine it. And suddenly
> he found himself saying aloud in rhythm with his horse's trotting
> feet, "I'm free, I'm free. I don't have to worry any more. I'm
> free. She's gone. She's out of me. Oh. Christ Almighty, I'm
> free. . . ."
> "I'm free, she's gone," he chanted aloud.[10]

The character of Kate in *East of Eden* now appears to have been created by Steinbeck's perceptions of the worst qualities of his first and second wives, Carol and Gwyn. Steinbeck's *Journal of a Novel: The East of Eden Letters* had to be edited to delete unpleasant and libelous references to his second wife Gwyn.

Steinbeck's letter of the 15th is remarkable, not because he used the same episode so clearly later in *East of Eden,* but because he was able to confide so deeply to Pascal Covici. Why? From the earliest to the end of their relationship, Covici wrote carefully-structured letters, attempting to explain Steinbeck to himself; as in Covici's letter of November 15:

> Whatever was ill-tempered about it was welcome to me. You are best when you do the things you know best. You often stray in alien places. You can't always help that because of your restless and creative spirit. When done with one thing you must immediately tangle up with something else, . . .

Covici's invasion of Steinbeck's psychic territory was a characteristic he had, as editor, not shared by Max Perkins, nor indeed, by other first-rate editors. Covici consistently attempted to view Steinbeck as he saw himself; this effort, while not always successful, allowed him an intimacy not shared by other editors. Covici's cataloguing of Steinbeck's personality, consistently, over the years, was no doubt what Thomas Guinzburg meant when he said that "Covici was an extraordinary guy—he was some part psychiatrist, some part lawyer, some part priest . . . Covici didn't work on books, he worked on people." And although Steinbeck perhaps didn't understand Covici's methods, he did appreciate them; he later called Covici:

> . . . father, mother, teacher, personal devil and personal god. For 30 years Pat was my collaborator and my conscience.[11]

VI

"IT'S YOUR OWN HOME GROUND, SOMETHING YOU KNOW ABOUT AND HAS BEEN IN YOUR BLOOD ALL YOUR LIFE."

January, 1949 to June, 1949

Steinbeck continued to return to emotional stability. His letter of January 22 marked a watershed; his psychological stability and the added convenience of new eyeglasses gave him a better perspective on life. That letter also was his longest; thereafter his letters to Covici became shorter and shorter, and during the spring of 1949, their correspondence slowly resumed normal proportions.

Jan. 22

Dear Pat:

I have my glasses now and print jumps out of the page at me. It has been creeping up on me for years and I didn't know it. I only know that it was getting increasingly difficult to work. I thought I was getting lazy and old and ill and now I think it was mostly eye strain. My distance eyes are still 17% better than the best norm. So I only need the glasses for reading and writing. And speaking of reading—there are some books I need Pat to fill out my library. You see when I want to know something the local libraries either don't have it or are closed. There is no particular hurry and I don't care whether the books are new or not but I need some volumes in medicine, a Grey's Anatomy, fairly new edition, 2. a Pharmacopea (can't spell it). This should be a new one because of the many new drugs. 3. The best standard volume in Toxology. In this field the encyclopedia is not of much value. My books are supposed to be on the way but of course I don't know what she will let me have.* I'll fill in the gaps when they arrive, but I don't know until then. Also I will probably bring up most of the books from the lab which will make all in all quite a good reference library. I brought up the safe, in which I will put any raritys so that when I go away they will be safe from fire anyway. These glasses are wonderful. It is a pleasure to write again and I was getting to dread everydays stint. Maybe I can work again. I hope. I was getting deeply worried—thinking my willpower was gone.

Here then is a health report. I am only interested because I must be well to work. I can see again. That is #1. That means none of those sick symptoms nausea, etc. that kept me pretty worried. I am tough and mean after quite a housecleaning. My closets were full of dust, of little fears, of half felt emotions. If I am to be a son of a bitch, I'm going to be my own son of a bitch. I kicked out the duty emotions. They will snap back of course but decreasingly. I get the despondencies still. But I have learned that if you are not right with a person, nothing can make you right and if you are right then nothing can make you wrong. There is some anger at me here because I no longer have the money to solve my friends' difficulties. I stumbled on a phrase to take care of that situation: it is Fuck it! I have been the soft touch for too long. Still would be if I had it but I haven't. And probably am never going to have again. Second—out of some kind of pride or weakness I have never wanted to accept anything. It gave me some self-indulging feeling to be the giver not the receiver. It is going to be hard to learn to receive and to accept but I am going to learn. Thus when a girl in Mexico wanted to hustle for me, I wouldn't let her. She would have had some good thing if I had let her walk the streets for me—some kind of fulfilling. Maybe if I had learned to accept instead of constant giving, Gwyn might have been fulfilled. But not (*sic*), I don't really believe that. Some other factor is there that I don't know

---

* When his wife Gwyn got her divorce, she took most of Steinbeck's books with her. She promised to return many of them.

about and am learning not to care. Third is the whole idea
of virtue. I have never wanted to be good. I must and am
learning that this is the really egotistic thing. If I can get rid
of that, I will have gone a long way. I also wanted to be just
which is another self indulgence. Dignity I never wanted so I
don't have to worry about that. Have I gone over all of this
to you before? Am I repeating myself? The thing is this—I am
about ready to be able to do anything I wish good or bad
without any reference to self. The next two years are going to
show whether all the training was worth doing and I must be
particularily clean to give it the chance. I must be clean of all
virtue and all pride. I must be as low as possible to be before
I can conceive highness. And I must hear the ugly sounds before I can hear beauty. It is not new at all but there are two
kinds of knowing—the mind and the whole body. And there
can't be any fakes in this new thing. Maybe I'm too old to
learn but I'm not too old to try learning. You are the poor
victim at whom I throw all of these things. Well, you will have
to receive these vaporings but you don't have to read them.
This is your freedom.[1]

It is a great fine storm in the air, wind and rain and fresh
cold. It is my kind of weather and it gives me a good feeling.
The rain is lashing the windows like whips and I have a good
fire. Later a girl will come in and I shall function well in
that department. You can't want more than that—a cold night
and a warm girl.

But good lord the fine thing is to be able to sit and write
with a pen and not have creeping exhaustion. I really have
liked to write and I had got to hate it because it hurt. Why
was I so stupid as not to know what was hurting.

My Arabia Deserta was down at the office. . . . I am so
glad to have it. I think it is the greatest secular prose in
English that I know. Doughy makes the language a great stone
with designs of metal and out croppings of preciousness,
emerald and diamond and obsidian. It is good to have here
to see what can be done with the language. I do not think it
was easy for him to write. No such sense of ease and flow ever
came without great and tearing effort.

I have some new snapshots of my children. They are growing so rapidly. And they look fine. We shall have great fun this summer. I think I have located a boat for us to go cruising in. I told them we would sleep and cook our dinner on a boat and that seems to excite them very much as it excites me still. What better thing is there than that?

Pat, I'm getting the old ecstacies back sometimes. Thinking about a boat made the hair rise on the back of my neck. You say a good piece of writing does that to you, a chacun son gout I guess. I have to hold on for five more years and after that I shall not care. I will of course but that is the way it seems to me now.

This long and pointless letter will draw to a close with this page. And about time, you say. But I have good out of it. And so you must take it.

I went out to find little pine trees to plant about my house and they aren't up yet. But some other things are. As soon as the rain stops I will take a shovel out and get some yerba buena and some wild iris for my garden. Yerba buena is a grown crawling mint from which the old ones use to make a curative tea. I remember drinking it when I was little. It is a stomactic and it smells wonderful when you crush it—a sweet but sharp odor that pierces way back of your nose clearly.

And this is the end. But I think you will agree that this propped up life is—what? I don't know. It still has some savor and what more could I ask of it.

Women are still beautiful and desirable and things smell good and sometimes the flame still burns jumping the nerve ends like little boys jumping fences.

So long

John

In January 24, Covici replied to Steinbeck's earlier letter, in which he writes of his psychosomatic cold, brought on by seeing his first wife:

Frankly, I doubt whether seeing Carol brought on your cold. Seeing her brought on a sadness and something within you snapped, and I am not so sure you know what it is and I had better not venture any explanation. It is good that you feel what you feel and are not building up another psychosis. Breaking through barbed wires, as you are doing, is a difficult process and believe me you are not free yet. But you have gone a long way.

The weakness in most of us falling for easy friendships, and rather be led than leading, lacking the discipline relentlessly to keep chipping our own stone, often leads us astray with our own energy spent and nothing accomplished. The miracle of creative work as you well know is just one long heart-breaking discipline. . . .

You say Carol hasn't changed in six years. Do you know anybody who does.

On January 29, Steinbeck left for Mexico, to work on *Viva Zapata.* Covici's reply to Steinbeck's long letter of January 22, reached Steinbeck in Cuernavaca.

11 February, 1949

I meant to write to you for days. I just couldn't get around to it. Gene Fowler just left for home. He has been here for the last four weeks cutting and changing the galleys and finishing his last chapter. At last the book is going on press. Advance sales are good. Then came Arthur Miller's new play, DEATH OF A SALESMAN, and that had to be rushed to the printer. The play opened last night and it was tremendously moving. It is a slice of life without a false note in it. The critics this morning all rave about it.

I hope your going to Mexico to do Zapata proves good and does not take you as long as you think it will. You have spent a terrific amount of time and energy on it already. I do hope that it's good and worth all your effort. . . .

. . . I shall also get you a Gray's anatomy pharmacopoeia and a volume on toxicology and will hold these, too, until you are home again.

How you could have gone on for two years without realizing that you need glasses is beyond me, but thank God you have them at last and see normally. That must have had a great deal to do with your nervous tension. I am so anxious for you to get back home and start on your novel. I am convinced that this will bring you back to yourself again and do the work that you mean to do.

Never worry that your letters are too long. When you are writing you are alone and on your own and that's when I see you and understand you best. Your philosophical and emotional outpourings touch me deeply and I think I understand. Please let me hear from you.

Love,

Whenever Covici felt Steinbeck could use some rest, he would offer him a quiet room in New York. Said Dr. Pascal Covici, Jr. late in 1975, "I remember Lewis Corey, Gene Fowler, Steinbeck, Arthur Miller, Saul Bellow and Lionel Trilling. They were family friendships. They were people we had at the house. Only when I became older did I recognize that they were all writers. I remember them as friends. Up to the very end (of his life), father took writers into our home. All were extremely engaging personalities. I don't remember any writer who was not a real contribution to our (dinner) table."[2]

Mr. John Steinbeck
147-11th St.
Pacific Grove, Calif.

Dear John,

You are more difficult to follow than Hamlet's ghost. Here I was all set to hear from you from Mexico when presto you are back at Pacific Grove. The Gods move in devious ways and so do you, but I think I understand you better. . . .

I suppose you know that Arthur Miller's DEATH OF A SALESMAN went over like a house on fire. Such rave reviews I haven't seen for a long time. We are publishing the play March 10th. I saw Miller today and he asked me about you. I didn't know that you ever met. He is a very agreeable, sincere, and compassionate person.

It will be a great day when you tell me that you are finished with ZAPATA. If you get another longing for travel, why don't you fly to New York for a week or ten days?

I have a large beautiful room unoccupied and you can be there unmolested and unknown as long as you want to. Maybe this is what you need.

Love,

Finally, Steinbeck's creative imagination again began functioning:

Washington's Birthday
and nearly mine

Dear Pat;

Here it is again, another year and the first one I haven't dreaded for a long time. I just finished my day's work. It is finally going like mad, or did I tell you that? And now that it is going I don't thing it will take long. And as always when I am working I am gay. I'm terribly gay. I'm even gay about what I'm going to tell you. And I want you to keep this to yourself.

I'm asking Gwyn for my books. I asked for the anthologies, poetry, drama, classics, etc. which I have collected over the years. Well I didn't get them. I got an absolute minimum. I wish you would get me, if you can, complete catalogues of Everyman, Random House, and the other libraries that do such things because I do want to replace the things I actually need for work. Isn't it odd that having stripped me of everything else, she also retains the tools of the trade from which she is living? A funny girl and I think she is headed for trouble—not from me. I did get the dictionary and the encyclopedia and a few others.

I don't know what has happened but the dams are burst. Work is pouring out of me. I guess maybe I am over the illness. Who knows? But at least there seems to be some opening at the end of the street.

Please let me hear from you. And don't tell any one about this book thing. I don't want to fight with Gwyn unless the children are involved and sooner or later I think they will be.

So long now
affectionately

John

On the 27th of February, Steinbeck wrote to Covici:

. . . I think people get exactly what they deserve or maybe
what they unconsciously want. If I was a stooge to two sick
women then that is what I deserved. It was their fault that
they were sick but it was my fault that I chose them and
stayed with them. I can't find any silly excuse for myself
there. But the main thing is that I don't want any more of it
on any terms: Hell, I want women—lot of them or one dam
good one but I want well ones. With my long lived ancestry
on both sides and barring accidents, I have probably 20 years
of life and work to do. Dam near half of my life has been
devoted to being nurse maid to neuroses and I'm through with
it. Maybe I'm a neurotic myself or maybe I have become one
but I don't think so. The fact that I am getting well by the
hour indicates—to me at least that it was only a temporary
illness. I know more about my life now that I ever have known.
I know what happened and when (although I didn't know
then.) And I am trying to set warning posts so that it may
not happen again.

I am not working today. I'm sitting and taking inventory.
The work flame is rising again and even more the joy,
pleasure flame out of which good work must come (Privately)
I'm afraid all hell is going to break loose in New York.
Gwyn is apparently getting worse and worse and I don't want
my kids to be little neurotics and I can't see how they can
escape it in that diseased atmosphere. I don't want to fight
but if I have to I'll fight like hell. And I have the strength
to do it now and the hardness not to be hit in return—except
through the kids. I don't know what to do but maybe I'll find
a way. I don't want to write these kids off—I love them no
matter what Gwyn says in her self-justifying rationalizations.
One of the things I have discovered is that I am a man and a
damned good one. It is odd but not really odd—that the
whole approach of both of my wives was to convince me that
I wasn't much of a man. And they damned near succeeded
—but not quite. And so I am looking forward to the next years

with a kind of burning. I don't deserve anythings but I am going to get them just the same. I feel curiously reborn.

This may sound like whistling in the dark to you but it isn't. I just noticed my handwriting. Compared with that of a few months ago. Crabbed and nervous and sick. I think there is confidence even in it. I know there will be relapses but they will be less and less. The old thing is objective now and outside of my guts and I can look at it and see what it was.

I can assure you that this feeling is the nicest birthday present I could possibly have. I am grateful to you for sticking by in the dark time when everythings was tattering and falling away. I, for one, expected to get out of it.

> Love to you
>
> John

Anything you may hear about me is probably true.* At least anything can happen and isn't *that* a good thing. There are no limits to feeling, or achievement any more and I'm not afraid of anything—anything. It would be well if certain people understood that very clearly.

Again, Covici felt moved to analyze Steinbeck. This letter is another example of Covici as psychologist, interpreting Steinbeck:

> March 4, 1949

Mr. John Steinbeck
147-11th Street
Pacific Grove, Calif.

Dear John,

To say that one gets what one deserves or what one unconsciously wants is too simple a statement and not necessarily true. I think that circumstances and mere chance or accident have

---

* A reference to printed gossip about his love life and possible drinking during this period.

a great deal to do with the matter. As somebody said, if we were all to get what we deserve we would all be in jail, or something like that.

All this speculation leads nowhere, of course. What is important I am happy to say is that you are certainly getting back your equilibrium and your sense of reality. Even your handwriting is clearer, firmer and less nervous. I think you know what you want to do and I am sure that you will do it, and you are again experiencing joy in your work. You have had enough of bitterness and disappointment.

Of course, I know that you are concerned about your kids. I am with you on any count, but please don't jump at conclusions. Wait and see and cogitate long and carefully and I am convinced that in your creative work, when your flame burns brightest, you will have found answers to your troubling questions. This may sound far-fetched and as chaotic as hell, but believe me that it isn't: great intensive vision brings prophetic illumination. I hear no rumors about a diseased atmosphere at Gwyn's and I understand that your kids are well and doing as nicely as one could expect. You are going to have them for the Summer, aren't you? You can tell a lot when you see them.

Again I want to emphasize that you have gained confidence and strength of purpose but these, as you well know, will be of no avail unless you use them with intelligence.

What do you mean by your mystic and enigmatic phrase, "Anything you may hear about me is probably true?" I don't want to believe anything I hear about you and shouldn't have to. I am still kidding myself that I could help you some in your need but not unless you tell me what is happening to you or what is probably going to happen. Don't let me depend on hearsay.

I am enclosing the Modern Library and Everyman's catalogues. I am also expecting the Oxford Classical Library one and will mail it to you when it comes. Have you received the medical books, your father's book, "The Red Pony" and "Tortilla Flat" that I want you to autograph?

Please keep me informed. Love,

Yours,

Covici's deep feelings about Steinbeck in his letters of March 4, caused Steinbeck to explain his earlier enigmatic letter:

(No date. Postmarked 8 March, 1949)

Dear Pat:

Thanks for your letter and the enclosures. I am not going to do anything in a hurry, even order books. The medical books and the bound children's books arrived. Many thanks. The plastic covering is very fine and will probably keep for all time.

Work on the script continues every day. I am trying to get the draft finished by April 1st and with out accidents I probably shall.

The line about anything being true was a joke. Probably not a very good one. I hear the most fantastic things about myself. That's what it was about. As for my private life—there hasn't been one. I have hardly been out of the house since I got back from Mexico. As for my romantic life, I know you wouldn't ask about that and I should not tell you if you did. I can only say that it is various and satisfactory. That I need and that I am going to have.

I think this script might be excellent. The dialogue has a good sound to me. I am putting some of it on records for typing now. And the speech sounds like talk.

Next day: I went to bed at that point. This simple life is getting to be a habit. I go to bed about 9 every evening and get up at 7:30. I have been visiting a friend. I have excitements again. Maybe it sounds as though I'm protesting too much but I'm not. I have the two necessities, work and women. It's time to start my day's work now.

love

John

By this time, Steinbeck's emotional world seemed stabilized; his letters to Covici and Covici's replies were slightly less intense, and became less frequent as Steinbeck's need for a confidential ear became minimal.

On the 18th of March, Covici sent Steinbeck a brief note:

. . . How are you? When you are finished with the ZAPATA movie wouldn't it be a good idea for you to come to New York for a few days? I have a nice big room for you, strictly private.

Love,

Steinbeck replied:

(No date. Postmarked 22 March, 1949)

I have about two more weeks on this script. At least I think so. But I can see the end in view. And it will be a pleasure to have it done. Then we shall see what. I am quite tired. This has been a very tiring job and it went on too long. A year now. I could have written a four volume novel in the same time.

My critics . . . are still waiting for me. They are going to be very angry with the Salinas Valley because it will be even more unlike Mice and Men. They catch up very late. . . .

I feel good.

When I finish then we'll see about New York and other things. I'm still very broke and it is going to be difficult to get around for a while as I used to. But I'll try to build up a reserve.

. . . I want to rest and contemplate a little and go to bed with very pretty ladies. I've not been out of the house in a month and normal juices have gone on accumulating. And I thoroughly believe that any man who is not deeply affected by a beautiful woman is queer, gelded or a liar.

My anchoritic life is beginning to tell you see. And what a liar I am.

Have not planted my garden yet. But I will as my work is done. I am going to put in flowering bushes that take care of themselves. I've been starting them all winter and they are about ready to set out.

There are some great scenes in this Zapata script. I don't know whether they will ever get on film but they are there.

So long. I'll loosen up as soon as I get through

affectionately
John

Saw Carol not very long ago. She was pretty tight. She said she had turned down 20 thousand dollars for the Grapes mss (a lie of course). Said now she wanted to sell it and did I know a buyer. I said I did not but maybe you did. So if you get a letter about that, you will know how it happened. She never was offered anything like 20 or even 5 thousand or even one or she would have taken it in a minute.

And again, Covici encouraged Steinbeck to return to his Salinas Valley project. This letter and the one following indicate Covici's deep conviction that the Salinas Valley manuscript should be Steinbeck's great work ("It's your own home ground, something you know about and has been in your blood all your life.") :

April 1, 1949

Mr. John Steinbeck
147-11th Street
Pacific Grove, Calif.

Dear John,

I, too, will be glad when you have finished with the ZAPATA script. As you say, you could have done, during this time, quite a hefty novel and been much happier for it. Remember years ago when you objected to my having your picture in the papers or your appearing in public? Your reasons were that you didn't want to be conscious of your reading public and so feel that you'd have to write with the public in mind. You were right then and you are still right, if you still think the same. In order to do a commercially successful movie you have to think of the millions you want to attract. You are not happy when your mind is chained.

Never worry that the readers will be angry with the SALINAS VALLEY. That, as you yourself have often said, is not important, even if true. When you write with honesty and conviction, with an eye on your own heart, your work will find the esteem it deserves in the mind and soul of man. As you know, the light of the body is the eye, let it be clear.

I still think it would be good for you to come to New

York. You don't need money. I have a perfectly good room
for you and also a car at your disposal—and I will furnish
the gas and oil. What do you say?

Love,

Steinbeck's vision apparently continued to bother him and Covici
was still concerned:

April 22, 1949

Mr. John Steinbeck
147-11th Street
Pacific Grove, Calif.

Dear John,

I have learned to disregard the stories about you in the
papers. For my own peace of mind they are not true until you
tell me otherwise. Yes, I also heard about your heavy drinking and sleeping with Goddard.* Both are possible but in your
case not fatal only a temporary disruption. Your sense of
values sooner or later will assert itself. You see, I have great
faith in your ultimate achievement.

I am so glad that you are satisfied with your script. Can
you spare a copy? I would love to read it.

Don't, please, be your own doctor where your eyes are
concerned. It is all together possible that you have the wrong
glasses. I don't believe that this is just nervousness. Let your
doctor examine your eyes again as well as your glasses. They
are sometimes improperly ground. It has often happened to me.

When you have finished planting and rested a bit I still
think you should come to New York for a while and see your
kids. My house and car are yours whenever you come; then
upon your return I hope that you will go back to your novel.
It's the one book of yours since "The Grapes of Wrath"
that I am banking on big. It's your own home ground, something you know about and has been in your blood all your
life. It can't miss being an important piece of writing regard-

---

* A reference to Hollywood gossip linking Steinbeck with actress Paulette
Goddard.

less of its possible sale. You can always make money in some way or another if you have to, but this novel you must do, you know that, and don't put it off again. You will be much happier.

It would be good to see you.

Love,

Late in April, Steinbeck decided to journey to New York to visit his children. The visit, which necessitated seeing his ex-wife, Gwyn, was too much. The emotional trauma of his divorce was too recent for a meeting with her then. Steinbeck returned to California, shaken. He wrote to Bo Beskow, a friend:

Three weeks ago I had a compulsion to go to New York to see my children and I did so thinking I was more well than I was. It struck me hard, all of the unhappiness arose again but it will not be very long before I am back where I was so that will be all right. My boys were well and healthy. I shall have them with me this summer and get to know them again.[3]

Covici, who had seen Steinbeck while he was in New York, was confused about Steinbeck's condition and subtly chided him for ignoring Lewis Gannett, the critic. Gannett had written the introduction to *The Portable Steinbeck,* which The Viking Press had published six years before.

May 5, 1949

Mr. John Steinbeck
147-11th St.
Pacific Grove, Calif.

Dear John,

It was good to see you, even though you seemed emotionally shattered and mentally confused. I say "seemed," for I long ago came to the conclusion that our opinions of others are mostly wrong. At any rate, I think that you have reached some sort of equilibrium and being back home again should help.

I was desperately sorry that I couldn't be of help to you when you were here. I felt, frankly, completely useless, like a wet hen not knowing how to come in out of the rain. I still can't figure it out.

I had lunch with Lewis Gannett the other day and he asked about you. I explained that you didn't want to see anybody and he understood. He is very fond of you and wants to be remembered. Sometimes I wonder whether we ever know who our real friends are. However, human nature is such a cockeyed conglomeration of contradictions.

Be well and let me hear from you.

Love,

Later, Covici analyzed Steinbeck's temperament, during his turbulent days after the divorce from Gwyn.

May 24, 1949

Mr. John Steinbeck
147-11th Street
Pacific Grove, Calif.

Dear John,

I have just finished reading a brilliant essay on Goethe by J. P. Hodin and I kept thinking of you persistently in the following paragraph:

"The mature Goethe, who has achieved inner balance after a hard struggle, was in very decisive opposition to everything diseased, decadent, nihilistic and pessimistic. He avoided it as though it were a plague. The great secret of his personality is the capacity to array the elements of life, strength and fertility, against the destructive forces in his own psyche and in his environment and so always to maintain inner harmony. So he conquered time with eternity and personal fate with the idea of necessity, accepting reality and not letting himself be tricked by any illusions. He lived in reality, and for him reality was the whole, not only the 'difficult' present, but the whole of creation."

You, too, are going through a terrific struggle with the forces within you and those surrounding you. What has been chaotic, however, is growing clearer for you and you are gathering strength and greater energy. When you again can lose yourself in creative work, it won't be with venom or hatred or vengeance, but it will be like Goethe, in an Olympic way.

Annie Laurie brought in the quitclaim papers* the other day for Wayward Bus for signature. That should help your finances a bit. But, as Harold told you, you can always draw on the firm should you need additional money, and no questions asked. You know that.

What about Zapata? Any decision? There is a good movie there and fascinating material for the book. A very moving story.

Lewis Gannett's CREAM HILL got excellent reviews. I think it will have a longish sale.

It was good to hear that Beth was with you. She loves you very much, and quite unselfishly.

Love.

After several weeks without letters from Covici, Steinbeck finally answered.

May 27

I had not heard from you and I was beginning to think that my beastliness in New York had angered you as it should. But then your letter arrived yesterday.

I do mostly ponderous, meaningless things now. The growing of certain plants becomes important for a moment. The girls are a channel I know—but a creative one. They are allright and very nice. I like the pretty ones best.

It is a very curious time. There is a great struggle going on but I don't even rightly know what is fighting what and which will win. Meanwhile I like it here better all the time. I

---

* Annie Laurie Williams, who handled dramatic rights for McIntosh and Otis, had sold the film rights to *The Wayward Bus*. The film of the novel was released in 1957.

only hope it does not become too strong a symbol of retreat
and retirement. I should not like that.

You see I am going to be all right financially. But the
constant drain of most of the resources to Gwyn worries me a
little because it makes it nearly impossible to build up any
reserve. I don't really need one though. I live very simply
and very cheaply. But if I want to take X years for a novel,
I must have a reserve for Gwyn and the children. For myself
I need very little. That is the only financial worry I have and
I don't worry very much about it. Not very much at all. I
forget to worry.

I wrote to Lewis Gannett and this morning had a very kind
and good letter from him. He is such a good man.

They tell me that in the columns I am in Mexico again.
My double life is interesting. I wish I had time for it. But perhaps I can enjoy it vicariously via the papers. And maybe
that's the best way.

It's a lovely day. I'm going out and walk in it.

Love,

John

Steinbeck's thoughts to have "a (financial) reserve for Gwyn and the
children," struck deeply at Covici, who became convinced that Steinbeck was avoiding the progress of the Salinas Valley manuscript. His
next letter was a deep plea to Steinbeck to begin work on it, and
avoid thoughts of a financial reserve which he didn't need. Apparently
Steinbeck had ignored Covici's previous letter of May 24, in which Covici reminded him "But as Harold told you, you can always draw on the
firm should you need additional money, and no questions asked. You
know that."

June 9, 1949

Mr. John Steinbeck
147-11th Street
Pacific Grove, Calif.

Dear John,

I just got back from Cambridge where I spent a few
days with Pascal. He was having his end-year exams and he

really worked. It was a grueling process. Can you imagine six hours of math? I'm afraid I couldn't take it. He is through for the year and came out very nicely. What's more he likes it at Harvard. On July 2nd he will be going to France with his French teacher and will be gone for about eight weeks.

The papers find it difficult to decide where you are going next or whom you are going to marry. They certainly keep you occupied and constantly changing.

Maybe you are going to resent this, but I have to say it. It seems kind of sad to me when I read that you must build up a reserve for Gwyn and the children before embarking on writing your novel. You wrote, if you remember, GRAPES OF WRATH on a hell of a lot less money. You needed less then, of course, but the opportunity of your getting money, should you need it, is infinitely greater now. Please believe me you have no financial problems. These are the least. What you need to my way of thinking is peace of mind and a great urge to do your novel. It is a terribly important piece of work, you know it and you feel it, but you are side-tracking it, pushing it away from you. Maybe in fear or confusion, maybe you are not ready for it. I don't know, but I am not wrong when I say this is the only work that will bring you back to yourself and your greater realization. In your ZAPATA there were many passages of beauty and tenderness and dramatic impact. I am not mistaken. All you need is the will to do it, but that I know is asking for a lot in your present mental disturbance. You have gone a long way in this respect; you have done a great deal with yourself in the last six months and I really have no fear. As tender and sensitive as you are, you are of the earth earthy and your roots are strong and deep and you will weather any storm.

Love,

Eventually, John Steinbeck returned to emotional normality after his second divorce, largely brought about by two major forces in his life: Pascal Covici's introspective and valuable letters of analysis and support and Steinbeck's own association with Elaine Scott, which was soon to begin.

VII

"THE CRITICS MURDERED US."

June, 1949 to January, 1951

Early in June, 1949, Steinbeck met Elaine Scott, whose marriage to Zachary Scott, a western film actor, was breaking up. Steinbeck's interest in her was intense; she too, became interested in him. Despite his earlier protests that he never would become deeply involved with another woman, they began to see each other frequently, as soon as her separation from Scott became legal. From early June, through the end of December, Steinbeck's correspondence to her was regular and intense; Covici and his other friends did not receive their usual letters from Steinbeck with his former regularity.

On June 17, Covici wrote Steinbeck a summary of events at The Viking Press:

Mr. John Steinbeck
147-11th Street
Pacific Grove, Calif.

Dear John,

Maybe your WAYWARD BUS is not one of your masterpieces, but it certainly keeps on selling. While Grosset is still publishing the $1.49 BUS, Bantam will bring out a 25¢ edition after January 1950 and are guaranteeing us $6,000. This means that they expect to sell a minimum of 300,000 copies. That is a lot of copies in any country of any book. At any rate, your coffee and cigarettes are well taken care of.

Anything happening with your ZAPATA?

When you see Carol will you tell her that a friend of mine is interested in buying the GRAPES OF WRATH manuscript, if her price is reasonable. I can't give her the name of the party but that is a fact. Or do you think I had better write to her direct? If so, will you give me her address?

Things are quiet around here with DEATH OF A SALESMAN and CREAM HILL still selling fairly well, but nothing exciting. Harold is leaving for Europe the first week in July and Huebsch probably some time in August. Marshall and I, I guess, will be the watch-dogs.

Right soon I take it you will be busy with your boys. That should be a real experience both for them and for you. Nothing else now.

Love,*

Later, Steinbeck had thoughts of re-publishing his part of *Sea of Cortez* separately. Covici replied:

I am sending you six copies of THE SEA OF CORTEZ. Frankly, I am not at all certain that it would be such a bright idea to bring out at this time your part of THE SEA OF CORTEZ in a regular edition. Wouldn't it be smarter to publish a 25¢ edition? If they accept it it might mean five hundred thousand to a millon sale. Think it over and let me know, and in the meanwhile I want to read the book over— I haven't read it in years. I remember it as exciting reading.

Love,

P.S. Would you want to call your part A JOURNEY INTO THE SEA OF CORTEZ?

On July 3, Steinbeck replied in a short note: "I see no reason why the Sea should not go as you say to a reprint house. And the title you suggest is all right with me." Covici seldom mentioned Steinbeck's reviews to him (he perhaps did not wish to be the bearer of any bad news). But he did write to Steinbeck about an essay which had just appeared:

* Covici's references are to colleagues at The Viking Press: Harold Guinzburg, president; Ben W. Huebsch, a senior editor; Marshall Best, managing editor.

August 17, 1949

Mr. John Steinbeck
147-11th Street
Pacific Grove, Calif.

Dear John,

I hesitated to send you the enclosed STEINBECK: ONE ASPECT by Blake Nevius, appearing in the *Pacific Spectator*. As you know I do not trust critics who pounce upon one shade of meaning in an author's work and play with it to death. When one exclusively emphasizes a particular aspect of a creative piece of work, that is, without considering all other aspects, good or bad, to my mind it seriously misrepresents the sum total of the author's creativeness. But here it is. Nevius, whoever he is, has some acute observations, nonetheless. The piece will interest you.[1]

At last the heat has broken and New York is liveable again. I do hope that it will stay that way when your boys come back.

I just got a letter from Gene Fowler telling me that he sold his Spanish castle and has now moved to a small apartment next to an old ladies home. He thinks that this is quite symbolic and that he truly belongs in humbler quarters.

Yours,

Still later, in the fall of 1949, Covici forwarded Steinbeck information about a special issue of *The New York Herald Tribune,* which contained an essay citing Steinbeck:

September 28, 1949

Mr. John Steinbeck
147-11th Street
Pacific Grove, Calif.

Dear John,

I expect you home by the time this reaches you. It must have been an ordeal for the children to leave you. It is very sad that they can't feel equal joy being with her as with you. I hope no great harm comes of it. They should be made to feel happy when they are with either of you.

Did you see the Herald Tribune anniversary number of September 25th. It contains a number of interesting articles. One is by Lloyd Morris on "The Heritage of a Generation of Novelists": Anderson, Dreiser, Hemingway, Faulkner, Farrell and Steinbeck. Here is what he has to say about "The Grapes of Wrath":

"Steinbeck's two novels about the agricultural workers prepared him for the epic subject which he undertook in 'The Grapes of Wrath.' This was the mass migration to California of the 'Okies,' the hundreds of thousands of families who had been dispossessed by the 'black Blizzard' which, in 1933, devastated the central prairie region. Steinbeck's book proved to be a twentieth century equivalent of 'Uncle Tom's Cabin,' a story that so poignantly challenged the conscience of the nation that there arose a swift demand for prompt remedial action. The book was, in a sense, a kind of allegory. For the trek and tragedy of the Okies represented a general process of social deterioration of which the Great Depression was a spectacular symptom. The Joad family were not merely victims of an isolated catastrophe; they were symbols, symbols of the probable fate of a large segment of the American people. In Steinbeck's view, this fate was made inevitable by the perversion of the American social system. Initially dedicated to the welfare of all, it had been warped to serve the interest of a few. Steinbeck's novel painted a massive picture of the human toll which the warped social system exacted. And it flatly stated the conviction that, for Americans, it would be better if the system were to be destroyed. Published in 1939, 'The Grapes of Wrath' marked the culmination of a movement of conscience that had begun twenty years earlier. In it, protest against things-as-they-are, and moral indignation that they should be

so, reached an intensity, a degree of exacerbation, without precedent in American fiction."[2]
I have it from busy rumor that you are coming East. Any truth in it or what are your plans? A number of things have been brewing in your mind, anything compelling enough?

Love,

Without mentioning Elaine, Steinbeck wrote to Covici, thanking him for sending the *Herald Tribune* article. Steinbeck's only comment was: "It is interesting."

A week later, he told Covici, "I'm about ready to go to work. My emotional life is balanced and full and all I need is the work. And I think I have it. This time I shall not talk so much about it. Maybe that isn't good."

In a letter to Elaine Scott, in Brentwood, California, that same day, Steinbeck described what he was doing and what he was planning. He had been keeping a day-to-day diary, but had forsaken it; he now planned to continue it. Later his diary would take the form of letters to Covici, during his work on *East of Eden*. He also told Elaine that he was working on *Everyman,* an early title for his play-novel, *Burning Bright.*

Darling—

You know sporadically I keep a kind of diary day book. It is written in a kind of Pepysian shorthand. It is valuable sometimes. Looking back through it I came to the reference to your first trip here. And it is amazing how quickly I knew. Almost immediately. I put things in it I don't even know, and only much later do I realize that they are in there. Actually it is a kind of warm-up book. When I am working it is good to write a page before going to work. It both resolves the day things that might be distracting and warms up my pen the way a pitcher warms up. It's a matter of long practice. I have made no entries all summer but now will begin it again. Very soothing to raw nerves.

Last night in one of the times I awakened I got a flock of
foreknowledge that was like a landscape on a dark night
suddenly created by a flash of lightning. There it was. Maybe
I'll write it and put it away. But it was all there. And it was
good.

Everyman continues to grow in my mind. My Christ! it's
a dramatic thing. Now it has beginning, middle and end and
that's what three acts are and that's why there are three acts.
The 5-act play is still three acts, and the form was imposed
by the human mind, not by playwrights or critics. This
doesn't mean that external reality has beginning, middle
and end, but simply that the human brain perceives it so.
This letter is growing pedagogic, isn't it?[3]

On October 18 Covici responded with great enthusiasm to Steinbeck's brief comments about his progress: "The one great gleam in
your letter is your telling me that something is really jelling in your
mind and you mean to tackle it soon. That to me is most exciting—
your creative self coming back."

In early November, after Elaine Scott received her divorce, she
and Steinbeck made plans to move and begin their lives together.

Covici sent Steinbeck a copy of Viking's edition of Chaucer. Steinbeck took the time to return his thanks, in a typewritten letter:

Dear Pat:

I received yesterday the Viking portable of Chaucer. Haven't
had a chance to glance into it yet except to see that I liked
the Modern English approach very well. You know, some day
I'm going to get all of the Viking portables. I think it's an
excellent library.

I'm working quite steadily now on the ZAPATA script and
I hope to finish a draft so that I can be in New York early
in December, and of course we will foregather then. I think
this is going to be a good script and that you will not be
ashamed of it.

If you have time, I wish you would look up for me the
biggest, goddamn atlas in the world. I don't know whether
there is one but I should like a huge one with detailed maps

of nearly everything in the world. It is something that I have
always wanted.

Frank Loesser will probably call on you to ask your advice
concerning booksellers, because he wants to stock a library
having to do with the history of music, and I know that you
know every bookseller in New York.

Isn't it an interesting thing to have a letter from me properly
typed and with all the words spelled correctly? I took a short
course and now I'm able to do this.

I'll see you soon

John

Steinbeck had not yet mentioned Elaine to Covici. It was a mark
of the communication between them that Steinbeck occasionally became
secretive about his affairs, as he did earlier when he went camping in
the woods with Gwen. He perhaps sensed that Covici might not approve. This secrecy seldom lasted long—he eventually told Covici what
needed to be told. Covici's last letter before the Christmas holidays
mentioned a new confidence; he observed that Steinbeck was apparently beginning to regain his self-determination.

Dear John,

Your typing is so good now that I am certain I can get
you a typing job any time you say.

Whatever happened to you in the last months I know
is for the best. There's a healthier and more vigorous ring
in your letter. Determination and self-assertion are the
keynotes. I can almost feel your smashing away the cobwebs
and poisonous tentacles that have been feeding on you. It
will take a while yet for you to get rid of all the poison and
bile you accumulated and which you are still spitting out.
That will come, too. You have a long way yet and you will
never know how anxiously I have been watching the
whole road.

What about Christmas eve? If you won't be at Gwyn's,
why not my house? There will be a big tree and you and the
boys can help decorate it. You could all sleep in my house.
If not Christmas eve, then you and the boys can come

Christmas day. I shall furnish plenty of fun for them. It will be good to see you whenever you come.

I shall be looking for the "biggest God damn Atlas in the world."

Enclosed is a Portable Library list. Please check the Portables you have and return the list to me. Maybe I shall give you a Christmas present. Maybe.

Love,

After the holidays of 1949, Steinbeck rented an apartment at 145 East 52nd Street, in New York. He was full of plans; he was working on his script for *Viva Zapata,* working on his play-novel, *Everyman,* and had thoughts of writing a long introduction to his narrative from *Sea of Cortez.* The introduction would be a memoir of Ed Ricketts. On February 24, Steinbeck wrote Covici:

Dear Pat:

I hope you had a nice vacation. I just talked to Harold and he said you would be back sunday so I will miss you. But I'll only be gone for a week I hope.

I have talked to Harold several times. And I have made some changes in Forest * but have not sent them over. Harold says there is no hurry so I will get them to you as soon as I get back. They are minor changes but since they will be in the play, it is just as well if they are in the book too. Transitions and one change of emphasis and one extension.

I hope to be in Hollywood only two days then I will go up to see my sisters, ship my dictionary and come back and I hope to get back a week from Sunday or Monday. I hate to go but it seems to be necessary.

I'll call you as soon as I get back.

love to you both

John

* Steinbeck was, at this point, indecisive about the title of his play-novel. He had tentatively used *Everyman,* then *In the Forests of the Night;* it was ultimately titled *Burning Bright.* Steinbeck had more problems with this title than he did titling any of his other material.

Later Covici observed that both of them would probably work better if they would continue to write each other, rather than telephone regularly or meet.

Dear John,

By all means let's indulge in letter writing. It's good to know that you can be reached by phone, but I often hesitate for fear of disturbing your flow of energy. Besides, I am more often at ease with you in a letter. I am shy and often hesitate when confronting you. In a letter I need not be spontaneous and, therefore, so frequently merely smart. I can be deliberate in my attack and, if you move me, heap honorable praise. . . .

You are not really worried how and when you will get all this work done; you are just amazed how much you want to do. And you will, never fear.

Love,

Covici then wrote, juggling all of Steinbeck's works-in-progress:

Dear John,

Don't forget to let me have a carbon copy of your new version of *Zapata*. With slight changes I think it could be published fairly successfully. Movie scripts that have been published were too technically written and were confusing to the average reader. Yours won't be. It always seemed to me that a picture on the screen is more like a novel than any form of writing.

I am anxious to see how you are handling the turbulent saga of Ed Ricketts. If ever there was a man who was an intimate with the God of metaphysics and pursued the activities of Priapus, it was your friend Ed, a fascinating and contradictory individual.

"In the Forests of the Night" is now at the printer's. Galleys should be in within the next two weeks and then you will have to give me a few hours to go over the editorial queries. Don't be frightened—I shall hold your hand.

Love,

Here was Thomas Guinzburg's Covici: ". . . some part psychiatrist, some part lawyer, some part priest. . . ." ("Don't be frightened—I shall hold your hand.")

Steinbeck later rented a farm for the summer which belonged to Henry Varnum Poor, the artist, and apparently told Covici of his relationship to Elaine Scott personally, for Covici mentions her in his next letter:

Dear John,

Henry Poor's farm should prove a glorious vacation for you all, but what disturbs me is your telling me that you will plant tomatoes and string-beans and you don't mention golden bantam corn, the one vegetable I love best. How about letting me plant some?

I am delighted, of course, with your enthusiasm for the Ed Ricketts saga but not astounded at the flow of your pen. I know how you work when you are keenly interested and have something to say. It will be good too, and when Elaine says so then I have no doubts whatever.

It all seems so exciting your good work with Kazan, your stealing time for the Introduction, your thoughts on gardening with Elaine and the boys—all healthy and earthy and heartwarming. . . .

Love to you both.

As ever,

At the end of May, Steinbeck wrote Covici from Cuernavaca. He and Elaine were there working on *Viva Zapata* and *In the Forests of the Night*.

Dear Pat:

Elaine and I worked all night last night and got the Forests rewritten in the third act. It is going off to Elizabeth today and she will give you a copy when she has it typed. There are many changes. In fact the whole third act is rearranged. I hope you are not upset. It is much better I think. The dramatic structure is tighter.

Kazan is due today but I'll believe that when I see it. It is very beautiful here but I am in no mood for a vacation. I want to get to work.

love,

John

Covici answered after an absence from Viking offices because of illness. Steinbeck had returned to the Poor farm, for the rest of the summer.

Dear John,

Thanks for thinking of me. I am much better.

I just re-read your profile of Ricketts. I think it is a most penetrating and at the same time most affectionate portrait of a friend. The ease and relaxed way with which you tell it, the seemingly artlessness, as if you were telling the story to a bunch of cronies over a bottle of beer—all of it is delightful reading. Now I shall start reading the log of THE SEA OF CORTEZ. I suspect that you will want to make a few changes and deletions—maybe not too many. Be sure and let me have Ed's picture. The two bearded sailors on the same page would be most effective.

I received a note from Carl Sandburg regarding the Ernie Pyle book and he ends the letter on this note: "I am sorry there was never a book of the Steinbeck newspaper pieces during the war. I clipped some that still are good reading." So there you are.

Love to Elaine,

Yours,

It was almost a month later before Steinbeck wrote Covici, and indicated that he was still worried about the activities of his ex-wife Gwyn. He was also working on a musical adaptation of *Cannery Row*, a project which he eventually abandoned. The sequel to *Cannery Row, Sweet Thursday,* was ultimately staged as a musical, titled *Pipe Dream*.

Dear Pat:

Thanks for your letter. I'm glad you like the story of
Ed. At any rate it is different.

The boys are fine, and it is being a good summer. The
furnace went off—so for the last four days we haven't had
any hot water. With kids, this is a problem. But we hope to
get it going again. I'm going to try to get back to Cannery
Row next week. We have had a very busy time and I'm glad
I stopped for a while. It was going too fast. Kazan was
here three days last week and we did the final on Zapata.
Actually we rewrote the whole thing. I'm pretty sure this was
the last.

According to the Grape vine, Gwyn is really making a
fool of herself in the west. Her lies about me get more and
more fantastic. I have a feeling that her mental difficulties
are getting worse all the time. Between you and me I hear
that she has finally done something to Harold and Dorothy,
but I don't know what. Do you? They were about her last
friends. I'm sure she is crazy—and headed for tragedy and
I'm sad about that but I have Elaine.

So long

John

In an undated letter, Steinbeck told Covici how the title, *In the
Forests of the Night,* was changed to *Burning Bright:*

Dear Pat:

A number of things to discuss with you so I'll write them
because on the telephone I forget everything. First about Sea
of Cortez. Please note the things you might want to cut or
change so I can do it all at once.

Second part—Forests. There is one disadvantage to the
play-novel form. The novel has to go to press and stay that
way but little changes take place in the play right up to
opening night. One big change took place yesterday. Neither
Rodgers, Hammerstein nor anyone in this office thought In

the Forests of the Night was a good title for a play. Too long,
they thought and too literary. They suggest and I have agreed
to the title Burning Bright. I wish I had thought of it long
ago. I don't know what you will do about this since you
have started the process and the thing is in page proof.
Maybe just a note on the title page. I can tell you that
Mielziner will do the sets. He is crazy about the play. I am
very glad of this because I think he is the very best of all.

The summer is half over and I don't know where it has
gone. Nothing ever went so quickly. Elaine has to go to
town to meet her daughter but she will be back tomorrow.
I miss her and the boys miss her. My sister went home. I
think she was frightened. She has been living alone so long
and in the past that she scuttled back. But I think she will
come back and soon. It usually takes two tries when you
have been boarded up so long.

If I do not mention the war* it is because I try not to
think of it much. It seems a screaming hysteria to me—a
thing of nightmare and madness. The pattern is too recent.
We seem to be forcing ourselves into a war. I do not think
the Russians will fight nor will they have to. We will bleed
white and all die of apoplexy.

I guess this is all. It is still cool and lovely in the country.
Who could have thought it? But I am getting restive and I
shall not be unpleased to be back in my little apartment
with the yellow pads laid out.

I'll talk to you soon.

love,

John

Covici followed closely the changes in the title of Steinbeck's play-
novel, and Steinbeck's long memoir about Ed Ricketts for the new
edition of *Sea of Cortez.* Neither Steinbeck nor Covici seemed upset at
the change of the title from *In the Forests of the Night* to *Burning
Bright;* Covici did not influence him one way or the other.

* The Korean War.

July 26, 1950

Mr. John Steinbeck
c/o Mr. H. V. Poor
South Mountain Road
Rockland County
New York, N.Y.

Dear John,

I understand your title will be changed to BURNING
BRIGHT. I think it's a snappy title and I suppose easily
remembered. As far as I am concerned I still like IN THE
FORESTS OF THE NIGHT. It has a lovely rhythm and a
certain literary quality which I like. Somebody suggested
that you call your play TYGER TYGER. That to me has
more meaning than BURNING BRIGHT. However, your
producers should know and I would not argue against their
decisions. You are only the author, we only the publishers
but they are the producers. We will sell the book under any
title. I am glad that we decided to do a new jacket. Your
suggestion to try the drawing of the French edition of MICE
AND MEN still appeals to me. When can I have a copy to
show to the manufacturing department? We should start
going on it.

Your news about Gwyn is disturbing but not surprising,
although I always did think she had fairly good common
sense. Obviously anger and disappointment changes the
picture. I did tell Harold about her shenanigans on the coast
and asked him whether he ever hears from her. He said he
does not, he seemed very sad but said nothing more. I
couldn't very well pry any further. Thank God for Elaine
and tell her that I love her more and more. . . .

Love to you,

July 28, 1950

Mr. John Steinbeck
c/o H. B. Poor
South Mountain Road
Rockland County
New York, N.Y.

Dear John,

About 1928 or before E. Knoblock *(sic)* published, what
is probably a play, a book under the title "Tiger Tiger."
Under the same title in 1930 a biography by Honoré W.
Morrow was published, and in 1920 a novel by C. A. White.
If you were to use that for your title I would keep Blake's
spelling—"Tyger Tyger." I am not convinced, mind you,
that "Burning Bright" is not a good drama title even if it
hasn't the right connotation, at least for me. But that is up
to you and your producer.

I am delighted that Mielziner will do the sets. He has
imagination and is not afraid to play with it.

I am reading "Sea of Cortez" for possible changes. I
still feel that you should do a paragraph or two telling why
the profile, why the journey and Ed's influence in the
undertaking.

The war could be a dreadful thing for many youngsters.
And I am thinking of Pascal who will be 20 years in
September.

It will be good to see you again.

Yours,

In reply to Steinbeck's earlier statement that "But I am getting
restive and I shall not be unpleased to be back in my little apartment
with the yellow pads laid out," Covici wrote:

That is really exciting—I don't believe you can possibly
realize how exciting it is to me that you will start on your
novel. I must admit that I am not really perturbed or
disappointed that you are not going on with dramatizing
"Cannery Row." Within its limitations you have done a

beautiful piece of work, imaginative and tender. Undoubtedly
you could have made it into a charming comedy of
character and situation but, as you say, it still would be old
work.

Later in the month, Covici sent Steinbeck criticism of his long
memoir of Ed Ricketts.

August 28, 1950

Dear John,

I had Marshall Best read your portrait of Ricketts. The
stuff, he says, is all good but he came through with one
reaction that gave me pause. "Somehow, and I am quoting
him, "I get the feeling that Steinbeck, though unconsciously,
is really painting the portrait of a man who wasn't a success
sexually and was overcompensating."

Marshall also feels that there is no indication he really knew
marine biology. No mention, he says, of his own book,
"Between Pacific Tides." The personal stuff is all good he
thinks if balanced with some indication that he also had a
right to be taken seriously.

Of course I know that you always took Ed quite seriously
and it never occurred to me that you didn't in this paper.

The above reaction may be worth considering. . . .

Pascal is coming home Wednesday and the fattest calf
is being prepared, except for a different reason.

Love to you both,

On August 30, Steinbeck wrote Covici about the forthcoming stag-
ing of *Burning Bright* and commented on Marshall Best's analysis
of Steinbeck's portrait of Ed Ricketts.

We have only a little time now. Tuesday we go into
rehearsal. We will commute all that week. Then on the 11th
which is the following Monday, we will take the boys in and
we will stay—only coming out here for week ends until
we go to New Haven. So, there are our plans.

As to Marshall's observations about the Ricketts paper. I always felt a little that he protests too much but I will not put that in the paper. If that is what comes through then it must. As for his work in biology—that too must be a matter of other record. His publications were very few —he had no degrees except a B.S.—he belonged to no learned societies and had no honors. He was respected by the best men in his field but this is not that kind of a paper.

He kept Covici posted regarding the progress of *Burning Bright:*

Oct. 9

Dear Pat:

I'm going to take time for a short note. The show is getting smoother and it will come in well prepared I think. The second act which worried all of us—now plays and has a dramatic rise. Best of all attendance picks up every night. Saturday night we had standees. And today—Monday—we'll fill the house. R & H says this is rare. *Season in the Sun* did not. This means nothing in New York of course.

Norton did a recap yesterday which amounts to a rave. This makes a great difference.

We are a little tired but we are happy. I am told that Winchell said Sunday that Elaine and I were getting married this week. I won't tell him that we can't until December. I think that is what he wants me to do.

No news here. I am still chained to the radiator.

So long,

John *

But Steinbeck's play did not succeed. It was perhaps his worst failure. To Eugene Solow, a friend, who adapted *Of Mice and Men* for the screen, Steinbeck later wrote:

---

* Elliot Norton, theater critic of *The Boston Post;* Walter Winchell, the columnist; Steinbeck's reference to the radiator meant that he was still in his hotel room, making last-minute changes to the *Burning Bright* script.

October 21, 1950

Dear Gene:

The critics murdered us. I don't know how long we can
stay open but I would not think it would be long. But there
you are. I've had it before and I will survive. But a book
can wait around and a play can't. We are disappointed but
undestroyed.

Now I'll get to work again. One good thing about these
things—they keep you from getting out of hand but they
promote no humility in me. I'll not change my address.

I wish you could have seen the play because it is a good
play. I think it will do well in Europe where people are
neither afraid of the theme nor the language. The sterility
theme may have had something to do with the violence
of the criticism. Our critics are not very fecund. Then, the
universal, mildly poetic language seemed to enrage them.
Garland * never quite balanced—wrote a notice of unmixed
gibberish. Simply nuts.

Well—there it is anyway. It can happen to anyone—and
does.

John[4]

Stung by the generally negative criticism of his play, Steinbeck
contributed one of his longest and most perspective essays, "Critics,
Critics Burning Bright," to *The Saturday Review*. In that essay, he
wrote:

If a writer likes to write, he will find satisfaction in
endless experiment with his medium. He will improvise
techniques, arrangements of scenes, rhythms of words, and
rhythms of thought. He will constantly investigate and try
combinations new to him, sometimes utilizing an old
method for a new idea and vice versa. Some of his experiments will inevitably be unsuccessful but he must try them
anyway if his interest be alive. This experimentation is not

* Robert Garland, drama critic of the *New York World Telegram*.

criminal. Perhaps it is not even important, but it is necessary if the writer be not moribund.

And sometimes the experiment, which at first seems outrageous to the critic and the reader who have not been through the process of its development, may become interesting and valid when it is inspected a second and third time. The structure of literature is not endangered thereby in any case and the growth of literature spring from no other source.

The unpleasantness Steinbeck suffered from the closing of *Burning Bright* passed quickly. On November 28, he wrote Jack and Max Wagner, two friends:

> . . . I am not the least bit angry or upset. In fact I am hard at work on my new novel—the perennial Salinas Valley and this time it is going to be good. Only amateurs are destroyed by bad notices. And more and more I grow to dislike amateurs and love professionals. There are so very few of them in the world.[5]

On December 28, 1950, Steinbeck and Elaine Scott were married in the home of Harold Guinzburg. After a wedding trip to Bermuda, they returned to New York, where Steinbeck began his *Salinas Valley*.

VIII

"AND STILL THE BOX IS NOT FULL."

January, 1951 to January, 1952

John and Elaine Steinbeck spent their honeymoon in Bermuda. From there, Steinbeck wrote one letter to Covici, January 5, 1951:

Dear Pat;

I haven't slept so much since I was a child—about 12 hours a day not counting naps which are pretty often. For two days now we had a baby hurricane but now it is warm and calm. Isn't it amazing that this place can be only 3½ hours from New York. The Gulf Stream is a strange instrument.

Maybe I am getting too relaxed. So much to do when we get back. I might learn to like this kind of thing. But I don't really believe that. I think we were both tireder than we knew. We struggle from bed to dining room to beach to bed and end up pooped. It is wonderful. And the dreams at night have been strange—a kind of autobiographical motion picture going way back and, curiously enough, in sequence, almost more accurate than most dreams. Today is very warm. Elaine is on the beach getting some sun. I have to see someone from a newspaper. I've put it off for a long time and now I have to do it I guess. I don't feel much like talking right now, but I will.

Our pockets and clothes were full of rice. When we got to the St. Regis we were dripping rice. Certain nieces of mine were responsible. You know I almost wish you *had* tried to trail us that night. Our bags had been taken to the hotel much earlier. And we went from a long ride in the park before we went to the hotel. It could have done it but it would have been difficult. Didn't even have to register. I had done that earlier and had the key in my pocket. And the hotel would not have admitted we were there. It was fun, I must say.

We only have a few more days here but it will be enough. I can only take so much rest and then I get restless. I'll want to get back to New York. I thought the boys conducted themselves very well at the wedding, didn't you? There was one tragedy when they discovered that Waverly * couldn't go home to live with them. They had worked that out for themselves. They were upset by that. They thought she was going to move in with them.

We'll be leaving next Monday and will be in late that night. So we may be back before you get this letter.

However, now I'm going to the beach and let the reporter find me if he can.

So long
John

When the Steinbecks returned to New York, they moved into a house at 206 East 72nd Street, where they lived for the next thirteen years. Late in January, Steinbeck began the day-to-day work on his novel. Wrote Charles Madison:

Early in 1951 Steinbeck was ready to begin the novel that had been gestating in his imagination over the past two years. His association with Covici was by then so close that he felt impelled to include him in the actual process of writing. What he did was to begin each morning's stint by addressing Covici, as sort of alter ego, on the separate left-hand page of a large pad supplied to him by Covici, pencilling freely what came to his mind as a means of "warming up" for writing the novel on the right-hand page. Three weeks after this was started, on February 22, 1951, he wrote self-consciously: "I am not going to have much time to visit with you. Has it struck you that this is a crazy kind of thing? Writing you what amounts

---

* Waverly Scott—Elaine's daughter by her previous marriage.

to a letter which you won't even see in under a year. It's fun in a way too."

These "letters" were in a sense outpourings; Steinbeck jotted down whatever came to his mind as he sat down at his writing table: trivialities, clichés, current incidents, momentary reactions, the minutiae of his most personal activities, but also sensitive and incisive feelings and ideas as well as discussions of the content of his novel as he was developing it.[1]

Steinbeck's material from his daily jottings to Covici ultimately appeared as *Journal of a Novel: The East of Eden Letters.** By early April, with approximately one-fourth of the book completed, Steinbeck again discussed his daily notes to Covici.

It is too bad that I write these long letters to you. I might be better employed in just sticking to my book. But I think I have explained by reason for it to you many times in an attempt to understand myself. Actually I do think I lose much time with these letter pages. I think I would either be staring at a blank wall or writing to someone else. I do know that I have always needed some kind of warm-up before going to work. And if I write to someone else I will be bored because I would have to tell things that happened last week or a month ago and I am not interested in those things. On the other hand, in this, there is rarely anything that did not happen mentally or physically within 24 hours. And in such things I still have an interest. So you see, I will continue with the letters. See how far I have got from the opening line—the week is gone.[3]

During the progress of *East of Eden,* Steinbeck would mail a week's manuscript to Covici, who would have it typed in the Viking offices, and return the typescript to Steinbeck for later correction. Covici would also send back his detailed criticism of that portion of the book. By

---

* Most of the letters from Steinbeck mentioned here were not included in his daily journal and appear for the first time. Written replies from Pascal Covici regarding *East of Eden* also appear here for the first time. According to Marshall Best, they were deleted from *Journal of a Novel* at Covici's request, before his death. He died in 1964; *Journal of a Novel* was published in 1969.[2]

the middle of April, Steinbeck said that Covici should not continue his criticisms; it only confused him. In his daily letters, Steinbeck emphasized this point:

> I hope you don't feel that I was short this morning on
> the phone, about the criticism. Right now, when I am only
> thinking ahead, it will do me no good. So write it all down and
> we'll go into it when the book is finished. As you remember
> I am pretty good about criticism. I want to warn you of only
> one thing. This is a different kind of book and you must
> be sure that you do not dislike it for its difference. Also be
> very careful that you are sure that the thing you intend is
> not a carefully planted matter. I think you must save any large
> criticism until the book is done or else you may find your-
> self trapped in this technique.[4]

Steinbeck also felt it necessary to remind Covici that, although he had achieved great popularity in the past for his works, he still maintained the position that he would not write solely for an audience or solely for money.

> You said this morning you had to sell X thousands of copies.
> I am sure, after all our years together, you will not ask me to
> make one single change for the sake of sales except in terms
> of clarity. I am not writing for the money any more now
> than I ever did. If money comes that is fine, but (if) I knew
> right now that this book would not sell a thousand copies, I
> would still write it. I want you to remember that, Pat. I have
> not changed in that respect even a little bit. . . .[5]

During his relationship with Covici, only one previous book had not been a success, *A Russian Journal,* and only two later would not be successful, *Once There Was a War* and *Burning Bright.* The other books produced from their relationship were financial successes, yet were books which Steinbeck and Covici accepted as artistic successes. Steinbeck's statement of warning here may be a result of the struggle of the work-in-progress.

The next week, Steinbeck repeated his problems of attempting to work with Covici during the creative period of the novel. Steinbeck repeats the idea that criticism of the book will be accepted at the right time—after the book is done, not during the process. On April 16, he wrote in his daily journal to Covici:

> I want to ask and even beg one thing from you—that we do not discuss the book any more when you come over. No matter how delicately we go about it, it confuses me and throws me off the story. So from now on let's do the weather or fleas or something else but let's leave the book alone. In that way we'll have some surprises. I know you won't mind this once you see why. Once it is done you may tear it to shreds if you wish and I won't object, and I'll go along with you, but but right now both you and I forget the delicate sets of balances involved. There are no good collaborations and all this discussion amounts to collaboration. So, we'll do that, if you don't mind. And let's stop counting pages, too. I am not being difficult I hope. It is just too hard on me to try and write, defend and criticize all at the same time. I can quite easily do each one separately. Let me keep the literary discussion on these poor pages. Then we will have no quarrels. . . .[6]

On April 30, in his daily journal to Covici, Steinbeck explained how his son Tom won a prize for designing a safety poster in school:

> Tom's winning the prize was a fine thing. He pretended he didn't care about it but when they called out his name he cried "Here I am!"[7]

Later Steinbeck used this exuberance as part of a sub-plot in *The Winter of Our Discontent.*

On the 10th of May, Steinbeck began having second thoughts about his title, *Salinas Valley.* A distant relative of his wife Elaine, told Steinbeck that Salinas Valley would mean nothing to people who had never lived there, or did not know where it was. The relative, Lawrence Hagy, suggested that Steinbeck call the work, *My Valley,* which Steinbeck first liked, because of the two Y's and the L's in the title. Steinbeck would continue to worry about his title for some time, until he chose *East of Eden* later.

On the 15th of May, when Steinbeck was told that Covici did not like his title, he wrote:

Now, although it is still very early, I shall get to the book.
You don't like the title MY VALLEY. I have never been a title
man. I don't give a dam what it is called. I would call it Valley
to the Sea which is a quotation from absolutely nothing but
has two great words and a direction. What do you think of that?
And I'm not going to think about it any more.

On May 22, Steinbeck again suggested another title for his book,
Cain Sign, from Genesis, denoting life and death, goodness and evil. He
told Covici that the story of Cain and Abel:

. . . has made a deeper mark in people than any other save
possibly the story of the Tree of Life and original sin. Now
since this is indeed my frame—is there any reason to conceal
it from my reader? Would it not be better to let him know even
in the title what the story is about? With this in mind I went
back to Genesis. I do not want a direct quotation but if I can
find a symbol there which is understood on sight and which
strikes deep, I will have my title.[8]

On June 11, Steinbeck finally came to the title for his novel which
was permanent. He wrote Covici, in his daily letter:

And now I had set down in my own hand the 16 verses
of Cain and Abel and the story changes with flashing lights
when you write it down. And I think I have a title at last, a
beautiful title, EAST OF EDEN. And read the 16th verse
to find it. And the Salinas Valley is surely East of Eden. I
could go on and write another page and perhaps it would
be good, who knows. Or maybe not. What a strange story
and how it haunts one.[9]

About this time, Steinbeck realized that his supply of pencils was
disappearing. He asked Covici to supply him with more. The editor,
happy to do favors for Steinbeck sent them. He never questioned why
Steinbeck couldn't keep himself supplied. Steinbeck wrote:

My pencils are all short now and I think I will celebrate
by getting out twelve new pencils. Sometimes the just pure

luxury of long beautiful pencils charges me with energy and invention. We shall see. It means I will have to have more pencils before long though. Would you send me another box. They are Mongol 480 #2 ⅜F round.[10]

Pascal Covici, Jr. has observed, ". . . My God, Steinbeck was a fanatic about pencils. They had to be exactly the right kind, and round." Over the weekend of June 15, 16 and 17, the Steinbecks moved for the summer to Siasconset, Nantucket. As Steinbeck's work on *East of Eden* became smoother and as he progressed with the novel, his letters to Covici became more frequent. On June 18, he sent Covici a second letter, in addition to the note before the day's work, which appeared in *Journal of a Novel*.

Dear Pat:

It wasn't such a bad trip. Didn't take as long as we had thought. Got in to find the lights on, beds made and fires lighted. Very pleasant. It was cold the first couple of days but now delightfully warm but not hot and no fires at night so far.

The boat is not here.* If it is not in a very short time I am going to be angry and start burning up the wires.

Went to work this morning and got my quota done by 1 p.m. Boys and Elaine are at the beach. I am going to do a few duties and then join them. I shall be happy here if my work goes as it should. And I see no reason why it should not. Started the sequence about Tom Hamilton this morning. It will take most of the week. I will send ms. registered mail every Saturday or perhaps Friday afternoon. In any case it should be in on Monday.

We shall be glad to see you when you come. Just give us a warning.

I miss the phone calls but will have to get over that.

Take your medicine and I think it is about time for you to go back and see Juan.† Call for an appointment. I have

---

* Steinbeck had placed an order for a small yacht.

† Covici had been ill and had seen a neurosurgeon, Dr. Juan Negrin, whom Steinbeck recommended. Covici had not yet told his wife Dorothy about his illness.

meant to discuss this with you. I think you should tell Dorothy about this. I can understand your wanting to save her worry but such things usually don't save anything. I thing you owe it to her to tell her. A woman marries a man for the worry as well as the other things. And now that it is better, she need not worry. But even if it weren't, she deserves to know. Just imagine how it would be if she kept something like this from you for whatever reason. It's part of trust and sharing. You think it over. You don't really spare her anything and you rob her of something that is her right. I hate to lecture you but I think I am right about this. Love to you both and all three and remind Pascal that we expect him here this summer.

John

On the 19th, Steinbeck described his own creative processes, in his daily note to Covici:

> . . . after everyone is asleep there is such quiet and peace, and it is during this time that I can explore every land and trail of thinking. Conjecture. Sometime I will tell you about this in detail if you are interested. I split myself into three people. I know what they look like. One speculates and one criticises and the third tries to correlate. It usually turns out to be a fight but out of it comes the whole week's work. And it is carried on in my mind in dialogue. It's an odd experience. Under certain circumstances it might be one of those schizophrenic symptoms but as a working technique, I do not think it is bad at all.[11]

Central to the structure of *East of Eden* was the story of Cain and Abel. As Peter Lisca writes:

> As the title suggests ("And Cain went out from the presence of the Lord, and dwelt in the land of Nod, on the east of Eden."), the vehicle for this theme is a reworking of the Cain and Abel story, told through three generations of the Trask family. Steinbeck sees this story in Genesis as a true account of man's condition, especially as made clear in the

Lord's words to Cain after rejecting his sacrifice: "If thou
doest well, shalt thou not be accepted? and if thou doest
not well, sin lieth at the door. And unto thee shall be his desire, and thou shalt rule over him." Steinbeck grounds his
interpretation of the story on a new translation of the Hebrew
word *timshel,* which the King James version renders as "thou
shalt." He proposes that the word is more meaningfully and
truly rendered as "thou *mayest,*" for this gives man responsible
moral choice, the dignity of free will—"thou mayest rule over
him (sin)."[12]

During the next few weeks, Steinbeck and Covici shared the research necessary for understanding the various interpretations of the
Biblical story. Steinbeck cites this study of "thou shalt" and "thou
mayest" in his daily entries to Covici, in *Journal of a Novel,* as well as
in additional notes and letters which were not made part of *Journal of
a Novel.* For his part, Covici, who remembered a little Hebrew, enjoyed this work and was happy to aid Steinbeck in this interpretative
analysis.

On June 21, Steinbeck wrote in his daily log, to Covici:

Your new translation of the story has one most important
change. It is the third version. The King James says of sin
crouching at the door, "Thou shalt rule over it." The American
Standard says, "Do thou rule over it." Now this new translation
says, "Thou *mayest* rule over it." This is the most vital
difference. The first two are 1, a prophecy and 2, an order,
but 3 is the offering of free will. Here is individual responsibility
and the invention of conscience. You can if you will but it
is up to you. I would like to check that phrase over. Will you
do it for me? The exact word—because if it is incontrovertibly,
"thou mayest" I must put this in my discussion, because it
will turn out to be one of the most important mistranslations in
the Old Testament. Get me the Hebrew word, will you? The
word that has been variously translated "do thou," "thou
shalt," and "thou mayest." This is important. This little
story turns out to be one of the most profound in the world.
I always felt it was but now I know it is.[13]

The next day, in his diaries, Steinbeck again asked Covici for help with the translations:

> Now in the work today or tomorrow I am going to need that Hebrew word which has been variously translated "do thou," "thou shalt," and "thou mayest." I need the word and I want you to get me a good scholarly discussion of it. I have a charming scene to use it in and I can write it all only leaving out that one word to be filled in later.[14]

The Hebrew word that Steinbeck needed was "timshel," which Covici supplied.

Steinbeck later showed Covici his gratitude for Covici's help by presenting him with the manuscript of the book, in a hand-carved box, with the Hebrew characters of the word "timshel" carved on the lid. The dust jacket for the first edition of *Journal of a Novel* shows the box. He gave the manuscript and box to Covici as a present at Christmas, 1951.

On the 26th of June Steinbeck again observed that he had to work around words which Covici would supply, but which had not yet been mailed to him:

> Some of tomorrow's work is going to be very funny, I think A really amusing venture in scholarship. But I must leave space for certain words which I have asked you to give me. I'll fill the word in later together with the definition and you will find for me. And that is all for today and I am satisfied with today's work.[15]

On June 27 Steinbeck wrote Covici an additional daily letter, also not included in *Journal of a Novel:*

Dear Pat:

> Just a note. Work goes well—very well, I think. I went over my quota today in a passage which I will want to hear whether you like. It's Lee's work with the Cain Abel story and it will be the last reference to the story in this whole book. But it

is pretty definitive. I have left a space for the Hebrew work
and its possible translations when you send it to me. I suppose
in this passage is the meat of the things I believe.

We have fishing tackle now and Elaine and I are learning
to cast and we will be very good at it. It is a little raw and
cold today but my how I love it. You know I hate heat. The
yellow pads came as you can see.

The enclosed letter to Pascal I would like you to address
and forward. It will get there quicker that way and meanwhile
please send me his address. I have left the envelope open
and you can certainly read it if you wish.*

I guess that's all. I'll probably hear from you in today's mail.

love to you all.

John

Steinbeck occasionally used the imperative ("I would like you to
address and forward") when requesting errands from Covici, as seen
elsewhere in their relationship.

In his daily journal to Covici for June 28, Steinbeck wrote:

There needs today to be the end of the kind of music
which is Samuel Hamilton. It has to have first a kind of re-
capitulation with full orchestra, and then I would like a little
melody with one flute which starts as a memory and then
extends into something quite new and wonderful as though the
life which is finished is going on into some wonderful future.
I want Samuel to go out with wonder and interest. . . .
Now tomorrow I will take up the little flute melody, the continuing thing that bridges lives and ties the whole thing
together, and I will end in a huge chord if I can do it. I know
how I want it to sound and I know how I want it to feel and
I know how I want you to feel when you have read it.

---

* Pascal Jr., then in college, was working at a summer co-ed camp for the
second year in a row, with boys the age of the Steinbeck sons. Steinbeck's sons
were still living with Steinbeck's second wife, Gwyn. Pascal Jr.'s wife-to-be, Joan,
was also working as a counselor at the same camp and helped frame the reply to
Steinbeck. Steinbeck later acknowledged his response. In a subsequent journal
entry, Steinbeck mentioned "a good letter from Pascal."

On July 3 Covici wrote Steinbeck about the translation of "timshel," Steinbeck's use of that word, and the last chapter of the novel. By now Steinbeck no longer found fault with Covici's comments on the book-in-progress.

July 3, 1951

Dear John,

What a superb chapter. A whole orchestra with every instrument playing its part. Don't worry about length now. Certainly it doesn't seem long to me. Samuel's telling of his secret life came as a shock, although you hinted at it at least twice, but you did it beautifully and subtly. Lee's parting from Samuel was painfully exquisite; it was a breathless night.

Your scholarly discourse I found fascinating but I am a little afraid that you are getting into deep waters. I just heard from Dr. H. L. Ginsburg of the Jewish Theological Seminary, one of our outstanding rabbinical scholars, and he told me that the word *tinshol,* a pure future tense, means "shall." He translates the line as follows: "Thou shalt prevail over it," meaning assurance that he will do it. I have yet to hear from other scholars. I have written to one in Israel.

Please don't belittle your notes. They are wonderful and anything but dull. I certainly remember your agonizing struggles at the Bedford Hotel.* You knew and I knew that you were rejected but you would not say anything. I also knew how painful you felt about the false starts on the novel. I wanted so much for you to be free and happy. Yours was a terrible struggle, but thank God now you have Elaine and what a difference that makes.

I hope with all my heart that you will want Elaine to rule the roost as far as the boys are concerned. She's tender and kind and understanding.

I shall visit Abercrombie and see about the bow and arrows and will write you soon.

Love,†

* Steinbeck made a false start on the book during his divorce from Gwyn.

† A birthday present for Elaine, which he was buying for Steinbeck in New York.

Again, on July 6, Steinbeck, still worried about the word "timshel," wrote in his daily journal:

Don't forget that in the Jewish translation you sent, they did not think "timshel" was a pure future tense. They translated it "thou mayest." This means that at least there is a difference of opinions and that is enough for me. I will have to have the whole verb before I will finish, from infinitive on through past, subjunctives and compounds and futures. But we will get it. We may have to go outside of rabbinical thought to pure scholarship which may be non-Jewish. What American university has a good Hebrew department? Dr. Ginzburg, dealing in theology, may have a slightly different attitude from that of a pure etymologist. We know that the other translations were warped by what the translators wish to be there.[16]

On the 10th of July, Covici again responded to Steinbeck's work-in-progress, with a long letter about the book. He had given Steinbeck a copy of *Bartlett's Quotations* and Steinbeck had reluctantly asked for another, to give as a gift. Covici had to reassure him that small favors and gifts which he had given to Steinbeck were given in joy ("You seem to forget that what you are asking of me is nothing compared to the riches of mind you are giving me").

July 10, 1951

Dear John,

Your last chapter on Adam and Kate was a real inspiration. The first part, the funeral, is moving poetry. The whole chapter held me like a vise. The tensity was almost unbearable right to the end. The motivation of Kate, though horrible and hateful to contemplate, becomes clear and almost logical. Her telling about the man who committed suicide on her account and of her seething, murderous hatred, quite justified, for Edwards, were strokes of genius on your part. This is drawing character in revealing flashes. It was a necessary and very important chapter, brilliantly thought out and wonderfully written. By way of parenthesis, I must tell you that the reading

of it gave Dorothy a terrific headache and the muscles
back of her neck were tighter than a drum.

Harold at last spoke to me about your book. I deliberately
wouldn't ask him. He will write you as soon as he reads the
Samuel chapters which are now being typed. But I can tell
you that he is awed, delighted and highly puzzled.

I am ordering another Bartlett's QUOTATIONS for you.
Tell me the name and number of the pencil you use. I had
better get them for you right away.

One way for you to get me really mad is for you to hesitate
asking me to help you in any way at all. You seem to forget
that what you are asking of me is nothing compared to the
riches of mind you are giving me. . . .

Love,

On Friday, July 13, Steinbeck wrote another letter to Covici, like-
wise not in *Journal of a Novel*. He realized, perhaps for the first time,
how deeply involved Covici had become in the creation of this book.

Friday, July 13, 1951

Dear Pat:

The mss. which I am putting in the mail at the same time
I post this will be one day short. I took Thursday off and went
fishing. However, I am going to try to work tomorrow so
that next week there should be an extra day. I know it doesn't
really matter that I keep to ten pages a week but it is a kind
of good feeling that I can do it.

The fishing trip got no fish and I got a painful sunburn,
but out of it I got a whole new extension of the book. I guess
I never really do stop working. I am not going to tell you
that extension now but it will gradually be incorporated in
the notes. It is not new, but simply a method for making
this book well rounded.

I am sorry about Dorothy's headache. It could be a little
like part of the litany—"the various parts of the body,
curse thee." It is a new field of criticism—criticism by neck,
by wrist, by line.

Yesterday, out on the water, I got a funny thought about

you. I am going to tell you and if it doesn't amuse you, at least it will amuse Dorothy to whom I hope you will read it. You have been publishing things for many years and there must be a special feeling a publisher has for a book, a continuation of proprietary, creative, etc. but very especially a publisher's feeling. The failure, or denunciation or attack or praise of a book would arouse an emotion but it would be a publisher's emotion. Now, I think, for the first time, although I may be wrong, I think you will have to experience writer's emotions. I think you are so close to this, to the making of it, that an attack on the book, even a raised eye, will send you into a rage. See if this is not true. You are not used to writer's emotions as I am. I think you will be more deeply hurt by attack and more proud of praise than I will be, because it will be your first experience. See if I am not right. And I am sure you will tell me if I am.

In your last letter, you said you liked to do the errands I ask. Will you do one more very silly one for me? Again it concerns Abercromie & Fitch. First I would like you to go there and ask whether they have a section or a personnel which takes care of queries by mail. In other words, if I want to ask about something, to whom do I write. Second—in either the boat department or the gun department, probably the latter, they used to have small cannons used for starting yacht races. They were pretty little things and they fired 10 gauge shotgun blanks. I would like you to go and inquire about them—whether they still have them. How much they cost, and how much the blanks cost. Then I would like you to put this information on a separate page in your next letter to me so that I may put it aside and not show it to Elaine. My reason is both absurd and good. On her birthday I would like to fire her a 21 gun salute and I don't want her to know about it. Her birthday is August 14 and she puts great stock in it. I shall have other things to request before then. If A & F do not have these little cannons, will you find out where I can get one. They will know. They used to have them. There it is—now back to work.

Covici continued to research "timshel," for Steinbeck, as well as running the errands at Abercromie & Fitch, in New York, as Steinbeck requested. In his next two letters, Covici supplied further information about "timshel," and the additional information "on a separate page" about the birthday cannons.

July 16, 1951

Dear John,

The five books of Moses, which I now have, with Hebrew on the right side and English translation by Isaac Leeser on the opposite, phrased the Cain passage as follows:

"If thou doest well, shall thou not be accepted? and if thou doest not well, sin lieth at the door; and unto thee is its desire, but thou canst rule over it."

Last Saturday I was out in Cold Spring * and I found a Bible in an old home which interested me very much. It's a large octavo. Part of the title page reads as follows:

"The Holy Bible, translated from the Latin Vulgate diligently compared with the Hebrew, Greek and other editions in diverse languages. The old testament first published by the English College at Douay, A.D. 1609. This edition was published in Manchester, 1812."

The translation of the Cain passage in this edition runs as follows:

"If thou do well, shall thou not receive? but if ill, shall not sin forthwith be present at the door? but the lust thereof shall be under thee, and thou shalt have dominion over it."

The phrase "over it" has the following note at the bottom of the page (which, of course, refers to the whole sentence):

"This is a clear proof of free-will. To destroy its force, Protestants translate 'over him' as if Cain should still retain his privilege of the first-born, notwithstanding all his wickedness, and should rule over Abel, who would willingly submit, 'unto thee his desire,' etc. But God had made no

---

* Cold Spring, New York, the home of Robert Ballou. Ballou, one of Steinbeck's earlier publishers, had joined The Viking Press as a consulting editor.

mention of Abel. The whole discourse is about doing well
or ill, and Cain is encouraged to avoid the stings of
conscience, by altering his conduct, as it was in his power,
how strongly so ever his passion might solicit him to
evil. The Hebrew is understood by Onkelos and the
Targum of Jerusalem, in the sense of the Vulgate."
I am looking forward to seeing you soon.

Love,

July 18, 1951

Dear John,

What you say about my reaction to praise and criticism
of your novel, E. of E. is not funny. It is too true for comfort.
Not only do I know the inception of it, the hell you went
through before the story took shape in your mind, but I have
made myself a part of the book as you put it on paper. The
father always believes he feels worse than the pregnant mother
when she gives birth. And because of my nearness to it I
so much dread the possible criticisms and am constantly
searching in my mind, after each chapter I read, for literary
generalizations and theories of art in general which could be
used against you. Something I have never done before. I am
fully conscious that this is your greatest creative effort and the
vaguest feeling of possible disaster fills me with horror.

Some smart alek, for instance, may probably ask, has it the
intense, moral preoccupation that any major work of art must
have, thinking undoubtedly of Dante, Shakespeare and Tol-
stoy? Or somebody might ask of the novel whether it stands
in some meaningful relation to recognizable life. A classicist
might ask, does the author know that in art half is greater
than one and hasn't he over-written and over-emphasized,
etc., etc.? So you see, what you said wasn't funny. But your
perspicacity is too damn keen.

The change in Adam when he is with Kate in the whore
house is good and sound and Samuel's influence is evident and
certainly felt. You almost hear Samuel talking through Adam.

The beginning of the third part must have been difficult

to write, and yet you tell of the economic change with great simplicity and lucidity. It seems almost too easy.

Love,

P.S. At last Dr. Negrin has rendered me a bill. I am much relieved.

The person to write to and who takes care of all queries by mail at Abercrombie and Fitch is Mr. Edward Shade.

The small cannon for starting yacht races, I mean the one they have on hand, cost $74.65.

The blank cartridges cost $3 for a box of 25.

They can get you a blue steel cannon for $40.25, which may take 10 days to 5 weeks after you order it.

The man to write to about this is Mr. W. Schroeder.

On the 18th, as Covici was writing to Steinbeck, Steinbeck was writing in his daily log, to Covici, again about the collaboration between author and editor. He wrote:

Your notes on other versions of "thou canst" came yesterday and I can see that you, even as I am, are like a hound on the scent. And isn't it interesting that this word has been a matter of such concern for so long. You are having fun, aren't you? This is a time of great joy. It will never be so good again—never. A book finished, published, read—is always an anticlimax to me. The joy comes in the words going down and the rhythms crowding in the chest and pulsing to get out.[17]

During August, Covici and his wife planned to spend some vacation time with the Steinbecks. On the 24th, Steinbeck mentioned the box he was carving for presentation to Covici, the box which would eventually contain the manuscript of the book:

I am going to work on the present I am making for you while you are here. I think you might like to watch the process of trial and error. You don't love tools and working with your hands as much as I do but I think you will like to watch it. So you shall and it will not interfere at all with conversation.

And again, on the 30th, Steinbeck repeated, in his daily journal, how much he wished Covici to understand the joys of woodworking and the hours of work he put in, on the box for the manuscript.

And I'm glad for you to see the carving of the box to hold this manuscript. Now you will know how much goes into it. If I had finished it alone you would not have known the hours and hours that went into it. It's a good thing to see. And maybe you will get some small tools to work with. I think it is good for both hands and brain, and when you finish, you have something and even if it isn't very good it is yours.

Steinbeck also felt compelled to write in his journal of August 2 that Covici might find him irritable and unpleasant during the creation of his novel. Covici undoubtedly knew that.

I feel a little mixed-up. Too many things happening I guess. I get confused. The single-track mind is overloaded. And the only danger is that I might turn mean. I almost always do when my pups of thought are endangered. You will probably regret that you came to the island because I am not very pleasant when I am working and sometimes I am downright nasty. I am not very large in that but I try.[18]

Pascal and Dorothy Covici arrived on July 27 and returned to New York on August 6, but Steinbeck had been right in his prediction; his concentration on the novel did in fact, ruin a dinner party, during the Covici visit. Steinbeck mentioned his rude behavior in a journal entry dated August 6, and in an additional letter to Covici:

Dear Pat and Dorothy—

I want to say that I am sorry for my beastly disposition. I guess I threw a pall over your nice dinner last night and I didn't want to nor intend to. My nerve ends were spurting hot little flames and sounds crashed on me like waves. It had nothing to do with anyone but me. And I have not Elaine's strength to cover and dissemble such a feeling. I was in a nervous collapse. I'm sorry if I made you sad. Last night all night I had it and

today it is better. Please believe that it had absolutely nothing
to do with anything but my own insides. It is some inner
confusion that comes on me sometimes with a frightening intensity. Forgive it please.

It has been good to have you here. I'm glad you gave got
to know the boys and they surely share our love for you both.
I hope, in spite of my ugliness that you had some joy and
rest here. It was a joy to have you.

A book is so long. It takes so much. It must be desperately
hard to live with and I do not envy Elaine having to do it. And
when it boils over, as it did last night it must have been pure
hell. I'm all right today. And I have no explanation.

Thank you both for everything, the lovely presents and
Thom's birthday and all.

Love to you both and happy landing.

John

In his journal entry for August 9, Steinbeck again commented on
the manuscript box and how he wished that *East of Eden* would never
end:

Everyone who sees it falls in love with your box. And
there is still lots of work to do on it. Lots. But if I get it done
when the mss. is done, that will be time enough. It gives me
lots of time. And I need lots of time.

Now the sun comes out. It is going to be a warm and lovely
day. And I'll have to stay in and work. I can see it is going
to be slow today—very slow. And I don't much care. It's
funny—I am reluctant to start on the last book because it
will mean I must go through to the end and I guess I don't
want to finish this book. I don't want it finished. It will be a
sad day for me when it is done. I have never loved my work
more, in fact never as much. And I don't mean the finished
work but the working. But now I guess I really must get to it.[19]

By the 16th of August, Steinbeck had completed the first Three
Parts of *East of Eden* and was ready to begin Part Four. To sustain his
own enthusiasm for the last segment of the novel, Steinbeck began to
number the pages, from #1, to add newness to this section in his mind.

He also summarized the remaining structure in his journal entry of August 19, to Covici:

> All of this is of course a kind of evaluation before going into the final section. I feel able to go into it. And I am now ready to discuss it in notes. It amounts to a whole novel in subject matter. I think it will be in the neighborhood of 80,000 words. Maybe a few less. It has three preceding books to fulfill and resolve. It will continue and carry out the design of the earlier two books. I know most of its incidents. I think it will have power and development. . . . So—now we are about ready to go. We have a new kind of a world in the Salinas Valley and our timeless principles must face a new set of facts and react to them. Are you interested to see what happens? I am.[20]

Two days later, Covici returned all of Part Three of the novel, which had been typed in the Viking offices from Steinbeck's handwritten manuscript. Covici still felt compelled, compounded perhaps by Steinbeck's moody behavior during the Covici visit, to encourage him to continue and successfully complete his project.

August 21, 1951

Dear John,

Here is the end of Book III; 636 typewritten pages or about 172,000 words. No untyped manuscript on hand. I am not complaining, I am just stating a fact because you have written a hell of a lot of words in comparatively so short a time. You have earned a holiday, and what better time to take it than the week of Elaine's birthday. What shooting there must have been. I celebrated the week by reading again the chapters I am mailing you. I found them good and the Dessie chapter best of all. It was a fine feeling I had reading them over again.

I am awaiting the beginning of Book IV. Right now I feel like a man sitting on a mountain top, deliberately majestic, knowing full well that I may be sitting on a volcano.

We enjoyed tremendously Elaine's lovely letter. It was

thoughtful, considerate and affectionate. She's a great, little girl.

Love to you all,

Steinbeck was able to sustain his own enthusiasm for the book; in his journal entry dated August 23, he wrote to Covici:

The typescript came and I glanced through it. Pretty good in places, quite good but needs lots of delicate cleaning-up work. Well I will do it.

You know after the summer and boys and play and the days being too short, I am glad that my last 30,000 words will be done in New York. There won't be any distractions there. And I'll want full concentration for my ending. But I seem to be able to concentrate pretty well even here.

From the number of pages I guess my estimate was pretty accurate—between 240,000 and 250,000 words.

I do hope you like the return of Lee. I think it is pretty good and short enough. I need Lee, not only as an interpreter but as an active figure. I have a feeling of goodness about the book now but there is so much more to come. I don't for the life of me know how I got in what I have already.

On an impulse I just went back and read the opening notes addressed to you. I wanted to see whether I had failed in any part to carry out my intention and I do not think I have. The direction has not changed a bit and this book which seems to sprawl actually does not at all. It is almost as tight as a short story. And I am pleased about that.

Now—I have a little over three weeks left here. Elaine has more mss. here than she can ever get done before we leave. Therefore, I think you should not send any more mss. here, either original or typescript. Of course, as always, I will send you the week's work as I finish it. And do you realize that after this week, there will be three more 10's— 40,000 words nearly, counting this week's work. And about one more month in town will finish it.[21]

On August 28, Steinbeck got a welcome surprise—first copies of *The Log from the Sea of Cortez*. He wrote in his journal:

The *Log* came and it is a very good-looking book. It would not seem to me that it would sell very well but these are curious times. I think it will in Europe. And it is barely possible that it might catch on a little here. When, I wonder, does it come out? It is a curious time for books. People do seem to like thoughtfulness—or do they? Maybe they only want reassurance.[22]

The Log from the Sea of Cortez was officially published 17 September, 1951, with a relatively small first printing for a Steinbeck book: 7,500.

On August 28, Covici commented for the first time about the last Book of *East of Eden*:

August 28, 1951

Dear John,

You need not worry about the beginning of Book the Last. It is very well thought out together with the scheme of the whole book. The beginning is a refrain of Book I— slow and majestic as it should be. The Lee episode is delightful and heart-warming into tears. The Abra and Aron colloquy is an illuminating, moving and intricate piece of child psychology, perfectly convincing and frightening with its tragic undertones.

It was very lonesome last week without your week's work. What slaves habit makes of us and how I love that kind of slavery.

It will be good to have you back again. I feel fine.

Love,

Early in September, Covici received another portion of Part Four from Steinbeck, read it, had it retyped and sent the typescript back with his comments. That Steinbeck based the character of Kate on his worst-perceived faults of his first and second wives, Carol and Gwyn, are seen in this letter from Covici, in which he wrote, "All the ancient wounds were opened; disappointments and fears and a kind of pain of what may come gripped your mind and heart."

September 6, 1951

Dear John,

After I read the conversation between Cal and Lee, upon
Cal's return from the whorehouse, I knew what had happened to you the week of your writing this chapter. All the
ancient wounds were opened; disappointments and fears, and
a kind of pain of what may come gripped your mind and
heart. A terrible darkness must have been yours. The writing
of it has great tensity and sharply compressed feelings. And
again you hint at greater tragedy to come.

It is too much for any human being to do so exacting a
piece of work, draining as the work does so much energy out
of you, and still have other worries, too. I hate to think what
would have happened without Elaine.

It will be good for you to get back. I am counting the
days.

Love,

By the middle of September, Steinbeck was beginning to show the
strain of constant work on his novel. In addition to his journal entry of
September 11, he wrote Covici an additional letter:

September 11, 1951

Dear Pat;

I am so punchy that I forget whether I have written to
you or not. I'm saturated with story and with many outside
matters. The really deep tiredness is creeping up but I'm
pretty sure I have two or three months more of this kind of
energy. And it is a very curious kind of energy. I have never
used so much of it for so long a period. I have worked more
wordage for shorter periods. I have been much longer on this
for instance even now than I was on the Grapes of Wrath. I
am fascinated with this week's work. As you are becoming
aware, I hope—Cal is my baby. He is the Everyman, the battle
ground between good and evil, the most human of all, the
worry man. In that battle the survivor is both. I have been
trying to think how long it is since a book about morality has

been written. That is not to say that all books are not about
morality but I mean openly.

Now the summer closes. We will get up at four in the morning on Sunday and tool our way homeward. And we have had
our triumphs this summer in addition to the work. Thom has
taken great jumps. Elaine almost despaired a number of
times but at the end of the summer Thom can read and do
his arithmetic. He will start ahead of his class, and more
important, he knows he can start. The block is gone. Catbird
is the one who might have the trouble. He is so gifted in charm
and cleverness and beauty that he will not have to go through the
fire for a long time, if ever. Poor Thom has it early and
will have it long. But he will be fired and there is no fire
without heat. We have done well this summer if you were to
make a score. I do not feel ashamed. Now if I can only get
a good book too, it will be fine.

Your letter came, Pat, and we'll have to take a rain check
on that dinner Monday night. The boys won't be with us and
we'll be so tired after moving and unpacking that we will
probably fall into bed. Besides, I am going to try to get back
to work on Tuesday so that I will only lose one day. The book
isn't done, remember. I wish the move were over. I kind of
dread it.

Anyway—we'll probably talk to you when we get in.

John

The length of the novel-in-progress continued to make Steinbeck
weary. In his journal entry for September 12, he noted that:

When I get home I am going to put new blotters on my
writing table and sharpen absolutely new pencils and open a
new case of paper and I'll be going into the last part of the
book. And God knows how long that will take. I just really
don't know in spite of my brave words about Oct. first. I just
don't know. It stretches on and on. . . .

On October first, Steinbeck was stalled at his work, and needed to
talk to Covici by telephone. Covici happened to be out of his office when
Steinbeck needed his support and guidance:

I am stuck this morning because I don't know exactly where
I am and what was in the work. You aren't in your office. Of
course I know you are out for coffee. But I will have trouble
starting until I can talk with you. But that's all right.[23]

This may be one of the episodes Covici was referring to when he told
Charles Madison, "I had to hold his hand . . . he seemed unable to
do anything for himself."

Steinbeck continued on, with increasing weariness and completed
his first draft of *East of Eden* November 1, 1951.

For Christmas, 1951, Steinbeck presented Covici with the original
manuscript of *East of Eden,* in the presentation box.

                                                    December, 1951

Dear Pat—

Do you remember you came upon me carving some kind
of little figure out of wood and you said—

"Why don't you make something for me?"

I asked you what you wanted and you said—

"A box."

"What for?"

"To put things in."

"What things?"

"Whatever you have," you said.

Well here's your box. Nearly everything I have is in it
and it is not full. All pain and excitement is in it and feeling
good or bad and evil thoughts and good thoughts—the
pleasure of design and some despair and the indescribable
joy of creation.

And on top of these are all the gratitude and love I bear
for you.

And still the box is not full.

                                                    John *

This letter appears as the dedication to *East of Eden.*

* The manuscript box which Steinbeck gave Covici is now owned by Pascal
Covici, Jr.

Steinbeck's letter of August 9, in which he writes of the manuscript box and how he wished that the work on *East of Eden* would never end, perhaps indicates Steinbeck's lengthy work on the manuscript, and his reluctance to complete it. He is apparently using the work on the manuscript box to delay completion on the manuscript itself (when the box is finished the manuscript is finished) although he is working on the writing every day. ("It gives me lots of time. And I need lots of time.")

To Pascal Covici

Dear Pat:
I have decided for This, my book, East of
Eden, To write dedication, prologue, argument,
apology, epilogue and perhaps epitaph all in
one.
The dedication is To you with all the
admiration and affection That have been distilled
from our singularly blessed association of
many years. This book inscribed to you because
you have been part of its birth and growth.
As you know, a prologue is written last
but placed first To explain The book's short-
comings and To ask The reader To be kind. But
a prologue is also a note of farewell from the
writer To his book. For years The writer and his
book have been Together — friends or bitter
enemies but very close as only love and
fighting can accomplish.
Then suddenly The book is done. It
is a kind of death. This is The requiem.
Miguel Cervantes invented The modern
novel and with his Don Quijote set a mark high
and bright. In his prologue, he said best what
writers feel — The gladness and The Terror
"Idling reader," Cervantes wrote — "You may
believe me when I tell you That I should have
liked This book, which is The child of my brain,
To be The fairest, The sprightliest and The
cleverest That could be imagined; but I have not
been able To contravene The law of nature which
would have it That like begets like —"
And so it is with me, Pat. Although some
Times I have felt that I held fire in my hands
and spread a page with shining — I have never
lost the weight of clumsiness, of ignorance, of
aching inability.
A book is like a man — clever and dull,
brave and coward, beautiful and ugly. For
every flowering thought. There will be

A typical handwritten note by Steinbeck

IX

"I AM STILL DAZED AND INARTICULATE SINCE READING YOUR DEDICATION . . ."

January, 1952 to June, 1952

After the Christmas, 1951, holidays, the Steinbecks accepted an offer from *Collier's* magazine: John would write articles about European countries; Elaine would take the accompanying photographs. They left America early in March, 1952, and John left *East of Eden* behind him. For the next few months, production, design, and promotion of that book would be Covici's responsibility; Steinbeck need only approve the dust jacket and read the galley proofs. Early in April, Steinbeck wrote Covici:

Friday

Dear Pat,

We're getting into Casablanca tonight. I have slept almost solid since I came aboard. Got your cable and am very glad you still like the book. I have just about forgotten it. That is probably a good thing. Like child birth, if there were memory, women wouldn't do it again. I don't know whether I have slept so much because I was tired or because I was lazy but I haven't touched pen to paper for 11 blessed days.

Our plans are changed. The ship doesn't go to Greece. We will get off in Marseilles and drive down the coast of Spain to Seville and after holy week to Madrid then fly to Egypt and then to Israel and then to Greece.

I guess there will be letters tonight when we get to

Casablanca.
This is just a note. Expect little else. I am magnificantly
lazy.

love to all
John

Steinbeck's wife added a post-script to that letter:

Darling Pat—We are anchored in Casablanca harbor—and
we have just heard a donkey bray—the first land sound in
11 days. J and I stood on the forward deck for 3 hours, from
the first moment of spotting the mainland till we dropped
anchor—we came into port at sunset & now the city lights
are all around us & the sky is full of stars—the trip has
been *perfect*—and I never use that word loosely! John's letter
above may sound sparse—but he is so *expansive & happy &
sweet*. I can't tell you how fine these 11 days have been—
we were so glad to get your cable—& we celebrated it
properly. Love to you & Dorothy & Pascal & Joan—and
especially to you from me.   E.*

Steinbeck had planned a long introduction to *East of Eden,* with
specific reference to Cervantes as father of the modern novel. Covici
suggested that a shorter introduction might be more appropriate. Steinbeck agreed from Seville:

Seville
April 10

Dear Pat:

Your letter re introduction came yesterday. Of course
do what you feel is right about that. It occurs to me that
what was good enough for Cervantes should be good enough
for me. But on the other hand there is no way of knowing
whether Don Quixote would go now. Surely Time would say
that it failed, just as Time and The New Yorker will say that
E of E fails. That is the modern criticism. "It's good but it
fails."

* Joan—Mrs. Pascal Covici, Jr.

We are going to phone Waverly† and she will have messages for you which will make this letter old hat. But I'll write it anyway.

We have changed our plans. Spain excites me as I have rarely been excited. I'm going to stay here a while and put Egypt and Israel farther back on the list. I feel that I want to do some work in Spain. We will probably go to Madrid Sunday and come back here the week beginning the 22nd. Then maybe go south and west. We came down the east coast then in from Valencia, and through Granada to Seville. It is the most exciting country imaginable. I want to see a lot more of it and I may get several articles here so it may be worth while.

Our health is good and Elaine is turning into a great little camera girl. She is really taking to it and learning all kinds of tricks of the trade. I am proud of her. Also she is a good sailor. We had really rough seas in the Atlantic and even worse crossing to Marseilles and she never turned a hair. We will never have to worry about her getting seasick. And that is a great relief to her.

I am pleased that the Viking people like the book. I'm sure that pleases me. And of course I hope a lot of people like it.

Gwyn wired Elaine that the boys were well and that she decided to let Tom go to camp and had written Josh Leiberman about it. I hope this is true and that Tom can go. I think it would make a great difference in his whole life.

I'll leave this open until after we talk to Waverly tomorrow night. She may have much more news. So long for now.

love,
John

Steinbeck's travels were a great relaxation to him after the long and arduous work on *East of Eden*. But he felt unhappy and depressed if letters from Covici were not waiting for him when he arrived at various points along his journey. As Madison writes:

† Elaine's daughter.

So dependent had Steinbeck become on Covici's letters when abroad, that he dreaded coming to a new place and not finding a letter, but in each place he found one awaiting him. And in each missive Covici fed him the admiration that buoyed his spirits.[1]

Steinbeck wrote to Covici again, on the 18th, from Madrid:

April 18

Dear Pat:

We've been nearly a week in Madrid now and go back to Seville for the great fiesta on Monday.

We have been seeing many pictures—at The Prado and today at Toledo to see the many fine Grecos. So many impressions. Maybe too many. Hard to take in a short time, a little stunning in fact. Come in dog tired.

We did not have mail forwarded so haven't heard much of anything. Letter from Kazan saying he had testified.* He had told me he was going to a long time ago. I wonder whether it made a sensation. He sent us a copy of his statement which I thought good. It must be a hard decision to make. He is a good and honest man. I hope the Communists and the second raters don't cut him to pieces now. But they can't hurt him very much.

About once a week we get a three day old copy of the Paris Herald Tribune which is our nearest approach to the news of the world. Spain is a curious and fascinating country. I am trying to get it sorted out in my head.

I haven't written anything. Going through a fallow time which, as usual, bothers me. Actually so much coming in there hasn't been time for much to go out. And my pen has gone rusty. Well—we'll just have to see how it goes.

News from home has been sketchy because of the loss of all the first letters which missed us on the ship. We spend next week at Hotel Madrid in Seville and then will make our decision on what to do next.

I'll try to write more often and meanwhile I hope to have
a letter from you waiting in Seville.

love to all
John

Covici's next letter to Steinbeck repeated the encouragement which
Steinbeck fed on ("You know darn well that you will soon write as
good as ever, if not better. . . ."). Covici had heard rumors of the
eventual decision by the editors of The Book-of-the-Month Club that
they would not take *East of Eden,* because of sordidness in the work.

April 23, 1952

Dear John,

Thanks for writing again in your natural way. It makes
me feel better.

Yes, I read Kazan's statement. It was a thrilling
experience; it was honest, brave and forthright. At the same
time there was also a story of his telling the history of his
joining the Communist Party. So far I have heard no reverberations from friends or enemies. I wrote to Kazan telling
him how proud I am of his statement.

As usual you worry unnecessarily. You know darn well
that you will soon write as good as ever, if not better. You
first have to absorb before you let go—you know that well
enough. Things must first mingle with your blood before
you can write.

I am terribly sorry that the jacket I had in mind for your
book fell through. We had a number of sketches and they
just completely failed. So I am afraid it will have to be a
type jacket or something with a Salinas Valley background.
If Matisse were here I am sure I could have what I want.

Arthur Miller telephoned the other day to inquire about
you. He said he was envious of your trip. He is working
hard on a new play, that's the second one this year, laid in
Salem in the year 1690; a very timely piece of work. He read

---

* Steinbeck's friend, Elia Kazan, the director, had testified before the House
Un-American Activities Committee, in Congress.

a scene to me over the phone and he seems to have a new, beautiful cadence in his prose. I never realized that that was in him.

All your birthday books from Beth, Elizabeth* and me just came in. I hope that they will excite you.

Just vague rumors that two of the judges of the Book-of-the-Month Club were worried that they could not possibly send EAST OF EDEN to their subscribers. The doings of Katie in the whore house, I am afraid frightened them. Life still frightens them. Their attitude is certainly bewildering to me. Not that it matters in the last analysis whether they take it or not; GRAPES OF WRATH did very well without benefit of any Club. It's their attitude that makes me mad. Well, you predicted that a long time ago, so you are right again.

Love to you both,

In his next letter to Steinbeck, Covici was able to apprise him of the estimated first printing of *East of Eden:* 100,000 before publication. The actual first printing was 110,000.

May 8, 1952

Dear John,

Your last letter arrived today, Thursday, May 8th. Spain is slow though undoubtedly fascinating, judging from your enthusiastic eagerness to write about it. You weren't nearly as excited about Russia or any other country, to my memory. I sure want to read what you have to say about this land of pride and dignity and cruelty.

I'd give anything to watch you and Elaine walking the streets of Paris, Elaine wide-eyed, alert to her finger-tips, striving with every muscle in her mind and body to see, smell and feel everything about her—joyous, receptive, inquisitive. She must truly be a wonderful companion.

The limited edition of EAST OF EDEN is promised to June 4 and about 750 of them will be immediately shipped

* Beth—Steinbeck's sister; Elizabeth—Elizabeth Otis, the agent.

out to the book trade to read. The regular edition will be
ready August 8 and publication date, September 19. The
first printing will be about 50,000 copies; the second
printing, also before publication, will depend upon our
advance. My guess is that the second printing will be about
75,000 copies since I am expecting an advance of about
100,000. I can see the lifting of your right eyebrow into a
perfect triangle and your face full of doubt. Nevertheless,
that's what I am figuring on.

I mailed you galleys by air today.

Pascal got all A's for the last term. He is now waiting
and wondering whether he will be called for a general oral
exam for honors. Graduation June 18 and we shall be there.
They are still very happy.

With love to you both,

Yours,

Steinbeck took time out, on May 12, to write two long letters to
Covici.

May 12, '52

Arrived in Paris yesterday but late at night after 28 hours on
the train from Madrid. It was a pleasant trip but toward the
end rather tiring. Now we are in this comfortable hotel. I
have slept myself out and tomorrow morning I am going to
start my first piece about Spain. I have been seeing everything
and writing nothing. It will be a pleasure to begin putting
some of it down. This is the longest stretch without writing
within recent memory. Have seen some strange and reversing
things. I hope I can make some sense of it when I start
writing it down. Spain wasn't what we expected. I wonder
what it was. I hope I can dig it out of my memory and make
it clear—even to myself. It is a completely contradictory
country. Anything you say or see or think is cancelled out by
something else you see. It is a country about which it is
impossible to make generalities. And yet how can you write
a piece about it if you don't think one way or the other.
Paradoxes as verities? That's the only way I can think of it

now. I think the best way is to set it down just as it happened, and to let the sense of paradox grow out of the material just as it has out of my memory. Anyway—that is what I am going to do.

Paris is always wonderful—both recognized and new everytime. This time the chestnuts are blooming and the trees are in full leaf and it is the core of spring. We walked for three hours this afternoon—from the Arch to the Concord and to the river and back. Sunday and sunny and everyone was out walking. The Champs was crowded with people all walking and not going anyplace just as we weren't.

I am going to try to do three* pieces while we are here before we move on to Italy. I hope to do them in two weeks or maybe two and a half weeks. I can if I will work because I have all my material very close to the surface. And still I know that it is very hard to start writing. I always think it will be easy and it never is.

We were sad that there was no letter from you waiting for us. And I would have liked to see a galley. I have forgotten the book. I'd like to see what it looks like and sounds like. And I've forgotten the work and all of it. Always it is that way. How strange it is. The memory goes so fast. Maybe that is a good thing—otherwise one would never write another book.

Here I plan to buy a little French car (to be sold when we leave Europe) to drive to Italy and all over. Renting cars is ruinously expensive. But I want to drive myself anyway. I never trust other drivers really. Feel much better if I have the wheel. Also you can stop when you want to. So that is what we are going to try to do.

We have been so out of touch in Spain. Some letters were lost when the ship did not go where we thought it would. And some took so long to come that we must have missed them. We have heard practically nothing for quite a long time. I hope I will hear from you in a day or so. It would make me feel much less cut off from the world. Spain is

* Steinbeck may have written *"these* pieces".

really the middle ages. After a time you lose all sense of the outside world. But Paris is of the world and of this year of our Lord. Here we expect to be in contact. In Spain we did not.

One thing will interest you. I had been told that my books were not permitted in Spain. This is not true. All of them are in and they have been printed in Barcelona with new Spanish translations because they did not like the Argentine and Mexican. And it seems that they are very popular. Isn't it crazy how misinformation creeps around. Maybe it is because we want it to and so expect it. Maybe I got a sense of self-importance by thinking my books were banned in Spain. Maybe a kind of martyr complex. Well, they aren't, so there's a good hair shirt ruined.

When we drive up and out of Italy, maybe we can get down into Greece before we return. I would like that I think. And it would be a very pleasant thing to do. Anyway we are going to try.

Guess that's all for tonight. I do hope I'll hear from you soon and I hope you'll send me a galley. Galley hell! you'll have books in a short time. But I'd still like a galley.

love to all,

John

Steinbeck then picked up his mail and received Covici's letter dated May 8. He had to comment on Covici's estimate about the 100,000 first printing before publication of *East of Eden:*

Before I had mailed this, your letter came in this morning and I was very glad to get it. Your description of Elaine on her first day in Paris is accurate to the last degree. She is wild with excitement. She will know more about Paris in a week than I will ever know. You are right about the impact of Spain. I can't remember ever being so knocked over by a country. Now I am trying to sort out the impressions and

set them down. I started my first piece this morning.* Should
finish the first one this week. Hope so anyway. Then another
piece on Spain and a third about Paris before we start for
Italy.

You are right. My eyebrow did go up at your mention
of a hundred thousand advance. I am torn by hoping so and
not believing it. This book could become a rage or it could
fall on its face. I truly believe that people now need and
maybe want an affirmation but I can be wrong so easily.
They may also want (because of the conditioning of psycho-
analysis, etc.) the easy way of no responsibility which is
what predestination amounts to. And this book lays it on
the line. However, it does say that responsibility is only for
the strong. And I believe that this is so also. It is not an
afraid book. And it is not equivocal. People may hate it for
that reason. . . . I gather from your lack of mention that the
book clubs have turned down Eden. Do you remember when I
argued that the book clubs were bound to be hindered by the
prejudices of so many readers? When the reader tells you
what to write and publish, you can't have very good books.
Maybe that is our trouble now. Writing for readers instead of
ourselves. Anyway, I will be glad to see the galleys which
should be in tomorrow.

I must say the pen feels very good in my hands again. For
the time since I left it has been clumsy but now it is getting
that at home feeling and I like it. That means I am going to
get some writing done and I am glad of that. I am never really
happy without it. Get very restless without it in fact.

Covici was able to turn the rejection by the book clubs into an advantage for The Viking Press, telling the booksellers that they would
have the complete market to themselves:

May 14, 1952

Dear John,

Your love of Spain is giving me a vicarious thrill; something
good must come out of it. For you to experience such unadulter-

* For *Collier's* magazine.

ated joy is something new and rare.

Marshall just showed me the draft of his blurb on EAST OF EDEN; it is beautifully conceived and executed. I shall send you a copy as soon as it is in print. We are also publicizing the fact that EAST OF EDEN will not be handled by any Book Club, nor serialized, nor digested in any magazine this year, thus giving the booksellers the complete market for the sale of your book. I know that they will greatly appreciate that. I am quite satisfied with the way we are handling pre-publication publicity. . . .

Please let me know as soon as you can when you receive the galleys, and please remember that these are not corrected; you will find many an error there but pay no attention.

Now I shall tell you a secret: I am beginning to miss you both a hell of a lot.

Much love,

As the publication date of *East of Eden* drew nearer, activity grew at The Viking Press and Covici's letter contained more publication information.

May 20, 1952

Dear John,

It is all excitement here. Our sales conference is on June 5th at which time copies of your Limited Edition are expected. Proof of the jacket should be ready then, too; I'll airmail one to you. I am enclosing the catalogue blurb. Since catalogue copy doesn't go to the printer until June 6th, please airmail any changes that you may wish to have made. In case you don't remember, the quotation at the end is from your daily journal which, by the way, is full of wonderful writing.

I hope Elizabeth Otis will let me have a copy of your article on Spain. I have a vague idea of how you will handle it, but I am eager to see how you really do it.

Kazan wants us to publish his pronouncement against Communism which he recently incorporated in a lecture he gave at Harvard. It is very good and moving, but I don't believe important enough for publication in book form. Besides,

it is only 40 typewritten pages long and book stores don't
want to sell pamphlets. I am sorry we have to turn it down.
Do you mean that Cat bird is going to the same camp with
Tom?
Much love,

Yours,

East of Eden was published with a dedication to Covici.* This pas-
page appeared at the end of Steinbeck's daily journal (ultimately published as *Journal of a Novel*):

To Pascal Covici
The dedication is to you with all admiration
and affection that have been distilled from
our singularly blessed association of many
years. This book is inscribed to you because
you have been part of its birth and growth.

The next day, Steinbeck reported that *East of Eden* would probably have a good beginning with his French publisher:

May 21
Dear Pat:

Well I just finished the second Spanish article and am
moving on to other subjects. Going to Rheims on Sunday
for a cathedral and champagne binge. There is a festival
there. Monday or Tuesday we will drive south stopping the
second day . . . and maybe staying several days there in the
vineyards. I think I will get my story of French farmers there
because I have access to them.
It might interest you to know that the reader for my
French publishing house read the galleys of E of E and reported with great enthusiasm. I am glad to hear this.†

* The dedication is printed at the end of Chapter VIII.

† The foreign rights to Steinbeck's works were negotiated separately and sold
on a country-to-country basis by his literary agency. Because Steinbeck was already a popular success in Europe, it is unlikely that his French publisher would
have rejected *East of Eden.*

I am getting so loaded with impressions of everything that I am almost sick like a kid in a cherry orchard. I don't know where to turn next.

Let me hear any news. This hotel will forward.

love to all,

John

Covici was happy to report to Steinbeck that Steinbeck's English publisher, Heinemann, also was enthusiastic about the sales possibilities of *East of Eden*. Covici, however, had become confused about Steinbeck's itinerary, which was not unusual. Covici had become confused years before when Steinbeck journeyed back and forth from California to Mexico.

May 23, 1952

Dear John:

Your continental trip is beginning to puzzle me. I thought you were heading towards the Near East—Arabia, Egypt, Iran, Israel and so forth, the countries full of dynamite and rocking news, where values are changing right under your nose and the dust of ages is turning into the garden of tomorrow. However, since I don't know your plans I can't judge your devious ways. It was good to hear that your French publisher is enthusiastic. Elizabeth just told me she heard from Heinemann's and they too are quite excited. News items are beginning to appear all over the country telling about EAST OF EDEN. The interest is keen and widespread. We mean to keep it that way.

Did you know that Elizabeth Ainsworth * is going home the end of June? I'm afraid she feels lost in New York and, therefore, growing lonesome. . . .

Just received a post card from Kazan telling that he is almost through reading EAST OF EDEN. "It's very good. Will get in touch with you when I finish." He also informs me that he decided against publishing his Harvard lecture.

Much love to you both.

* Steinbeck's sister, who had a home in California.

Five days later, Steinbeck appraised Covici of the change in travel plans—they would not be going to Egypt or Israel on this trip. Steinbeck also told Covici that *Collier's* did not buy his first travel article. The magazine, did, however, buy his subsequent pieces from Europe.

Paris—May 28

Dear Pat—

(Received) Your letter yesterday in which you are annoyed that we have not gone to the near east. Our plans have changed and I am not at all sure we will get there this time. I can't see everything even if sometimes I think I can. I don't think that is the center of the world. I think the world's future is here in France—in Italy and Germany. I will just have to do it my own way taking my own pace no matter what people think about it.

We have a little French car and we are going to stay in the Jura with a French family—wine growers. I want to know what they think and how they live. I'll stay until I know the economy of the country and the quality of the people—sorry if I disappoint you about Israel but I can't help it. I can only do so much.

I had the galleys bound because they break up so if you don't. Read some last night and I like the book. The blurb is very good. I would hate to try to describe the book in such a short space.

When you get the bound books—send one of them to us here at the Lancaster Hotel. We'll be back and this is our permanent address in Europe. Naturally I am anxious to see the special edition. Send one to Elaine for her own. And I shall be very anxious to hear what the book sellers think of it because they are the ones who will sell it. I think it is a brilliant idea to contact them. They are usually the last people to be contacted.

Collier's rejected my first piece about Spain. They specified a certain kind of piece and then didn't want it. That should teach me never to follow suggestions. I never will again.

Have not heard from Kazan. But I understand there is a great fuss and feathers over his statement as opposed to Hellman's. One can never know what one would do until it happens. I wonder what I would do. I'll never know I guess. And I don't even know what I wish I could do. Isn't that strange. I understand both Hellman and Kazan. Each one is right in different ways but I think Kazan's took more courage. It is very easy to be brave and very hard to be right. Lillian can settle smugly back in the kind of martyrdom but Kazan has to live alone with his decision. I hope I would have the courage to do what he did.

Paris is so lovely. Elaine is already making plans to come back before she has even gone away. Now and then we get to disliking the French until we realize that they made this country and no bad people could have done it.

My boys will have grown and changed before I see them. It is true that they are both going to the same camp but they will not be in the same groups. I could have insisted that Catbird come here but Gwyn says he wants to go to camp and I know how that is. Europe would mean nothing to him and my wanting him is purely selfish. I will try to see much of both of them in the fall. But I do miss them. I miss them terribly. But I will not impose that on them. Too often a parent imposes his own wishes on a child—and does it on high moral grounds when actually he is only pleasing himself.

Just at that moment some French reporters interviewed me. I wonder if any of it was true. I'll never know.

And I guess that is all for right now.

love to all
John

Covici acknowledged that wishing Steinbeck would go to the Near East was for his own interests:

May 29, 1952

Dear John,

I am afraid that you are right. It was partly selfishness my wanting you to go to the Near East. I wanted your reaction about Israel because, personally, I don't believe that it will last. If not for our interest in oil nothing would probably have

happened in the Near East. There is too much dust over Asia
to come back to life. Strangely enough I feel the same about
Europe. Maybe it has a few hundred years yet, but I think it
is done for. What is born, sooner or later decays. The Americas
is the only future I see and when that goes this little planet
is finished.

In the meanwhile life and living excites me. Jack Mullen,
our sales manager, just got back from a west coast and
middlewest trip. He saw practically all booksellers along the
way and the interest in your book is very keen, he tells
me. There is no doubt in their minds, even before reading
it, that you have a best seller in EAST OF EDEN. Of
course they want it to be. What's so nice about it is that
they all have a wonderful feeling about you. I am afraid that
the Limited Edition will give us trouble. We won't have
enough copies to supply the demand. One bookseller wanted
50 and we can't even guarantee him 10, since all
together we only have 750 copies to sell. There will be fun,
never worry.

I am still waiting for Kazan to call me and tell me what
he thinks about your book. He certainly is a slow reader.

Did I tell you that Pascal is graduating with a Magna?

Love to you both.

Yours,

Early in June, the Steinbecks made a short side trip to Geneva.
Steinbeck wrote to Covici from there on June 2 and June 4:

June 2

Dear Pat:

We are going to stay here a few days while I try to do a
piece of work on the Jura—very difficult because I must
do it so soon. We stayed . . . five days—met many people,
drank much lovely wine, talked to lots of people and
Elaine took lots of pictures. Now I must try to put it all
together and see what comes out. I have never been in
Switzerland before and what a neat and orderly little place
it is. We are dirty and tired from traveling so we will rest

and stay quiet here. Also bathe. It is amazing how important
bathing is to us. We can get along without it but we prefer
to do it. It is a luxury rather than cleanliness.

While there* we stayed with a man I have known before.
He is a teacher . . . and writer. For five years he has
been working on a critical volume on my work which he
plans to make the standard work. It is now over 400 pages
long and the most complete and careful work I have seen. He
has not only analysed my work but all criticisms of my
work. It is a formidable thing. He has not been able to get
Burning Bright and of course E of E. Therefore—as
soon as you get books, will you send him Burning Bright and
one East of Eden? I will print (his) name and address
on the other side of this page.

Books to Louis Gibey—60 Rue de Charcigny, Poligny,
(Jura) France.

It is Tuesday now and we plan to stay until Friday. We
will drive around and look around and Friday morning
we will drive to Italy. Will take several days to get to Rome.
Our address in Rome will be c/o Hotel de la Ville, Rome.
I would love to have a long and newsy letter from you there.
Indeed in the Jura I suffered the first pangs of homesickness.
It came about the right time. We have been three months
away but in addition, the houses were full of children and
it was very different from hotel life. I guess that's all.
Elaine wants to write a post script.
Elaine says she'll write a post card instead.

J.

Steinbeck continued his news to Covici, two days la·er, in a longer
letter from Geneva.

June 4

Dear Pat:

Geneva is a very quiet city and we have taken full
advantage of it. I did my piece about the Jura and I think it is

* In France.

pretty good. At last Elaine and I are working together
with pen and camera. She has learned an awful lot and learns
more everyday. And with knowledge she is enjoying it more.
We have slept, worked and walked. Went for a boat ride
yesterday. Lovely lake and cute little towns.

Tomorrow we drive slowly south. I forget what I have
written you. And I have not heard very recently from you.
But there may be word in Paris. We won't be in Rome
until June 14. That will give you plenty of time to get a letter
off to me. I'll want to hear about the sales meeting day
after tomorrow and if possible I would like to have a book
in Rome. Address me at the Hotel de la Ville in Rome.

I am learning a lot but not much French. My French is
still a scandal to the jaybirds. I don't think I'll ever learn
it. I think I'll get along better in Italian. It is closer to Spanish.

In the Jura we lived in a peasant home and talked with
peasant people. Went to the vineyards and to the wine
caves, tasted wine and ate and talked. I've tried to put the
essence of it in the piece I wrote. And Elaine surely
captured it with her camera.

I'm looking forward to Italy. Hope they aren't too mad
at Americans. But I'll have lots of contacts there. Anyway—
we're off. If modern Italians won't have us, we'll associate
with renaissance Italians. What have we to lose.

As a matter of fact, Pat—the trip is turning out very
well, maybe not financially because it is very expensive but
surely I am getting things and Elaine is in heaven. She knows
every street and building in every town. She reads maps
and guides. I just blunder through but not Elaine. She
knows—really knows. She says herself she is going to have to
buy a lot of lunches when she gets home for the
privilege of boring people about her trip. She never gets
tired. I guess she really meant it when she said she had been
poised 37 years waiting for this.

I am getting really anxious to see the book now and
to hear about it. I have been away from it long enough now
to lose the initial disgust that comes right after finishing.
So let me have little bits of news about what is happening. I do

hope the book will do well. I read some of it recently and I think I like it pretty well. I would really hate it if it were beaten to death by the sneers of our critics but, I would hate it more if people didn't read it.

Well, I guess that will be all for now but see that you get a letter off to me in Rome or I will put an Italian curse on you.

love to all,
John

Two days later, The Viking Press held its last pre-publication sales conference for *East of Eden*. Covici's letter of June 6 was the embodiment of all the letters Steinbeck wanted and needed to get from his editor, friend and confidant:

June 6, 1952

Dear John,

I am still dazed and inarticulate since reading your dedication.

Yesterday was Sales Conference day. When it came time to discuss EAST OF EDEN, our sales manager, Jack Mullen, turned to Harold and said, "What can you say that we don't already know? We have all read it and fully realize that it is the biggest book we have had since GRAPES OF WRATH. All you need to do is to buy yourself a bag of peanuts, sit on the rafters and watch the sales." Marshall piped up, "Well, then let me show you something." (I had brought your beautiful box with the manuscript down to the office and Marshall displayed it.) I never heard so many ahs and ohs. Then he read Pascal Jr's. appreciation of your book and to top it all he read a few excerpts from the Journal, which I gave him. The last passage he read I want to quote here:

"The writers of today, even I, have a tendency to celebrate the destruction of the spirit and God knows it is destroyed often enough. It is the duty of the writer to lift up, to extend, to encourage. If the written word has contributed anything at all to our developing species and our half developed culture, it is this—great writing has been a staff to lean on, a mother to consult, a wisdom to pick up stumbling folly, a strength in weakness and a courage to support sick cowardice. And how any negative or despairing approach can pretend to be literature I do now know. It is true that we are weak and sick and ugly and quarrelsome but if that is all we ever were, we would, milleniums ago have disappeared from the face of the earth and a few remnants of fossilized jaw bones, a few teeth in strata of limestone would be the only mark our species would have left on the earth."

When this was over there was absolute quiet in the room— I could hear a little fly buzzing over the ceiling. It seemed to me as if somebody were going to burst out crying. No word was spoken for I don't know how long. Never in my 30 years attending sales conferences have I ever experienced anything like it. Here we were assembled to talk about an important book and without saying a word, in complete silence as if in prayer, we all felt and thought alike. It was a memorable conference.

I am sending Louis Gibey a copy of BURNING BRIGHT and telling him also that I will send EAST OF EDEN as soon as regular copies are available. I am also asking him to let me see the manuscript when ready. Of course his book might best be suited for some University Press, but I would like to read it.

Well, this is too long a letter already.

Much love to you both,

The dedication of *East of Eden* to Covici was as specific as Steinbeck ever got during Covici's lifetime to acknowledging Covici's role in his career. Steinbeck later admitted Covici's support after Covici died, in 1964.

X

A BRINGER TO LIGHT . . .

June, 1952 and afterwards.

During the summer of 1952, preparations for the release of the trade edition of *East of Eden* continued. On July 8, Covici wrote to Steinbeck, who was then in Paris:

Almost daily we receive letters from booksellers all excited about EAST OF EDEN, and the orders are very good. It is all I expected and hope for. I had lunch with Lewis Gannett the other day and we talked about the book, of course. He changed his vacation plans so that he would be able to review it. He will receive a copy of the limited edition and so will a number of other important reviewers. The excitement about the book keeps up. It is really unprecedented.

In the middle of preparations for the release of *East of Eden,* Covici reported to Steinbeck that all the supplies for the birthday party for the sons had been sent, and received, at their summer camp:

July 21, 1952

Dear John,

Four packages were mailed last Friday to Mr. Stainback *
and should be there not later than July 25th.

Tom will receive a very nice and simple-to-operate camera and 12 rolls of film, one bomb-a-ship float, ore Moby Dick float—both big enough for him to sit on.

* Mr. Stainback—manager of the summer camp the Steinbeck boys attended.

Catbird will have a rubber locomotive float, also big enough for him to ride on the water.

For both the boys and their bunk-mates there will be 24 chin whistles, 24 balloons and 24 water guns. Enclosed from Dorothy are two under-water masks for the boys and two boxes of cookies. It was impractical to send cakes. I think they will have a wonderful time, so you have nothing to worry about.

I just talked to the sales department and today's orders, July 21st, are almost unbelievable. Kroch has already sold 50 copies of the limited edition and he is now ordering 75, which he is not going to get. Some book shops who have ordered only 100 are already reordering, doubling their original amount. A. C. McClurg of Chicago ordered 5,000 copies for early delivery.

So please tell Elaine she needn't worry about finances and to buy everything she wants.

Love to you both.

Yours,

On the 23rd of July, Steinbeck wrote a short letter to Covici, mentioning the large first edition of the book, and thanking Covici for the birthday presents. In part, he wrote:

I am so greatly relieved that you will get the things to Tom in time for his birthday.

110,000 is one hell of a big first edition. I hope you don't get left with them. But I have always felt that this book will either hit hard or not at all. I still think the promotion idea of sending out the book is the cleverest in years. The French publishers are so excited about it that they are having half a dozen translators send in competing translations so they may pick the best. I don't know that this has been done before and I must say it is very flattering. . . .

I guess that is all. And I am terribly relieved that you are going to do the birthdays. I felt dreadful about that.

Love to all

jn

East of Eden sold well for The Viking Press, but it did receive mixed reviews. The idea of the history of the Trask and Hamilton families grew from Steinbeck's original idea of tracing his own family background. Peter Lisca's analysis of *East of Eden* suggests that critical acclaim for the book was tempered by the observation that Steinbeck attempted to do too much within the framework of his original idea of the book. Lisca believes that:

> Steinbeck's attempts to impose an order on his diverse materials proved unsuccessful, and many reviewers pointed out that because he tried to say too many things at once, Steinbeck failed to achieve fictional concentration. As the reviewer for *Time* so succinctly put it, "perhaps Steinbeck should have stuck to his original idea of telling just the family history. As it stands, *East of Eden* is a huge grab bag . . ."[1]

However the critics may ultimately place the value of *East of Eden,* by the time the public and the critics had received the book Steinbeck and Covici no longer discussed it at length. Steinbeck continued to discuss the book and the critical reception it received, in letters to friends, until the end of 1952, but the last mention of the book by Covici was a short letter dated July 30, 1952, to Steinbeck:

Dear John,

I just received a letter from Mr. C. L. Stainback in which he reports that he got all the packages and states, "All the things sent were in good shape and we have them in Mrs. Stainback's log cabin away from the boys—and we are planning a good birthday party and presents for August 2nd." Well, that sounds very good. I am sure they are going to have a wonderful time. Mr. Stainback must be a good man.

It is still hot, hotter than hell and I do hope that it cools off before you get home.

The salesmen are back from the road and unbelievably enthusiastic. The book stores, they tell me, are all behind the book. New York and Boston have not been sold yet, and I believe we will reach the [financial] advance I promised you

a year ago.
Much love to you both.

Yours,

Steinbeck's last major discussion of the book with Covici was his letter dated July 23, in which he mentions the first printing of 110,000. Thereafter, Steinbeck turned to his sequel to *Cannery Row, Sweet Thursday.* His correspondence with Covici was virtually non-existent until the summer of 1954, when *Sweet Thursday* was released. Steinbeck continued to travel throughout Europe, to write magazine pieces and to do other journalistic work. Covici was busy with other authors and other book projects in New York and for The Viking Press. Covici and Steinbeck did not again work as closely as they did during the completion of *East of Eden,* nor was their professional relationship as productive as it was in 1952. In a short letter to Steinbeck after his annual summer vacation, Covici said somewhat plaintively: "I have caught myself two or three times since I came home picking up the receiver to call you. This is certainly some Freudian maladjustment. Maybe I miss you. I don't know."

In 1955, Covici again wrote the kind of letter that Steinbeck needed and responded to. Covici had not received a book manuscript from Steinbeck since *Sweet Thursday.* Because Steinbeck was selling his magazine pieces through his literary agent, Elizabeth Otis, Covici saw only the articles which appeared in subscription copies of the magazines which he received.

In his letter of July 14, 1955, Covici seems subtly to be urging Steinbeck to live and grow in America, rather than journeying extensively in Europe, which he had been doing.

Dear John,

I hope you are not bemoaning the fact of your writing short pieces. It is the little things that you do, what you once called the sharpening of the pencil, where some of your sharpest writing appears. The finest effects, somebody said, are hit off with the shortest strokes. The short, single word or phrase, a slight twist of your hand as it were, does the trick.

You obviously are not ready to go beyond the limits. You have been there before, struggling with the dark and dangerous, but you will venture forth again. The conflicts of today are

more difficult and numerous and the answers are too contradictory and of little avail. What saddens me so much is to
see our young men rush to Italy and France to finish a sonnet
or write a little novel about their moods or despairs or the
so-called welt-schmertz. By all means let them travel but
let them come back and stay long enough at home to com-
municate to us the new vigor and growth and excitement of
life.

The other day I dipped into D. H. Lawrence's *Phoenix,* and
here is what I mean to say: "But as far as it can happen
from a communication, it can only happen when a whole novel
communicates itself to me. The Bible—but *all* the Bible—
Homer, and Shakespeare: these are the supreme old novels.
These are all things to all men. Which means that in their
wholeness they affect the whole man alive, which is the man
himself, beyond any part of him. They set the whole tree
trembling with a new access of life, they don't just stimulate
growth in one direction." That is why your GRAPES OF
WRATH and EAST OF EDEN are great novels.

Well, the heat is coming back and we are promised a
scorching week-end, but undoubtedly we will survive that,
too. Dante survived purgatory!

Do you think it would be possible for you to give me copies
of the short things you send out? Maybe Elizabeth will let me
have carbon copies.

Love to Elaine.

Yours,

In late 1955, Steinbeck bought a house on the ocean, in Sag Harbor,
Long Island, which was to be his preferred home (he maintained a
brownstone house in New York City) for the rest of his life.

During 1956, in addition to covering the Democratic and Republi-
can conventions, Steinbeck began a short satirical novel, *The Short
Reign of Pippin IV.* He worked on it halfheartedly during the spring
and summer of 1956.

On July 30, he wrote a progress report to Covici, about the manuscript of *Pippin*:

July 30

Dear Pat:

It looks very much as though I am going to finish the Short
Reign of Pippin IV. I don't know how this is possible, but, it is.
I have all of this week to finish and I think it is drawing to
a close. It looks as though it would end up as somewhere
between 46,000 and 50,000 words. But that is only an estimate.
As for its excellence, I cannot give you an idea. I have been
so torn with tensions during its writing that I have no idea.
I think it may have some values but I can't tell. I'm pretty
sure a lot of it is funny as hell and I think a lot of it is es-
sentially true, but what its overall value is—I don't know. One
thing I do know however is that I shall be desperately glad
to get it done before I go away. Then I can do the convention
job with a clear heart and then I can come back to really
devoted work with an even clearer heart. And if we have
to throw out this book—well we have thrown out others and
probably will throw out many more but that has no emphasis
on the fact that I have to write them. And in the Short
Reign I think I have said many things that must be said that
should be said and that haven't been said. The spiritual father
of this book is Candide and while I do not write as well as
Voltaire I think I write much funnier. Anyway, I just wanted
to tell you that I think I'll have it done. We will come in on
the 8th. Maybe I can see you on the afternoon of the 9th.
We leave for Chicago the 19th.

That's all

Yours

John

Because Steinbeck and Covici met when Steinbeck presented the
completed manuscript to him, there is no written reply by Covici extant.

Although again a commercial success (it was chosen by the Book-
of-the-Month Club), *The Short Reign of Pippin IV* was dismissed by
many critics, including Peter Lisca who in his book *The Wide World
of John Steinbeck* wrote:

More important than what is present of the earlier Steinbeck
in *The Short Reign of Pippin IV,* though in terms of clichés,

is what is not present. There is none of the concern with technique and form. The materials are fragmentary, and the prose is that of a conventional storyteller. The humor is not that burlesque humor of *Tortilla Flat,* that Rabelaisin humor of "St. Katy the Virgin," that folk humor of *The Grapes of Wrath,* that tender humor of *Cannery Row,* that terrible Swiftian humor of *The Wayward Bus;* and it is nothing as good. It is a sophomoric humor of grotesque improbability and wordplay.[2]

After the completion of *Pippin,* Steinbeck turned to a project which he had held dear for years and years; back to the days of his youth when he received a juvenile version of *The Knights of the Round Table.* He would read and study and do research and re-write the Malory legend into modern English, suitable for American readers. He pursued the idea for years and when he finally got down to working on it, he discovered that it was an unsolvable puzzle. The book never took form. His dream lay unresolved. Eventually, in late 1976, a few fragments were published in book form as *The Acts of King Arthur and His Noble Knights* not by The Viking Press, but by a firm Steinbeck had not worked with— Farrar, Straus and Giroux. Thomas Guinzburg, president of Viking, said "It (*The Acts of King Arthur* . . .) just wasn't something we wanted to publish . . ."

In his letter of January 7, 1957, written at Sag Harbor, Steinbeck discusses the problem of the Malory project and the forthcoming publication of *The Short Reign of Pippin IV*:

Dear Pat:

If I seem to have run off and deserted, it is probably true. Moss Hart says in a letter I got from him yesterday, "It gets increasingly hard for a writer to write." He really has something there. Gradually the writing itself is shoved farther and farther back. It is easy to see why Christmas and social affairs and new baby are more important. They are the present danger of Oliver Wendell Holmes. The writing is the eternal danger and can be shoved aside for the crises. But when the crises become chronic, then something must be done about them. And in such cases, thank god for Sag Harbor. There is an abysmal peace and quiet out here. The bay is frozen over and a light snow is on the ground and nothing happens. A big blue heron flies up and sits on the ice. A flock of sea gulls settles on the pier. There are new rabbit tracks in the snow. I have a little smoke house going in the garage, smoking herrings. But nothing really happens. The phone does not ring with an hourly crisis. Sometimes as much as four hours passes without a report on the baby.* Five hours without a report would constitute a crisis.

I knew the Malory would be difficult. The stuff you have will have to be redone but I knew that when I did it. I just wanted to see whether I could do it at all or wanted to. Since Christmas I have been reading, reading reading and it has been delightful, like remembered music. I've gone back over my Anglo Saxon, unused since I was in college and into the old and middle languages, carefully and reading them aloud for sound. I've been back into Gildas and into the Anglo Saxon Chronicle, into Bede, and back into histories of Roman Brittain and Saxon Brittain and into the whole field of the myth and back and back to the Greek myth in which this thing has a strong plant and to the Buddhist myth which is full of it, and into the twelfth and thirteenth and fourteenth century in England—all not for background necessarily but to surround myself with the odor, the gas, the feeling, whatever you want to call it. And now I am about ready to go on. I have even gone into Jung's interpretation of the myth in a modern psychological sense. I rather think this has been necessary. But Malory was not writing myth. He was writing stories and stories about people whom he thought of as real people and of events which at least while he was writing them, were real events. And I am ready to go back to that approach. The myth grows out of all this but there must be an unequivocable sense of reality in the story out of which the myth may grow. Now language is a difficulty but I think for me less than for most people. I miss the open e which allows the rythm of the old sentences but I shall try to use some method for keeping that flowing rythm. And I shall continue with the connective

---

* Waverly Scott, Elaine Steinbeck's daughter, had married and given birth to her first child.

words which were used very like the greek kai to indicate a
continuation of idea.

You know it has been a long time since I have been able
to do a long course of uninterrupted reading. And it has been
good.

At that moment you called on the phone. I'll be interested
to know what happens in your sales meeting. If the salesmen
happen to conceive a love for this silly little book, they may do
more for it than you can think. The people in England are
crazy about it, but then the English have always had a greater
love for satire than the Americans. As for the French—they
will hate it or love it depending on how it is presented and on
how they feel at the moment. There are great numbers of
French who would love it if it were written by a Frenchman
but who may hate it if they get a sense that it is written by a
foreigner. But Graham Watson says, that the satire is so
gentle that in his estimation even those most sharply hit will
also be amused by it. And, he says, this is the most deadly
kind of satire, that which you must admit is true while you are
nursing your wounds.

I want you to send a galley, one of the very first you can
to Moss Hart, 1185 Park Ave., N. Y. with my compliments.
This is a must. I have promised it and he has recently done some
very kind things to me. Besides, this thing is eventually going
to be either a play or a movie as you very well know and he
is the first one I would like to see it. Just put in a card that
it is sent at my request and the quicker the better. At the
same time I want you to send a copy to Harry S. Truman at
Independence and one to Adlai Stevenson at Libertyville, Ill.
They are both expecting it and their liking of it will do no
harm. I have promised it to them and I want you to take care
of the sending. Critics are very fine but the word from these
men can get around to circles where critics do not dare to tread.
I think that is all for now. I'll get back to my reading for a
while.

And please do telephone me after the sales meeting. I shall
want to know what happened there.

love jn

Again, from Italy on May 3, Steinbeck wrote Covici; his letter helped formulate his feelings about Malory while at the same time serving as a form of self-analysis. Covici, perhaps the best audience Steinbeck could find, eventually was able to explain Steinbeck's reasonings in ways which had not occurred to Steinbeck, the explanations ranging from flat statements to hyperbole.

As for Malory—that work continues and I am digging out stuff all the time. I think I told you I got into the archives and library of the Vatican and I am putting a research person in there looking for something quite definite which may not be there but if it is not, it won't be anywhere. Meanwhile I have another girl working in the archives here in Florence. Florence controlled the economy not only of the world but of England and the great banking houses of Florence were deeply involved in the wars of the roses in addition to every phase of English life. Through money and trade they invaded the whole of northern Europe and being damned good business people, they kept records and the records are in existence today and as pretty a set of records as you could imagine. Florence was a highly civilized community when England was still in a state of semi barbarism. I am laying a whole background for my work on Malory, perhaps a better one than has ever been laid. I think you are quite wrong about him as being a scoundrel. I may be able to prove that he was much more than that, a man of conscience, a leader of certain groups against intolerable conditions, and a forerunner of the reform of the church which reached its peak in the Reformation of Henry the VIII. He grew up near the hot bed of Lolardy in Coventry and was undoubtedly influenced by Wycliff. I begin to believe that the Morte might have been perhaps unconsciously a criticism of his own time in the only way a writer could do it and not be killed. To my mind he is not a simple raider at all but a man with a principle and a direction. I am getting all kinds of leads as tempting as you can imagine. I think that my investigation is unique since I am approaching him as a novelist primarily and being a novelist I know more about the drives of such people than do most scholars who try to tie his work into pure history or pure myth. Anyway it is one of the most fascinating jobs I have ever undertaken.

I have changed my plans about coming home. I had planned to sail from Sweden July 9. I am not going to do that. I shall go back to England and walk about in Warwickshire to get the visual feel of the country. If I don't do it now I will have to come back to it and that would be silly when I am already so near. I can't write about a country I haven't seen. Anyway, that is the plan.

All well here. I feel a little crowded with work but I can't do anything about that. There is just more work than I can do.

And I have to go on with it now.

> love to all there,
>
> john

During the rest of 1957, Steinbeck was traveling in Europe and busy on other projects. The *Morte d'Arthur* was still a project he wished to complete. On his birthday, in 1958, he received a letter of congratulations from Covici. It was full of hyperbole, unusual for him; yet Covici did occasionally use hyperbole for effect, and homily, also for effect, when corresponding with Steinbeck, generally when urging him on to greater and better work.

Dear John,

I am sorry I won't be here to have lunch with you on your birthday. That you were born and in some small way I have been of use to you in bringing your books to light means a great deal to me, possibly infinitely more than you may ever realize.

When I look back at the long list of your books I am truly astounded. And if you don't write another book, you have written your name in American literature for as long as the human race can read. For you, too, have the poetry, the compassion, the laughter and tears that we find in Cervantes, and Dickens and Mark Twain. A reading of your work will always add something new to one's imagination and will always have something to say.

There are thousands upon thousands who are grateful to

you, but I have a very special cause to wish you a very happy birthday.

Love,

Late in 1958, another of Steinbeck's books was published by The Viking Press. *Once There Was a War* was a collection of reportage.

Why this volume was published; who made the decision to publish; who edited it; who decided that 1958 was the right time to release it: all remain something of a mystery. There is no correspondence from Covici which specifies publication plans. There are no letters before the publication date from Steinbeck indicating his approval for the project. Perhaps they agreed to this book in person, either in New York or Sag Harbor, and Covici did the editing, or left the job to an assistant in the Viking Press editorial offices.* In any case, there are only two letters from Steinbeck to Covici which mention the book: one dated only Friday:

Dear Pat;
I'm going through the usual turmoil of getting started. It's always a restless time but not an unhappy one. I'm going to stick to this like fly paper and I think I can make something good of it—think? I know damn well I can.

What a strange summer. It has actually been chilly up to a few days ago. But now I am watering and living and working in a bathing suit.

In the book "Once There Was a War," the whole story of the visit to Maurice and his being shot down is out. There are complaints about this including mine. Why was it thrown out and by whom. I would like the pieces put back in. They mean something to me.

---

* This happened later, to a Steinbeck book. Steinbeck's *America and Americans* was conceived in the editorial department of The Viking Press. Half photographic essay and half Steinbeck's thoughts on the social and political times, the book was partially completed by Viking editors before presentation to Steinbeck. Thomas Guinzburg, Viking's president, said, "We picked the photographs for the book in the offices because we knew that John had something to say (about politics and society). It was a busy-work project for him at the time, after Covici's death."

Surely they are emotional but so is war. Put them back—will
you? And if anybody kicks about it, say I instructed it.
I have a million things to do and even more to think.

Love,
John

Two weeks later, Steinbeck wrote a longer letter about the book.
He was right about "this curiously archaic set of reports." The book
went out of print with The Viking Press, as did Steinbeck's earlier book
of reportage, *A Russian Journal* (1948). Neither book is now available
from Steinbeck's American paperback publisher, Bantam Books,* although his earlier ones, including *Cup of Gold,* continued to be reprinted
periodically. Bantam did issue a paperback of each.

October 1, 1958

Dear Pat:

The box of books came through yesterday and I think they
are very attractive. Also the opening essay is better than I
thought it was. I can't really feel that many people will want
to read this curiously archaic set of reports. In a hundred years
they may have some value for their attitudes, but now I am
much afraid that they may only be found to be boring. I suppose
I still have some collectors who buy the books and keep them
in mint condition for some possible future resale value, but
those must have dwindled to a certain extent. It is a publisher's gamble anyway and I hope it pays for itself. I am not
spending the proceeds to my self in advance for wine or otherwise. But it is a good looking book as books go.

Wonderful changeable fall weather. Today pouring and
yesterday cloudy and the day before bright as a razor. It
is my favorite season. I am out in my little work house which
is being as battered as a ship in a storm and I couldn't want
to be in a better place. And there does seem to be some kind
of mental breathing going on which I am sheltering like a small

---

* In 1977, The Viking Press merged with the British firm of Penguin Books,
to form Viking-Penguin. Steinbeck's titles are now reprinted in paperback by Viking-Penguin. Throughout his active career, Steinbeck's paperback reprint publisher
was Bantam Books.

unvehement flame. Writing is so much a physiological process, with me at least. I can think it and plan it and lay it out all in neat little rows but unless I feel it in my bones and in my stomach it is no good. I know that our intellectual critics who also write with their stomachs only they don't know it, must take a feeble view of stomach writing but there it is. And I am beginning to have the stomach churn.

No fishing this week except for some scallops on Monday. It has been too stormy ever since. But that also is a good thing because there are always a thousand things to be done indoors. Right now Elaine is inside the house painting all of the floors. I avoid this by staying out in my little house and sometimes I do some work as I am about to do right now.

I only wanted to say that I got the books and that they look fine. And, since selling them is not my business, I have no ideas about that, or if I have, your organization would not be interested. But it is time I got to work. I've malingered enough for the time being.

yours

jn

Later, in December, Steinbeck rather painfully told Covici that a book which he was working on was to be scrapped and never published. He apparently did not want to follow the two previous short and relatively unsuccessful books with another. He wrote a letter to Covici, didn't mail it, and wrote another. In the second, he reaffirmed his decision not to publish:

December 20, 1958

Dear Pat;

I didn't send the other letter because I knew you would not be back from Texas. But also I wanted to inspect both the decision and the letter after an interval. And it is right. There is no reason to change a word. The frail and hackneyed story will not go down. I shall not be sorry for this cause. I said in the other letter that the story in a fresh form and in not more than 10,000 words might be worth doing. Anyway, during the time before England I will probably try this. In fact, I have already started but that doesn't mean that the new approach will not go down the drain also. I intend to the surgically selective.

Today is our anniversary. 8 years and good ones. Your big bunch of yellow roses came yesterday and made us very happy. As usual we will go along to a small restaurant and drink a bottle of red wine to the occasion. It was a very fortunate one for me.

Anyway, now the inspection is over and this letter can go. And I am sure you will agree with me. I'm not ready to be a hack—not yet.

Affectionately,

John

Covici again replied with a letter full of hyperbole, perhaps intended to encourage Steinbeck; the hyperbole so obvious as to be unmistakable in intent ("The fires within you . . ."):

January 5, 1959

Dear John,

I am glad, not just because of your decision but for the reasons of your decision. As Harold Clurman said in a recent review of his, "What is true of art in general is true of criticism as well: conclusions do not matter so much as the process by which the conclusion (if any) has been reached."

When I lunched with Shirley Jackson and she hinted at what you were doing, and that was three weeks before you told me, my spontaneous reaction was, "I hope it is not another small book. He cannot afford it." When you told me the story I was truly excited. It was something new and original. When I asked you how long it would be and you said between 40,000 and 50,000 words, I was somewhat tongue-tied. And then I read the first 100 pages and I was delighted. You were on solid ground on your own territory. Your wonderful American colloquilism and humor were all there. Then the thought occurred to me that if your interest should keep up, your imagination take fire, you might do a full-sized saga about the West in the manner of Don Quixote. That was, of course, wishing thinking, but not very clear thinking.

Your surgery I know was painful but your decision is sound, and I am glad of it. I do think, however, that the story has good movie possibilities, but then you and Kazan will know best.

The fires within you will be burning for a long time and good work will come out. But most of all I am as sure of grass being green next Spring that you will write a far greater novel than you have already fashioned. How do I know this? I was never wrong about you and your work and you are the only man in my life I can say this about.

Your GRAPES OF WRATH is a great contribution to American literature. There are weaknesses in EAST OF EDEN but it also has greatness. A still greater novel will come out of you.

Love to you.   Yours,

Steinbeck moved to England and spent most of 1959 living in Somerset, attempting to recapture the imagery and mood of Malory's England. Although he was happy and interested in the Malory project while he was in England, he returned to Sag Harbor late in the year, and began working on his next two projects, two salable books; *Travels With Charley* (1960) and *The Winter of Our Discontent* (1961).

Before Steinbeck returned to the United States, Covici, sensing his difficulties with the Malory project, sent him a lengthy letter, subtly suggesting how Steinbeck might approach the work. However, when Steinbeck returned to America, he eventually abandoned the idea and only fragments of it were eventually published. Covici's technique of being subtle with his authors is again apparent in his longest and last letter about the Malory project:

Mr. John Steinbeck   September 17, 1959
The Cottage
Discove, Burton
Somerset, England

Dear John,

Your last letter is certainly everything but optimistic. Your state of mental depression worries me far more than the fact that what you have been doing hasn't jelled yet.

Of course, I was never quite certain what you would finally settle on. You were talking for a time about doing a translation of Malory. Certainly a considerable and worthy undertaking and would be a real contribution. You could indulge yourself writing a very long introduction, telling of the origins and history of the stories, their remarkable inspiration and contribution to English as well as world literature. As a faithful translator you would follow, more or less the word of Malory, but you would undoubtedly have a scholarly and great rendering of a great book and translated into modern, impeccable and wonderfully cadenced English. It would also sell for a long time.

But I have been reading off and on for the last year Malory, and the more I read about Sir Launcelot, scattered throughout the book, the more I am convinced that here is the greatest outline for a novel I have ever come across. And frankly, I have been hoping that this ambivalent Knight would fire your imagination and that you would let your creative instinct go all out for him and fashion a novel about him and his period as was never fashioned before. You know the country, its smells and color, you know the people, you have a superb outline, and now if you would only let your genius play on the work. After that you may even want to do a novel on Sir Tristran and Isoud, and then one on Sir Galahad and the Sangreal.

Of course I am probably talking into the wind and this may not be at all what you want to do. But I have been having fun thinking about it and I had to tell you.

Whatever disappointment you have had in your writing you have no business to have such black thoughts. Of course you had them before—I remember them only too well. When we most desire to die we cling to life most desperately. Believe me, I have no misgivings about your ultimately coming through. But whatever you are groping for, do not lacerate yourself unduly. All wretchedness will pass, as they always do. You haven't done your best yet and you have much to give.

We had a wonderful time with Pascal and his little family at Swampscott. The swimming was invigorating and our two grandchildren were a great joy to be with. It is much fun when the ultimate responsibility is not yours. They have now gone back to Texas, and that is good, too.

Love to you both.

Yours,

In early and mid-1960, Steinbeck planned a trip throughout America in a pick-up truck, with a camper top. His experience in it would be the basis of his next book. Fearful—he was then 58 and planning the trip alone—he wrote Covici. Covici replied again, urging Steinbeck to make the trip and ignore the neglect of his friends and associates which would be part of the research. Mindful of *Don Quixote,* Steinbeck named the research "Operation Windmill," and called his custom-built truck "Rosinante."

Covici's next letter reveals him as psychological counsellor, interpreting to Steinbeck the problems and values Steinbeck must face— Arthur Miller's Covici, ". . . a mixture of slave-driver and . . . father. . . .

He had a way of whipping me along with everybody else he cared about to produce more and to demand work and in general acted like a mixture of a slave-driver and a very caring father. You had the feeling that somebody in the building (The Viking Press offices) gave a damn. . . ."[3]

June 23, 1960

Mr. John Steinbeck
Box 1017
Sag Harbor, L.I., N.Y.

Dear John,

I only want you to be good in your work, the rest of you will take care of itself. It is good too, and I am glad, that you count me among the few who knows something about creative work.

To my mind, the creative artist's whole operative consciousness, his unfolding of the story, is the most sensitive, delicate thing in the world. The ache of fear the writer must

experience, the principal of continuity, the felicity of form
and composition shaken—all must be most excruciating. Any
work of art, however small, if sufficiently sincere must oc-
cupy the writer's complete attention and energy.

Of course it is hard for those about you or friends whom you
neglect, but when you fail in the work that keeps you alive
you alone will pay the piper. Yours is a haunting anxiety to
go on. Any outside pressure and interference not only delays
your work but shatters that subtle intimacy that creativeness
demands.

It seems to me that only by ignoring the humdrum, the convenient, the daily social demands, can you, with passionate
determination, so fashion your work that it will have "the
intensity, lucidity, brevity, beauty, and all the merits required
for your effect." Your work is your life, so live all you can.

I love Rosinante. Who doesn't after reading DON
QUIXOTE. Whatever your solo journey does for you it
will be a rich experience. A new sun, wind, kaleidoscopic
change of scenery, new voices, new faces, intimate human contacts and strange reverberations. Your journey can be anything and all things.

Love,

PC/rw
P.S. I am not pushing, but I have a sneaking suspicion that
WINTER is not a novel.

Replying to this letter, Steinbeck defined the novel in his own terms:
". . . a novel is a long piece of fiction having form direction and rhythm
as well as intent. At worst it should amuse, at half-staff move to emotion
and at best illuminate. And I don't know whether this will do any of
these things but its intention is the third."

Surprised that Steinbeck would need to define the art of the novel,
Covici declined to define the novel himself. But he did encourage Steinbeck to proceed with his work-in-progress and believe in his own feelings.

Covici's letter of July 7, 1960 indicates his concern for Steinbeck's
progress:

July 7, 1960

Dear John,

My hunch was not a very happy one. I must admit that it contained an element of prodding. My first thought was that you were doing a high-minded polemic on our time and discontent. And you could do it superbly.

You completely flabbergasted me, however, when you asked for a definition of a novel. I wouldn't attempt it. It was simple for Aristotle to write what makes a good tragedy. All he had to do was to read the drama of his time, choose the ones he approved of, and make rules and definitions of what makes a good play. Then comes Shakespeare, Ibsen and Shaw and ignore most of the rules. And rightly so, since each generation sees life differently, and there is more to see and reveal, and cannot follow the old rules. What technical rules and definitions of a novel can you name that would apply equally to "Clarissa Harlowe," as well as to "War and Peace" and "Ulysses"? You know as well as anybody that every new adventure into novel writing, of any important consequence, must make its own technique and definition.

The novel is anything you like, and since it is also an adventure of the mind, for your purpose your own definition is right—a novel is a long piece of fiction having form, direction and rhythm, as well as intent. "At worst it should amuse, at half staff move to emotion and at best illuminate."

Have no fear about the outcome. I know you are following your creative instinct and, therefore, touching life. You remember Chaucer's wonderful line (Rumer Godden quotes it in her new novel): "Life is a thinne subtil knittinge of thinges," and so is a novel.

To say I am excited is to put it mildly. I shan't tell you my hunch now, since it has to do with the tremors of my spine. I am grateful for your very revealing and exciting letter.

Love

By August of 1960, Covici had read large portions of *The Winter of Our Discontent,* as they were sent to The Viking Press offices to be typed. His letter of August 11 is encouraging, guiding and questioning.

He says , however, that he does not understand the end of the book, in which Ethan keeps the family "touchstone." The talisman, symbolic of everything good, indicates, as Steinbeck later explains, "anything one needed."

August 11, 1960

Dear John,

I have been thinking quite a bit about your book and have been wondering, since talking to you over the phone, whether I made myself understood. I was delighted with it and think it one of the best things you have done in many years. I read it with great excitement and was so pleased that you had gone back to the theme of social justice, but seeing it now not from the side of poverty but that of money. It reminded me of Dante's treatment of userers in Hell. There are no messages of hope in it, and there shouldn't be. And it is in the most praiseworthy sense of the term subversive, and what it subverts are pieties of honesty, success, and the American way of life. There have been few writers who have attacked these with as much strength. In this decade no one but you has even tried it.

I know that you are now revising the book. When I finished reading it I had a number of queries. Please remember that other intelligent readers will probably have other queries. The point I want to make is that while you examine all revisions suggested, you should make none unless they convince you. You cannot afford to make somebody else's mistakes. In the last analysis you have to follow your own creative instinct.

For instance, I felt some of the action might be quicker, but that could easily be done by removing some of the "philosophical" passages—not all by any means, for some of them are really fine, and this is in its own way a novel of ideas. I think that the appearance of the Government man be-fore Ethan begins his job on the bank ought to be sharpened. I also think that the last conversation between Ethan and his wife ought to leave us with a clearer picture of her place in the story. The following is probably not important, but I think the intimations of incest between the children are, as they stand, frustrating and pointless. Ethan holding out $3,000 is correct, but what does he intend to do with the money? It seems that it is a mark of the corruption of secrecy in man who thinks he can put aside principle for one single day in order to give his life a new and practical direction. Ethan does not commit the crime he planned, his son does win the contest, and yet everything is turned around once more to show how filled with evil this traditional kind of victory must always be. And the ending did not seem right to me—I don't understand it.

Now, if the above thinking makes any sense to you and you are convinced, I am quite sure that you will make the right revisions.

This is a hell of a long letter, but I can't pass up Ethan's wife who is really the great surprise, tough as a boot. How amazingly you reveal her as the wifely mystery—smiling, sweet, patient, constant, sensual, and all the while an iron devil. She is going to upset lots of people. The surprise bitch of the year. And yet there seems to be no misogyny attached to the characterization. She is a combination of social and biological forces. Like the talisman itself, a stone resembling human flesh, her flesh turns out to be stone. But all this is done with so much fairness that we are left looking not "at a case" but at the human mystery.

You have a grand book John, and God bless you.

Love,

Steinbeck had worked on *The Winter of Our Discontent* and *Travels with Charley* during the same time, but had completed *The Winter of Our Discontent* first.

The correspondence suffers a lapse of nine months here; there is a break of that length in the extant letters until the approaching publication of *The Winter of Our Discontent.*

On June 12, 1961, he wrote Covici, in part:

Dear Pat;

I have a feeling that I got out of town just in time. It was really getting me down—the noise and the dirt and confusion. I didn't seem to have a reserve of strength to fight

back with. But now I am out on my point * overlooking the
water and it is early in the morning and the troubled world
isn't bobbing so much. This is good medicine for me. As soon
as the quake goes from my stomach I'll get back to *Travels
With Charley* and then everything will be alright.

Among other changes ascribable to advancing age is a mean
inability or at least a reluctance to write letters. I find I haven't
anything to say in letters and very few people to whom I can
say the nothing I have to say. For this reason, please consider
this and any to follow not letters, but those old fashioned
working notes with which I used to warm up my pen. It's a
little like a pianist who rips off a few scales before starting to
play. . . .

Well, we have another publication date. Do you know
how many we have sat out together? I just counted and it's 22.
Twenty-two times we've sat with the corpse. Wouldn't you
think we'd get used to it? But we never are. It's always the
same mystery. . . .

I think this book is going to gut shoot a lot of people who
can only react by hating it. The book even says it—only
other people are criminals. . . . The pen is warm now. I will
try to put it to use.

Yours,

John

Covici replied; in part:

As always I love your "warming note," or what I call
sharpening of the pencil. Your casualness often means more
to me than your full dress accouterments. . . .

It is strange that after all the books you have published,
each one has a new, exciting experience for me, and with all
the anxieties and fears and hopes—I love it all. And now I am
excited about the newest you are writing. What I read of it
I found rich and rewarding with humor, wit, and revealing
observations. It will be a good book. I also got a title

* He had built a gazebo to serve as a writing sanctuary on the ocean.

for your next book—"Traveling 'Round the World With My Sons."

On the 17th of June, Steinbeck's "progress report" informed Covici that he had turned down an offer of an honorary doctorate degree from the University of California.

June 17/61

Dear Pat;

This is a progress report.

Now as I understand the semantics of business and art, a Progress Report is what you get if you have made no progress whatever. If you are getting ahead you have neither time nor need for a Progress Report.

Is it possible that I detect in myself, not the usual despair, but a whisper of triumph in this statement? For twelve hundred years I have driven myself with whips over an imaginary road toward a non existent goal. What possible carrot has been able to draw me. Not money. And it can't be honors. Last week I refused a doctorate from the University of California. I don't need that little cape. I was not asked whether I wanted the Academy.* And I have never been near the place. My seat among the fifty stuffy Immortals has never been occupied. It surely can't be public acclaim because I run from such demonstrations. I can't believe that I have important information for the world since I can't even inform myself. Do I want to give pleasure to others? I don't think so. I'm much too selfish. Is it a problem to be solved? Can't be. I don't know the problem let alone the solution. Then if all these are negatives, I must look somewhere else. Maybe it's just a habit, a conditioning, a nervous twitch. Perhaps the hardest thing to achieve is a proper leisure. Of course, I am half way through a book. A hell of a time you will say, to cultivate leisure. But I am always part way through or just starting or nearly finished. No answer there. I guess there's no sense in any of it. I watch my boys go through the agonies of

---

* He was elected to the American Academy of Arts and Letters in 1948.

growing up not missing one single thorn. It takes a lot of searching to find out every possible hurt and indulge in it, and always the same ones. I'm too old to have had children. There's an intermediate age when inspection is not so close and memory perhaps not so sharp. Love has set in. Not joyous love but a ritual self appraisal with invariably the wrong answers.

Well, as you can see, I've made an early morning compromise. I am avoiding work by working. It's the oldest thing there is. The day is pure gold. And if I had any sense at all, I would go fishing. Maybe I can this afternoon or tomorrow. Fishing is very valuable. It is one of the verities.

Something that should amuse you. An English reviewer of *Winter* found the symbolism of the talisman obscure. Isn't that odd. He must not have read with much attention. That particular talisman was anything one needed. And that's not very obscure except to one who has never needed anything.

Well, the time has come to go to work and leave this chattering.

Yours,

John

Steinbeck's refusal of the University of California degree seems to have disturbed Covici. His reply is poignant.

June 21, 1961

Dear John,

I think you did wrong refusing a doctorate. The University of California did not mean just to honor you, but they had hoped to shed a little glory upon their meagre honor list. How many living authors can they claim on their rostrum who not only are internationally known but whose books are being read in every college in the country? I am sure that the University feels terribly disappointed. By honoring you they were honoring themselves. It would have been a nice thing to do.

Fishing is good for your soul; by all means indulge in it. I haven't fished for fifteen years. I was never a strenuous fisherman or a competitive one. I just liked to fish in a lazy, lackadaisical way. Now that I am growing older—and my, how fast—I should indulge in this pasttime. Take me out some time if you need company, but I am no Isaac Walton.

Now that the reviews are coming in I'm not in the least scared. The two worst ones I have already seen—the Saturday Review and Time Magazine. The first is a stupid one, the second is pure venom. We'll survive.

Best to you.

Yours,

Mid-1961 marked the time when Steinbeck and Covici saw some of their contemporaries begin to fall. Ernest Hemingway's suicide in 1961 disturbed both of them, no less so that a great man of literature was gone, but rather, in Steinbeck's view, his method of death. Steinbeck wrote, to Covici, "Surely a man has a right to remove his own life but you'll find no such possibility in any of H's heros."[4] Covici replied in kind, urging Steinbeck to consider his own career:

> Hemingway shooting himself was a terrible shock to me. Maybe it is my old Hebraic soul revolting against suicide. I have enjoyed reading him. He worked hard to create a style and I think that he succeeded brilliantly, but he applied it to a minor vision of life and I could never find any greatness of spirit.
>
> Of course you have written a number of books, and you will keep on. Can a tree stop bearing? As long as the tree has the creative juice of life it will blossom every Spring. Your hidden voice however is right—no reason for your struggling for or against. Go with the wind, your roots are deep enough.

Covici, who had been suffering from an ulcer, again wrote to Steinbeck, encouraging him to continue, to speak the truth as he found it:

August 2, 1961

Dear John,

> It is possible that the world could blow up, or that we could become a series of anthills. But I don't believe it. We have been going through a lot of material, mental, and emotional

depressions since World War I. We have been grabbing, thieving, and fortifying ourselves against all tragic hints in our little lives. And it isn't that we haven't gone through worse things in the past. But I am convinced that intelligence, science and moral rectitude will win in the end. Look through history from the beginning of time. How often we have been on the brink of perdition. Think of the thousands of acres that will be cultivated when salt water will be turned into fresh. We will be able to feed a hundred-fold of today's population. Think of the endless possibilities of reshaping our daily living with the new power we are developing. Who knows, but in the next fifty years we may even be starting to populate Mars, or the Moon.

Of course there is the possibility of some madman pushing the wrong button, but even then I do not believe it would be the end of the world. I strongly believe in the ultimate intelligence of man.

By all means say what you think is the truth, but don't shut out all rays of sunshine, no matter how dim.

You and I could explain, if we wanted to, some of your present pessimism which is, in a way, something of a personal nature also. I wish that you were here and we could talk it out.

Love,

In September, the Steinbeck family began what was to be an around-the-world trip. In September, also, Steinbeck was terribly shocked at the death of Dag Hammarskjöld, Secretary General of the United Nations. On September 19, 1961, he wrote Elizabeth Otis, "My hand is shaking pretty badly, isn't it? Guess Dag's death hit hard. I'm all shaky inside. Have been reading the appraisals of his character in the paper and I guess I knew a different man than they did. He was neither cold, cool, dispassionate nor neutral. He was a man passionate about what he was doing. He wrote letters all over the world to people he wanted me to talk to. . . ."[4] At the same time, Harold Guinzburg, founder and President of The Viking Press, was hospitalized with a serious illness. Covici was busy with the manuscript of *Travels With Charley,* and wrote Steinbeck, en route, of his thoughts:

Dear John,

The first and best news in your letter is that Elaine has been pronounced well. The rest doesn't matter.

I read the third part of your Journey and enjoyed every line of it. Your New Orleans episode is hair-raising, and I hope that Harold will not want to cut any of it. Your desert scene is delightfully fresh and enlightening, and full of poetry. Your meeting with the "enlightened Southerner" and your conversation with him is a masterpiece of subtle analysis. Back in my brain there are some reservations—maybe too many generalities, too much Texas, a little too long here and there— but I want to read all of the Journey two or three times, have others read it, then Marshall and I will compare notes and will give you the details. But there is nothing to worry about. You have a fresh, newly conceived book full of keen observations, wise deductions, informative, with the smell of the earth and of its colors, humorous, witty, gay, and it all makes delightful reading.

This book proves what a superb artist you can be in this form. Auden in his essay on Henry James says, "Of all possible subjects, travel is the most difficult for an artist, as it is the easiest for a journalist. For the latter, the interesting event is the new, the extraordinary, the comic, the shocking, and all that the peripatetic journalist requires is a flair for being on the spot where and when such events happen—the rest is merely passive typewriter thumping: meaning, relation, importance, are not his quarry. The artist, on the other hand, is deprived of his most treasured liberty, the freedom to invent; successfully to extract importance from historical personal events without ever departing from them, free only to select and never to modify or to add, calls for imagination of a very high order."

You have the genius for this kind of writing. And this trip, I do not hesitate to say, will prove of far greater importance than you ever dreamed about. Just take it in your stride, don't rush yourself, and when you are moved, and you will be, write to me.

I went to see Harold and I found him cheerful and looking

well, but he seems to me still very weak. His back annoys him terribly and when he talks a bit too long his breathing is not too good. Of course he's annoyed most that he cannot visit the office yet, but he will I am sure before too long, and that will be good.

My love to you both and please remember me to the boys and Terrence.*

Ever yours,

On October 17, 1961, Covici again wrote to Steinbeck, apprising him of The Viking Press editorial staff reaction to *Travels With Charley*.

All of us have read your Journal book and all are enthusiastic. The consensus is that you have a good, fresh, personal view of America today, pleasantly readable with narrative interest in the trip's continuity, and plenty of human interest in new adventures, your dog, and the people you meet and describe so vividly along the way. Not much cutting is to be done. The third part practically needs none. Most of us feel that it is the best and in a way gives the book its justification.

On October 23, his friend and colleague Harold Guinzburg died. Steinbeck had flowers sent, via his literary agency, to the funeral and sent Guinzburg's widow a short note of condolence.

The Steinbecks had moved from England to Paris and there, on November 6, Covici wrote to Steinbeck about the loss he felt in the Viking offices with the death of Harold Guinzburg:

Your Hamilton † was quite right when he said, "it takes a man to stand up." But you can't help feeling it like a man. I go to the office every day but something is decidedly missing. It would be good if you were here and we occasionally would retire into the corner of some cafe and over a cup of coffee

---

* Terrence McNally, who had recently been graduated from Columbia University. The Steinbecks hired him as a tutor for the boys. He later became a successful playwright.

† Samuel Hamilton, a character in *East of Eden*.

tell each other stories. It's no fun doing it by myself. But, as you say, we have to go on, and we will.

While traveling in Italy at the end of November, Steinbeck suffered what was later diagnosed as either "heart failure" or a small stroke. Since he eventually died of a stroke, a minor foreshadowing of that trouble may have occurred. Their around the world trip was cancelled and the Steinbecks settled in Rome, waiting for him to recuperate.

Early in January, 1962, Covici visited the west coast bookstores. When he returned to New York, he was told of Steinbeck's illness by Thomas Guinzburg, who had become president of The Viking Press. Covici immediately wrote to Steinbeck, hoping that he would quickly recover:

> When we got back from San Francisco Tom told me of your change in plans and the reason for it. It was quite disturbing, but he also assured me that you are rapidly on the mend which I want to believe with all my heart. It would relieve me greatly to hear direct from you. However, if you are still in no mood to write me, would Elaine please drop me a line?

While Steinbeck was recuperating in Italy, Covici, staff members of The Viking Press, the publishing company's attorney, and Steinbeck's literary agent continued final corrections and reading of *Travels With Charley*. Covici was forced to conclude that Steinbeck's original manuscript contained possibly libelous descriptions in the chapter devoted to anti-integration demonstrations in New Orleans. Covici, Elizabeth Otis and the Viking lawyers convinced Steinbeck to rephrase some of that chapter, which appears in Part IV, not Part III as Covici indicated in his letter of February 8:

January 26, 1962

Mr. John Steinbeck
Morgana Tiberio Hotel
Capri, Italy

Dear John,

I had lunch with Elizabeth Otis yesterday. She semed quite perturbed about the legal complications concerning TRAVELS WITH CHARLEY, and so am I.

Tom is sending you the corrected galleys with queries and an explanatory letter, which you may already have received.

What worries Elizabeth, and I think she is right, is that our attorney, although he feels that we can use the objectionable words in the last part, has asked us to delete the descriptive phrases of the women. Your attorney claims that anybody who wants to sue can use the descriptive phrases in *Holiday* to identify themselves. I know nothing about legal matters, as you undoubtedly know, but this I do know, that if somebody sues and wins you will have to pay through your nose. As much as I would like to see those phrases in the book I don't think they are worth all that gamble. So, if you are asked to decide, if I may be so bold in my ignorant way, I would toss it back to your attorney and Elizabeth and tell them to decide. Both your attorney and Elizabeth, I assure you, will act on the safe side.

The book will sell regardless. I know that's not what's worrying you and I would give a hell of a lot to leave those words in the book, but since the risk is all on your side I am not advising it.

Love to Elaine and you.

Yours,

February 8, 1962

Mr. John Steinbeck
Villa Panorama
Capri, Italy

Dear John,

Here is more cheerful news. Advance orders for the Travel books keep coming in and they delight my soul. The salesmen like the book better than anything you have done and they obviously conveyed that feeling to the booksellers. It leads our Spring list. I read it again with your new paragraphs and it is a good book. Your new version in Part III has all the bitterness and disappointment in people that one could possibly express, but to say I like it as well as the first would not be telling the truth. Nevertheless, you did right. The gamble was too great and probably not worth it. It is a good book for so many reasons. Almost everything that you ever thought, felt, smelled and expressed about people and things in your other books is here succinctly, trenchantly, vividly said, and with humor and infinite pain to yourself.

Again, we shall see what we shall see.

My prophetic soul was right that Elaine was your proper wife. She wrote us a very wonderful letter. God bless her, and you too.

Love to you both,

Steinbeck had made corrections necessary to avoid lawsuits over descriptions of the anti-integration demonstrators.

In a letter dated February 22, Covici congratulated Steinbeck on his sixtieth birthday. Covici's statement "when my future seemed darkest and my continuing with you quite doubtful," was a reference to the bankruptcy of his own firm, Covici-Friede, years earlier. The author, indeed, could have picked any major publisher in the country and left Covici to fend for himself, but he did not. Covici, after all the years and all of Steinbeck's books, did not forget his friend. It was Covici at his most humane.

February 23, 1962

Mr. John Steinbeck
Villa Panorama
Capri, Italy

Dear John,

Thousands of your readers are glad that you were born. You need not tax your imagination too much to realize my state of mind on your birthday. Firstly, of infinite importance to me and fraught with so many emotions, I did help bring your books to light (and by the way, the Hebrew word for publisher means just that—a bringer to light). What is even of greater importance from a human relationship point of view, when my future seemed darkest and my continuing with you quite doubtful, you extended to me the most friendly hand I ever knew. You who so emphasize in your books the dignity of man made me feel it. As somebody said, "Friendship sits high upon the forehead of humanity."

Your 60th birthday may have come around sooner than
you expected, but do you realize what you have accomplished?
Just naming a few of your books that are without doubt
a permanent contribution to American literature: PASTURES
OF HEAVEN, the first of your books I read and which
compelled me to search you out I consider one of your finest
books. TORTILLA FLAT, a wonderful, ironic, tragic-comedy
story. Here is where your three ruling characteristics are
foreshadowed—your use of allegory, your non-teleological
thinking, and your transcendentalism. Your first objective
work which raised great critical controversy, a bitter, brutal
satire and is gradually being considered one of your
important books—IN DUBIOUS BATTLE. Then the shining,
tenderest, moving story, OF MICE AND MEN. With what
warmth I can think of THE RED PONY—an illuminating
story in four parts telling of the growth of a boy into a young
man, becoming of age with understanding and compassion.
Now comes the publishing event of the 1930's, THE GRAPES
OF WRATH, a universal classic which will be read as long
as English is read. And with the same breath, if ever there
was a classic, I want to mention CANNERY ROW.

To have done all this and so much more which I haven't
mentioned is to have done a great deal at the age of 60.
You have another 20 years to write, and who knows what you
may yet accomplish. I only hope to be around and
celebrate your 70th and then your 80th birthdays—I shall
be content.

Happy, happy birthday and much love to Elaine in which
Dorothy joins me.

As ever,

On July 14 (Bastille Day), Steinbeck wrote a long letter to Covici.
In part, he observed:

I'm not the young man of promise anymore. I'm a worked
over claim. There may be a few nuggets overlooked but
the territory has been pretty thoroughly assayed. More
and more, young people look at me in amazement because

they had thought I was dead. Among writers it is becoming
very fashionable to be dead.[6]

Covici sent a long reply to Steinbeck in which he suggested that
Steinbeck's best work lay ahead of him and that age, of itself, should be
no barrier to creative activity:

August 2, 1962

Mr. John Steinbeck
P.O. Box 1017
Sag Harbor, L.I., N.Y.

Dear John:

I wish I could give you the exact form and color of my
reaction to your "Bastille Day" letter. What affected me most
was your lack of confidence in your work and your grave
doubts as to your future work. Of course it is not for you to
judge your work, successful or not. I recently came across
a quotation from James Baldwin which I copied in my
notebook and here it is:
"The effort to become a great novelist simply involves
attempting to tell as much of the truth as one can bear, and
then a little more. It is an effort which, by its very nature—
remembering that men write the books, that time passes
and energy flags, and safety beckons—is obviously doomed
to failure. Success is a word which cannot conceivably,
unless it is defined in an extremely severe, ironical and painful
way, have any place in the vocabulary of any artist."
After middle age most of us experience and suffer a
great change, but often we also experience a new birth.
As you well know, Sophocles wrote one of his best plays
at the age of 80, Anatole France a novel at 79, Goethe
finished the second part of FAUST at the age of 81. The
fact that you mean to do some long slow thinking is proof
that there are many more fish in your sea.
As to my personal peeve, I must confess I deserve your
gentle lashing. I was startled when I read that you thought
some kind of pattern would emerge in your letter. Strangely

enough I was looking for it, and under the fog that you
create I am sure there is one. The crux of the matter, in my
late afternoon of life I want to keep what I joy in most,
and want to make it last as long as possible. Selfish, no doubt.

My love to you both.

Travels with Charley reached the top of the best seller lists but
that did not particularly please Steinbeck. He retreated to Long Island
and his working gazebo on the Long Island Sound, with pleasure.
Covici remained baffled about Steinbeck's continued depression:

October 16, 1962

Dear John,

You certainly didn't sound right to me the other day
when you phoned. You seemed quite weary and tired, as if
you were going through the movements of life and not living
it. That is probably not true about you for I often had glimpses
into your deeper and darker recesses, where you mostly live
and where you keep connection with life and which is
quite unapparent. Having seen so little of you in the last
year or so I cannot say. But you sounded sad.

If this sounds like a tragic note I know you will bear
with me, since in the last couple of years I have been involved
in a few tragic happenings. What strange and incalculable
things life does to us, and I still find it interesting.

My curiosity is baffled, my spirit uneasy not being able
to know what is ailing you. Especially now when your book
is doing so well and praises coming in from every State
in the Union, both critical and popular. I also know your
lowest moments have been your greatest creative inspiration.
I sincerely hope this is so.

Love,

Late in the autumn of 1962, Steinbeck was watching television when
he learned that he had been awarded the Nobel Prize for Literature.
On October 25, 1962, he telegraphed his acceptance of the award to
the Academy. The award brought him both happiness and unhappiness,

perhaps in equal measure. It made him more internationally famous than he had been; yet the award aroused resentment and anger in many of his critics. The distress which Steinbeck encountered was obvious to his friends and colleagues. John O'Hara observed it, in a letter to James Gould Gozzens:

> Steinbeck has been a friend of mine since 1936, and last
> year he was badly wounded—trying not to show it, and
> showing it every minute—by the attacks on him following the
> Nobel Prize. He did not know what hit him. He had been
> (like you) accustomed to respectful reviews throughout most
> of his career, and when there was an occasion for jubilation
> THEY suddenly turned on him. Of course THEY are not
> the same identical THEY who were reviewing 25 years ago;
> but the old THEY did not defend Steinbeck as they could
> have. I happen to know that I have been up for, and
> passed over for, the Nobel four times. If I ever get it, I
> know what to except in the way of angry protest; but
> Steinbeck was taken completely by surprise.[7]

The award also made Steinbeck something of an elder statesman of letters, a position which he disliked. On the other hand, it helped him to continue his involvement with major American political figures, including the Kennedys and the Lyndon Johnsons. He later worked as a speech writer for Johnson, during the 1964 campaign, just as he had for Adlai Stevenson in 1952 and 1956.

On January 28, 1963, from Sag Harbor Steinbeck wrote a long, rambling, introspective letter to Covici, (another "warming note," or "sharpening of the pencil"), in which he attempted to analyze his own situation and the problems and the challenges of the day.

Thursday

Dear Pat:

> We came out here last Saturday and the time since has
> swept by. We must go back in town on Monday next and I
> wish we didn't. It is cold here and the bay is frozen
> solid and there isn't a soul on the point but us. We haven't seen
> anyone and since there aren't any papers, there has been

little reason to go to town. Elaine could rest her vocal chords because there is no one to talk to except me. So maybe she has benefited by it also.

I have been laying out some work hoping it can weather the flow and jog and rupture of town. After all, out here one has a chance to think without interruption. I wonder if that might not be an explanation of our times—interruption—nothing through because something else clamored for attention—no scene unbroken by a commercial.

Yesterday I got the copy of Publisher's Weekly you sent out, the one with my picture on the cover. I haven't read one for a long time but I read this one. And I found it very interesting. One of the things that sticks out is the fall of fiction as opposed to non fiction. Now I have read some of the non fiction that goes now and while it may be non fiction, it does not follow that it is factual. But this has set me to thinking in terms of fiction versus non fiction.

Fiction, it seems to me, in its inception was an attempt to put experience in a form and direction so that it could be understood. Not that fiction could be understood but that reality could. Now perhaps that has changed. Perhaps people can no longer find themselves and their neighbors in fiction and so go searching in non fiction for some likeness of experience.

There is one difficulty in this. Writers of fiction are usually better writers than writers of fact. This was not always true. But perhaps fiction writers are no longer fastened to reality. Maybe their "schools" have taken them away from their source. Are the Greek myths fiction? Are the Sagas fiction? Not in the sense that is understood today. Ideally—the fiction writer must be much closer to reality because he does not have the corraborations as proof that the non fiction writer has. You can write anything in the morning paper so long as it happened. The fiction writer wouldn't dare do this. What he writes must . . . not only have happened but *must continue to happen*. This makes it more difficult. The thing is a kind of challenge to me. I would like to write a piece of fiction as though it were non fiction and see what would happen to the reader. I apprehend that the difficulty does not lie in fact or fiction but in the form they have made for themselves. If this could be done well enough, who would be able to challenge it? One of the difficulties is the modern feeling grows out of the fact that the fiction writer must know the reason for everything that happens in his work. In reality we seldom know the reason for anything and do not expect to know. In other words the form fiction has taken is so far away from experience that we are no longer convinced by it. Fiction which one once used to be held up against life for validation at present would be invalidated if it mirrored or paralleled experience. The only fiction people seem to be buying is that which deals with material as far separated from common experience in time (historical) or place (exotic). Jones can write about combat convincingly because 99% of his readers have no access to the experience. The Ship of Fools has been so far removed from reality that it is a kind of reverse morality play.

The foregoing was written yesterday. It seems odd to be writing when I will be going into town on Monday and will be talking to you soon after. But I often forget to make notes of things I want to say to you.

This time in the country has been very good for me. I have been away from the damnable mail and the thrice damned telephone. It has been a good chance to get back some balance. Also it has brought back the old restiveness to get to work. I confuse pretty easily I guess, although the Stockholm experience is capable of confusing anyone, I guess. When it comes right down to it, nothing has changed. The English sentence is just as difficult to write as it ever was. I guess a whole lifetime of direction can't be changed by one experience. But I have had to make a couple of drastic changes in the time past. Once I thought I could successfully divorce everything about myself from my work, I mean, as far as the reader was concerned. I discovered that this, while it would be done if one had early written under a pseudonym, was impossible. So I had to split in two and establish two entities—one a public property and a trademark. Behind that I could go on living a private life

just as long as I didn't allow the two to mix. Now perhaps
there must be three—the Nobel person, the trademark and the
private person. I don't know how many of these splits are
possible. As far as I am concerned the only important
unit is the private one because out of that work comes and
work is to me still not only the most important thing but
the only important thing. The rest are unreal and have no
relation to the work as far as I am concerned.

Now, go back to the discussion of fiction as opposed to
non fiction. Ideally, fiction takes on a greater reality in (the)
mind of the reader than non fiction. Participation in
Crime and Punishment has a greater reality to most people
than anything that has or is likely to happen to them.

The next question is this: Has the present day reader
rejected fiction because the fiction is not good or because the
reader has changed and the fiction has not? Or could it be that
the present day reader *does not want* to participate—wants
rather the things he reads set apart and aside for inspection
but refuses to be involved or caught up in them. Mizener's
article in the New York Times[8] would seem to indicate that
this is so. He says, in effect, things are not like this and if they
are, I am uneasy. Now, does he say that there are no
relationships between people which he would call sentimental?
If this is his meaning, he is wrong or inexperienced or
unobserving. Or is he saying—"alright, such things exist but
they should not be written about." If he is saying this, then
he is defining what reality should be written about and what
should not. Let's say a writer is describing a battle scene.
There are some cowards, there are some heroes and in between
there are a large mass of insensitives who are fairly unaware
of what is going on. Now it seems to me that Mizener is saying
that the writer may mention only the cowards and the
insensitives but ignore the heroes. Has Mizener repeated (the)
dictum—that only Kings, Gods and heroes are fit subjects
for literature? It seems to me that this is so. And yet we
know that heroes exist. It occurs to me that Mickey
Spillane is writing for Mr. Mizener much more than I am.
Never will he catch a Spillane character in such abominations

as humor, love, compassion or thought. What it boils down
to is that everything exists; it is what you pick out of the
grab bag of experience that matters. I have known people who
for some reason or other bring out the worst in everyone they
meet. Maybe its a smell or an attitude—at least a psychic
order, maybe simply bad manners. Perhaps this is what is
wrong with Mizener. Whatever his virtues are, and he must
have some, he is certainly bad mannered. I didn't mean
to dwell on Mizener but it does seem to me that in the
thinking of fiction-non fiction, his attitude is important as a
kind of guide.

I have been reading Smollet the last few days and
thoroughly enjoying Roderick Random. Haven't read that
for thirty years. Can you think what our critics would
do to that if it was published today? You can almost hear
Kazin's and Mizener's guffaws of rage if a book should
come out called Moby Dick. They would do just what the
critics did when it was published.

However, these are only notes for consideration. We will
see what comes out of them. Brutally cold today. I have a small
electric heater in my house on the point. It warms up quickly
but outside it is about $+4°$ and went below zero last night. But
I wouldn't have missed coming out here. It gets me all rested
up.

I guess that's all about now.

See you soon
John

This was Steinbeck's last long, introspective letter to Covici. Perhaps
they discussed these ideas when they met next in New York. There is no
record of a lengthy reply from Covici about these questions. In June,
at Sag Harbor, Steinbeck developed eye trouble; an operation resulted
for a detached retina, and he had to make a long convalescence. Covici
again responded with the kind words that Steinbeck needed:

July 22, 1963

Dear John,

It was good to hear Elaine's words that you are recovering

so beautifully. I do know how impatient you must be wanting to be your whole self again. Of course you'll recuperate completely and sooner than you expect, but believe it or not I'm impatient, too. Somehow it seems all wrong to me for you to be laid up. You are not the kind to be ailing and confined, and I keep thinking of that all the time.

And so here is another prayer.

Love to Elaine and you.

As ever,

The Steinbecks spent part of September, October and November in Russia, on a cultural exchange trip. They were in Warsaw, when they learned of the death of John Kennedy, which he also took very deeply and personally.

During the winter and spring of 1964, Steinbeck devoted himself to other matters, including a possible book about John Kennedy, which never took shape or form. On July 1, Steinbeck was notified that he was to be awarded the Presidential Medal of Freedom, by President Lyndon Johnson. It is the highest citation awarded to civilians.

On August 6, B. W. Huebsch, one of the founders and, with Pascal Covici and Harold Guinzburg, a member of the reigning triumvirate at The Viking Press, died suddenly in London, during a business trip.

On October 14, 1964, an association begun thirty years earlier came to an end. Pascal Covici died in New York following major surgery. It was the only possible end for the Steinbeck-Covici relationship, which had endured and grown stronger over the years, based on mutual respect, cooperation and enthusiasm. The friendship, which had begun when Covici first bought and read a remaindered copy of *The Pastures of Heaven,* had survived twenty-two books, Steinbeck's three marriages, the dissolution of Covici's own firm, and deaths of mutual friends and associates. When his editor—his "bringer to light"—died, John Steinbeck's career in effect also ended. Steinbeck survived his friend and colleague by four years and two months and died in New York December 20, 1968.

APPENDIX

The following is a general chronology of the careers of John Steinbeck and Pascal Covici:

1885—Pascal Covici born in Botosani, Rumania.*

1896—Covici brought to America by his parents, who settled in Chicago.

1902—John Steinbeck born in Salinas, California.

1920-1925—Steinbeck attends Stanford University, but fails to graduate.

1922—Covici opens a bookstore in Chicago, under the name Covici-McGee; he begins publishing books under that name.

1924—Covici changes the name of the publishing firm to Pascal Covici.

1926-1929—Steinbeck lives in California, writing stories and novels.

1928—Covici moves to New York and begins publishing with Donald Friede under the company name of Covici-Friede.

1929—Steinbeck's first novel, *Cup of Gold,* published by Robert M. McBride & Co.

1932—Steinbeck's second novel, *The Pastures of Heaven,* published by Brewer, Warren and Putnam.

1933—Steinbeck's third novel, *To a God Unknown,* published by Robert O. Ballou.

1935—Covici publishes his first book by Steinbeck, *Tortilla Flat,* under the Covici-Friede imprint. It won the Commonwealth Club of California Gold Medal.

1936—Covici-Friede publishes *In Dubious Battle.* It wins another Gold Medal from the Commonwealth Club of California.

* According to Pascal Covici, Jr., his father usually gave his birthdate as 1888, which appears as the official date on his memorial volume prepared after his death by The Viking Press personnel (although officially privately printed). He was actually born in 1885. He gave the later date (1888) so he would appear to be no more than 50 when he joined The Viking Press.

1937—Covici-Friede publishes *Of Mice and Men* as novel and play and *The Red Pony*.

1938—Covici-Friede dissolved. Covici joins The Viking Press as senior editor. The Viking Press publishes *The Long Valley*.

1939—The Viking Press publishes *The Grapes of Wrath*.

1940—Steinbeck awarded a Pulitzer Prize for *The Grapes of Wrath*.

1941—The Viking Press publishes *Sea of Cortez,* by Steinbeck and Ricketts, and *The Forgotten Village*.

1942—The Viking Press publishes Steinbeck's *The Moon Is Down* and *Bombs Away*.

1945—The Viking Press publishes *Cannery Row*.

1947—The Viking Press publishes *The Wayward Bus* and *The Pearl*.

1948—The Viking Press publishes *A Russian Journal*.

1950—The Viking Press publishes *Burning Bright* as novel and play-script.

1951—The Viking Press publishes Steinbeck's *The Log from the Sea of Cortez,* with preface about Ed Ricketts.

1952—The Viking Press publishes *East of Eden*.

1954—The Viking Press publishes *Sweet Thursday*.

1957—The Viking Press publishes *The Short Reign of Pippin IV*.

1958—The Viking Press publishes *Once There Was a War*.

1961—The Viking Press publishes *The Winter of Our Discontent*.

1962—John Steinbeck wins The Nobel Prize for Literature. The Viking Press publishes *Travels with Charley in Search of America*.

1964—Pascal Covici dies.

1966—The Viking Press publishes *America and Americans,* edited by Thomas Guinzburg.

1968—John Steinbeck dies.

1969—The Viking Press publishes *Journal of a Novel: The East of Eden Letters*.

1975—The Viking Press publishes *Steinbeck: A Life in Letters,* edited by Elaine Steinbeck and Robert Wallsten.

1976—Farrar, Straus and Giroux publishes Steinbeck's *The Acts of King Arthur and His Noble Knights*.

BIBLIOGRAPHY

BOOKS

Astro, Richard. *John Steinbeck and Edward F. Ricketts: the Shaping of a Novelist*. Minneapolis: University of Minnesota Press, 1973.

Berg, A. Scott, *Max Perkins, Editor of Genius*. New York: E. P. Dutton Co., 1978.

Bruccoli, Mathew J. *The O'Hara Concern*. New York: Random House, 1975.

Bruccoli, Mathew J., ed. *As Ever, Scott Fitz—*. New York: J. B. Lippincott Co., 1972.

Canfield, Cass. *The Publishing Experience*. Philadelphia: University of Pennsylvania Press, 1969.

—————. *Up and Down and Around: A Publisher Recollects the Times of His Life*. New York: Harper's Magazine Press, 1971.

Carruthers, Clifford M. *Ring Around Max*. Dekalb, Illinois: Northern Illinois University Press, 1973.

Commins, Dorothy, *What Is an Editor? Saxe Commins at Work*. Chicago, The University of Chicago Press, 1978.

Covici, Pascal, ed. *The Portable Steinbeck*. New York: The Viking Press, 1943; 2nd Edition, with an introduction by Lewis Gannett, 1946; 3rd Edition, with an introduction by Pascal Covici, Jr., 1971.

Davis, Robert Murray, ed. *Steinbeck: A Collection of Critical Essays*. Englewood Cliffs, New Jersey: Prentice-Hall, 1972.

Fontenrose, Joseph. *John Steinbeck: An Introduction and Interpretation*. New York: Holt, Rinehart and Winston, 1963.

French, Warren. *John Steinbeck*. New York: Twayne Publishers, 1961.

Friede, Donald. *The Mechanical Angel*. New York: Alfred Knopf, 1948.

Gross, Gerald. *Publishers on Publishing*. New York: Grosset and Dunlap, 1961.

Hart, James D. *The Popular Book; A History of America's Literary Tastes.* New York: Oxford University Press, 1950.

Hayashi, Tetsumaro. *A New Steinbeck Bibliography.* Metuchen, New Jersey: The Scarecrow Press, 1973.

Haydn, Hiram. *Words and Faces.* New York: Harcourt Brace Jovanovich, 1974.

Jones, Howard Mumford and Rideout, Walter B., eds. *Letters of Sherwood Anderson.* Boston: Little Brown and Co., 1953.

Jovanovich, William. *Now, Barabbas.* New York: Harper & Row, 1964.

Kuehl, John and Bryer, Jackson, eds., *Dear Scott/Dear Max: The Fitzgerald-Perkins Correspondence.* New York: Charles Scribner's Sons, 1971.

Kujoth, Jean Spealman, ed. *Book Publishing: Inside Views.* Metuchen, New Jersey: The Scarecrow Press, 1971.

Latham, Harold S. *My Life in Publishing.* New York: E. P. Dutton Co., 1965.

Leggett, John. *Ross and Tom.* New York: Simon and Schuster, 1974.

Lisca, Peter. *The Wide World of John Steinbeck.* New Brunswick, New Jersey: Rutgers University Press, 1958.

Madison, Charles A. *Book Publishing in America.* New York: McGraw-Hill, 1966.

──────. *Irving to Irving: Author-Publisher Relations, 1800-1974.* New York: R. R. Bowler Co., 1974.

Mott, Frank Luther. *Golden Multitudes.* New York: The Macmillan Co., 1947; reprint ed. New York: R. R. Bowker Co., n.d.

Nowell, Elizabeth, ed. *The Letters of Thomas Wolfe.* New York: Charles Scribner's Sons, 1956.

Pascal Covici, 1888-1964. New York: The Viking Press, 1964.

Reynolds, Paul R. *The Middle Man.* New York: William Morrow and Co., 1972.

Steinbeck, Elaine and Wallsten, Robert, eds. *Steinbeck: A Life in Letters.* New York: The Viking Press, 1975.

Steinbeck, John. *Cup of Gold.* New York: Robert M. McBride & Co., 1929.

──────. *The Pastures of Heaven.* New York: Brewer, Warren and Putnam, 1932.

──────. *To a God Unknown.* New York: Robert O. Ballou, 1933.

──────. *Tortilla Flat.* New York: Covici-Friede, 1935.

—————. *In Dubious Battle*. New York: Covici-Friede, 1936.

—————. *Of Mice and Men*. New York: Covici-Friede, 1937.

—————. *The Red Pony*. New York: Covici-Friede, 1937.

—————. *The Long Valley*. New York: The Viking Press, 1938.

—————. *The Grapes of Wrath*. New York: The Viking Press, 1939.

—————. *The Forgotten Village*. New York: The Viking Press, 1941.

Steinbeck, John and Ricketts, Edward F. *Sea of Cortez: A Leisurely Journal of Travel and Research*. New York: The Viking Press, 1941.

Steinbeck, John. *Bombs Away: The Story of a Bomber Team*. New York: The Viking Press, 1942.

—————. *The Moon Is Down*. New York: The Viking Press, 1942.

—————. *Cannery Row*. New York: The Viking Press, 1945.

—————. *The Wayward Bus*. New York: The Viking Press, 1947.

—————. *The Pearl*. New York: The Viking Press, 1947.

—————. *A Russian Journal*. New York: The Viking Press, 1948.

—————. *Burning Bright*. New York: The Viking Press, 1950.

—————. *The Log From the Sea of Cortez*. New York: The Viking Press, 1951.

—————. *East of Eden*. New York: The Viking Press, 1952.

—————. *Sweet Thursday*. New York: The Viking Press, 1954.

—————. *The Short Reign of Pippin IV*. New York: The Viking Press, 1957.

—————. *Once There Was a War*. New York: The Viking Press, 1958.

—————. *The Winter of Our Discontent*. New York: The Viking Press, 1961.

—————. *Travels With Charley in Search of America*. New York: The Viking Press, 1962.

—————. *America and Americans*. New York: The Viking Press, 1966.

—————. *Journal of a Novel: The East of Eden Letters*. New York: The Viking Press, 1969.

—————. *The Acts of King Arthur and His Noble Knights*. New York: Farrar, Straus and Giroux, 1976.

Targ, William. *Indecent Pleasures.* New York: The Macmillan Co., 1975.

Tedlock, E. W. Jr., and Wicker, C. V., eds. *Steinbeck and His Critics: A Record of Twenty-Five Years.* Albuquerque: University of New Mexico Press, 1957.

Turnbull, Andrew. *Thomas Wolfe.* New York: Charles Scribner's Sons, 1967.

Valjean, Nelson. *John Steinbeck: Errant Knight.* San Francisco: Chronicle Books, 1975.

Wheelock, John Hall, ed. *Editor to Author: The Letters of Maxwell E. Perkins.* New York: Charles Scribner's Sons, 1950.

INTERVIEWS

Best, Marshall, senior consulting editor, The Viking Press. Interview, Sharon, Connecticut, 1 December, 1975.

Covici, Pascal, Jr., Southern Methodist University, Dallas, Texas. Interview, 19 December, 1975.

Guinzburg, Thomas, President, The Viking Press, New York. Interview, 24 October, 1975.

Madison, Charles A., former editor, The Henry Holt Co., New York. Interview, 12 February, 1976.

LETTERS

Austin, Texas. University of Texas. Humanities Research Center. John Steinbeck Collection.

All Steinbeck-Covici correspondence cited in this work is drawn from the Steinbeck collection. As cited in the Notes, some of these letters have been previously published in the Steinbeck and Wallsten volume, *Steinbeck: A Life in Letters.*

ARTICLES

Banker, Robert. "What Makes a Book Sell?" *Publishers' Weekly,* December 4, 1954, p. 2179.

Mizener, Arthur. "Does a Moral Vision of the Thirties Deserve a Nobel Prize?" *New York Times,* 9 December, 1962, sec. 4, pp. 4, 43-54.

Morris, Lloyd. "The Heritage of a Generation of Novelists." *New York Herald Tribune,* 25 September 1949, sec. 7, pp. 12-13, 74.

NOTES

I

1. Hiram Haydn, *Words and Faces.* (New York: Harcourt Brace Jovanovich, 1974), p. 308.

2. Ibid., p. 316.

II

1. Lewis Gannett, cited in Warren French, *John Steinbeck* (New York: Twayne Publishers, 1961), p. 21.

2. Ibid., pp. 21-22.

3. Elaine Steinbeck and Robert Wallsten, *Steinbeck: A Life in Letters* (New York: The Viking Press, 1975) contains maps indicating the locations of Steinbeck's homes in California.

4. Donald Friede, *The Mechanical Angel* (New York: Alfred Knopf, 1948), p. 80. This volume, now out-of-print, describes the partnership of Covici and Friede during the years of the Covici-Friede Company, including a brief mention of John Steinbeck's acceptance by the firm. A large percentage of the book details Friede's career as a west coast agent after the Covici-Friede firm went out of business. A portion of *The Mechanical Angel* which deals with the Covici-Friede Company is excerpted in *Publishers on Publishing,* ed. by Gerald Gross (New York: R. R. Bowker Co. and Grosset & Dunlap, 1961), pp. 326-353. Pascal Covici, Jr. says that his father was five feet, ten and one-half inches tall, not six feet three, as Friede says. Letter to author 5 January, 1977.

5. Letter from John Steinbeck to George Albee, dated only "1935" in Steinbeck and Wallsten, *Steinbeck: A Life in Letters,* pp. 101-102. Early in his career, his work was handled by Mavis McIntosh, but Steinbeck's work was turned over to Elizabeth Otis, and it was she who remained Steinbeck's literary agent.

6. Friede, *The Mechanical Angel,* p. 84.

7. Friede's *The Mechanical Angel* contains a summary of the publishing practices of Covici-Friede prior to Covici's discovery of John Steinbeck: *passim,* pp. 83-121.

8. Ibid., p. 129.

9. Ibid., p. 131.

10. Canfield, *Up and Down and Around*, p. 203.

11. Friede, *The Mechanical Angel*, p. 131.

12. Pascal Covici, Jr., Interview at Southern Methodist University, Dallas, Texas, 19 December, 1975.

13. Steinbeck and Wallsten, *Steinbeck: A Life in Letters*, p. 177.

14. Ibid., p. 183. Steinbeck's anguish over the flood of personal publicity can be seen in his letters to friends, pp. 178-196.

15. Ibid., p. 187.

16. Steinbeck and Wallsten, *Steinbeck: A Life in Letters*, pp. 196-197. Steinbeck and Ricketts were planning a short guidebook to the coastal waters north of San Francisco, as a warm-up to *Sea of Cortez*. Steinbeck's reference to "business at the lab is picking up" referred to Ricketts' Pacific Biological Laboratories, in Pacific Grove, California. Steinbeck would later disguise it in *Cannery Row* and *Sweet Thursday* as "Western Biological Laboratory." The trip to Mexico for *Sea of Cortez* was made during late March and April, 1940.

17. Ibid., p. 205.

18. The break-up of Steinbeck's first marriage and his marriage to Gwyn Conger are seen in Ibid., *passim,* pp. 213-251. A confusion has grown up in Steinbeck's criticism about her genealogy. In *John Steinbeck* (1961), Warren French notes in a chronology: "1943: Married Gwyn Verdon" p. 16, apparently confusing her with the Broadway star, Gwen Verdon. The mistake was repeated by Pascal Covici, Jr., in his Introduction and Chronology to *The Portable Steinbeck* (1971), and elsewhere. Steinbeck's second wife's last name was Conger, and she was not the star Gwen Verdon, Pascal Covici, Jr. acknowledged his mistake and described Warren French's in an interview at Southern Methodist University, Dallas, 19 December, 1975.

19. Elizabeth Otis, as his agent, was often sent sections of completed manuscripts before Steinbeck sent them to Covici, or to Viking Press. In this instance, Steinbeck forwarded sections of the illustrations to Covici, through Elizabeth Otis.

20. Steinbeck and Wallsten, *Steinbeck: A Life in Letters*, p. 228.

21. Ibid., p. 229.

22. Steinbeck and Wallsten in *Steinbeck: A Life in Letters* have deciphered Steinbeck's handwriting in this letter as "I told you once I found a great *paltry* in scientific writing." In view of his love of his work in *The Sea of Cortez* and his attempts to resolve his own philosophy through science, "I have found a great *poetry* in scientific writing" would

seem to be the correct interpretation. Lisca also translates the same passage as ". . . I have found a great poetry." (p. 181).

23. Lisca, *The Wide World of John Steinbeck,* p. 181. Lisca discusses the development of *Sea of Cortez,* pp. 178-184.

24. John Steinbeck to Webster F. Street in Steinbeck and Wallsten, *Steinbeck: A Life in Letters,* p. 242.

25. Lisca, *The Wide World of John Steinbeck,* pp .184-185.

26. Ibid., pp. 213-214.

27. John Steinbeck to Mildred Lyman, in Steinbeck and Wallsten, *Steinbeck: A Life in Letters,* pp. 276-277.

28. Dr. Pascal Covici, Jr. Interview at Southern Methodist University, Dallas, Texas, 19 December, 1975.

29. William Targ, *Indecent Pleasures* (New York: Macmillan, 1975), pp. 251-252.

III

1. John Steinbeck to Charles Brackett in *Steinbeck: A Life in Letters,* pp. 284-285.

2. Arthur Miller in a memorial volume, *Pascal Covici, 1888-1964* (no date, publisher or editor listed—printed by The Viking Press, 1964; limited to 500 copies—not for sale), pp. 9-10.

3. Malcolm Cowley in *Pascal Covici 1888-1964,* pp. 24-25.

4. Steinbeck and Wallsten, *Steinbeck: A Life in Letters,* p. 290.

5. Ibid., p. 296.

6. Lisca, *The Wide World of John Steinbeck:* "The frame story . . ." pp. 232-233; "None of (the) characters . . ." p. 241; "Although the journey . . ." pp. 242-243.

7. Charles A. Madison, interview, in his home, New York, 12 February, 1976. Madison worked as a college editor at the Henry Holt Company and knew Covici from 1933 to Covici's death in 1964.

IV.

1. John Steinbeck to Webster F. Street in Steinbeck and Wallsten, *Steinbeck: A Life in Letters,* p. 301.

2. Ibid., p. 303.

3. John Steinbeck to Edward F. Ricketts, April 1948, in Steinbeck and Wallsten, *Steinbeck: A Life in Letters,* p. 309.

4. John Steinbeck to Bo Beskow, 29 April, 1948, ibid., p. 310.

5. John Steinbeck to Bo Beskow, 22 May, 1948, in Steinbeck and Wallsten, *Steinbeck: A Life in Letters,* p. 312.

6. John Steinbeck to Ritchie and Natalya Lovejoy, ibid., p. 316.

7. Marshall Best, in an interview in his home, Sharon, Connecticut, December 1, 1975.

8. Dr. Pascal Covici, Jr. said that Steinbeck's *Journal of a Novel: The East of Eden Letters* had to be edited in the Viking Press offices prior to publication to delete unpleasant and libelous references to Gwyn. Interview at Southern Methodist University, Dallas, Texas, 19 December, 1975. Marshall Best stated the same thing in an interview 1 December, 1975, Sharon, Connecticut.

9. Marshall Best, interview, Sharon, Connecticut, 1 December, 1975.

10. John Steinbeck to Webster F. Street, 27 August, 1948, in Steinbeck and Wallsten, *Steinbeck: A Life in Letters,* p. 324. Neale's first (or perhaps last) name is not mentioned in *Steinbeck: A Life in Letters* and neither Pascal Covici, Jr. nor Marshall Best ever knew him.

V.

1. Steinbeck used the idea of music "beginning to turn in my head" as symbol; see *Cannery Row,* chapter 18, and in *The Pearl, passim.* Lisca discusses this fictional device in *The Wide World of John Steinbeck,* p. 228.

2. Steinbeck may have informed Covici of this episode by telephone; there is no letter from Steinbeck about this extant in the Humanities Research Center archives. No mention was made of this episode in Steinbeck and Wallsten, *Steinbeck: A Life in Letters,* perhaps because Gwyndolyn Steinbeck was alive at the time of the publication of that volume. Gwyndolyn Steinbeck died in Boulder, Colorado, 30 December, 1975. This is the first publication of this incident.

3. There is no known meaning for Steinbeck's statement "There is one more bit of terror but I'll face that when it is necessary . . ." This letter was awkwardly edited in Steinbeck and Wallsten, *see* pp. 338-339. For a further insight into Steinbeck's condition during this period, *see* Steinbeck and Wallsten, pp. 338-340.

4. Thomas Guinzburg, in an interview in the editorial offices, The Viking Press, New York, 24 October, 1975. Guinzburg joined The Viking Press in 1952, knew Covici and Steinbeck until their deaths.

5. Steinbeck and Wallsten, *Steinbeck: A Life in Letters,* p. 344.

6. Dr. Pascal Covici, Jr. said that "Steinbeck's first wife Carol refused to bear him any children because, as I was told, she told Steinbeck, 'You'd be a poor father.' " Interview at Southern Methodist University, Dallas, Texas, 19 December, 1975.

7. Much of this letter is illegible; it appears that some liquid had been spilled on Steinbeck's original ink and blurred it. This letter and the sub-

sequent discussion about Steinbeck's financial condition was not cited in Steinbeck and Wallsten, probably because Gwyn was alive.

8. Some literary agents acted as financial managers for their client-authors. F. Scott Fitzgerald's literary agent, Harold Ober, did so for many years. See Bruccoli and Atkinson, *As Ever, Scott Fitz—*, passim. The best analysis of the role of the literary agent is found in Paul R. Reynolds' *The Middle Man* (New York: William Morrow and Co., 1972).

9. The safe from Ricketts's Pacific Biological Laboratory is discussed in Steinbeck's *The Log From the Sea of Cortez,* pp. xv-xvi.

10. *East of Eden* (New York: The Viking Press, 1952), p. 329.

11. Madison, *Irving to Irving,* p. 212.

VI
1. The segment of Steinbeck's letter from the end of the section on the Mexican girl, to this note, was deleted from Steinbeck and Wallsten, p. 347. Here are the guilt feelings Steinbeck expressed in his earlier letters of January 15 and 16, 1949.

2. Interview, Southern Methodist Univ., Dallas, 19 December, 1975.

3. Steinbeck and Wallsten, *Steinbeck: A Life in Letters,* p. 352.

VII
1. The essay, which deals with *several* aspects of Steinbeck's literary craftsmanship, has been reprinted and appears in Tedlock and Wicker, *Steinbeck and His Critics,* pp. 197-205.

2. Lloyd Morris, "The Heritage of a Generation of Novelists," *New York Herald-Tribune,* 25 September, 1949, Sec. 7, pp. 12-13, 74.

3. John Steinbeck to Elaine Scott, 11 October 1949, cited in Steinbeck and Wallsten, *Steinbeck: A Life in Letters,* pp. 380-381.

4. Steinbeck, cited in Steinbeck and Wallsten, pp. 412-413.

5. Steinbeck and Wallsten, *Steinbeck: A Life in Letters,* p. 414.

VIII
1. Charles A. Madison, *Irving to Irving: Author-Publisher Relations 1800-1974,* p. 208.

2. Marshall Best, interview in Sharon, Conn., 1 December, 1975. Best edited *Journal of a Novel* for The Viking Press.

3. Steinbeck, *Journal of a Novel,* p. 50.

4. Ibid., p. 55.

5. Ibid., p. 55.

6. Ibid., p. 58.

7. Ibid., p. 72.

8. Ibid., on choice of titles, pp. 81-82; "Now, although it is . . . ." p. 86; ". . . has made a deeper mark. . . ." pp. 90-91.

9. Ibid., p. 104.

10. Ibid., p. 131.

11. Ibid., p. 106.

12. Lisca, *The Wide World of John Steinbeck,* pp. 261-262.

13. Steinbeck, *Journal of a Novel,* pp. 107-108.

14. Ibid., p. 109. Steinbeck's "charming scene to use it in" is *East of Eden,* Chapter 24, section two, pp. 302-304.

15. Ibid., p. 113. Steinbeck's "a really amusing venture in scholarship" is probably the end of Chapter 24, on pp. 307-309.

16. Ibid., p. 122.

17. Ibid., p. 132.

18. Ibid., "I am going . . . ." p. 135; "And I'm glad . . . ." p. 137; "I feel a little . . . ." p. 140.

19. Ibid., pp. 143-144.

20. Ibid., p. 146.

21. Ibid., pp. 149-150.

22. Ibid., pp. 152-153.

23. Ibid., "When I get home . . . ." p. 160; "I am stuck . . . ." p. 163.

IX

1. Madison, *Irving to Irving,* p. 211.

X

1. Lisca, *The Wide World of John Steinbeck,* pp. 263-264.

2. Ibid., p. 287.

3. Arthur Miller, letter to author, 3 August, 1976.

4. John Steinbeck to Pascal Covici, July 1961, in Steinbeck and Wallsten, *Steinbeck: A Life in Letters,* pp. 703-605.

5. John Steinbeck to Elizabeth Otis, 19 September, 1961, cited in Steinbeck and Wallsten, *Steinbeck: A Life in Letters,* p. 715.

6. For additional about this, see Steinbeck and Wallsten, *Steinbeck: A Life in Letters,* pp. 802-803. They specify that Steinbeck wrote his "Bastille Day" letter in 1964, but he did not specify the year. Covici has the year noted: 1962, on his reply.

7. John O'Hara to James Gould Cozzens, 4 August, 1964, cited in Matthew J. Bruccoli, *The O'Hara Concern* (New York: Random House, 1975), pp. 289-290.

8. Arthur Mizener, "Does a Moral Vision of the Thirties Deserve a Nobel Prize?" *New York Times,* 9 December, 1962, Sec. 7, pp. 4, 43-54.

INDEX

Abraham Lincoln: The War Years, 72
Abramson, Ben, 11
Acts of King Arthur and His Noble Knights, The, 197
Adler, Elmer, 15
Ainsworth, Elizabeth, 183
Air Forces Aid Society, 33
Albee, George, 12
America and Americans, 10, 202(n)
America Faces the Barricades, 15
American Academy of Arts and Letters, 92, 214(n)
Anderson, Sherwood, 16, 126
Aquila Films, 55
Aristotle, 210
Arnold, Gen. "Hap," 32-33
Artzybasheff, Boris, 36
Associated Farmers, 21
Astro, Richard, 10
Atheneum Publishers, 5
Auden, W. H., 28

Bailey, Temple, 42
Baldwin, James, 224
Ballou, Robert O., 9, 81, 158
Bantam Books, 123, 203
Bartlett's Quotations, 155-156
Beau James, 95
Bellow, Saul, 75(n), 108
Benchley, Marge, 98
Benchley, Nathaniel, 62(n), 98(n)
Benchley, Peter, 62
Beskow, Bo, 25, 73-74, 117
Bessie, Simon Michael, 5
Best, Marshall, 18-20, 75(n), 78, 124, 137-138, 145(n), 181, 189, 218
Between Pacific Tides, 138
Bombs Away, 10
Book-of-the-Month Club, 6, 13, 15, 32, 44, 58, 175-176, 196
Book Publishing in America, 11, 14
Bobbs-Merrill, 5
Boston Post, The, 139(n)
Brackett, Charles, 52
Brewer, Warren and Putnam, 9
Browning, Robert, 34
Burning Bright, 48, 127-130, 136-138; Steinbeck discusses sterility theme in, 139-140; 146, 187, 190

Cain Sign (East of Eden), 148
Candide, 196
Canfield, Cass, 4, 16
Cannery Row, 10, 35-38, 40, sales figures for, 41; 42-44, 74, 133-134, 137, 194, 197, 223
Canterbury Tales, The, 15
Capa, Robert, 59, 62-63, 65

Caswell, Paul, 67-68
Cervantes, 172, 201
Chaucer, 210
Christian Science Monitor, 38
Churchill, Winston, 54
Clarissa Harlowe, 210
Clurman, Harold, 205
Colliers, 171, 180, 184
Corey, Lewis, 108
Covarrubias, Miguel, 50, 52-54
Covici, Dorothy, 79, 97, 98, 134, 150, 156-157, 161-162, 172, 192, 223
Covici, Joan, 172
Covici, Pascal, Jr., 11, 17, 39, 41, 79, 91, 96-97, 108, 120-121, 137, 150, 153, 172, 177, 186, 189, 208
Covici, Pascal, Sr., actual and official birthdates of, 233; liquidation of Covici-Friede, 16; cites John Steinbeck as "my rarest experience," 29-30; death of, 231; denies Steinbeck repeats his style, 35-36; discusses creation of *East of Eden,* 159-160; early letters to Steinbeck lost, 16-17; early religious training of, 51; editor-author philosophy of, 43; encourages Steinbeck to learn to sketch, 35; first letter from Steinbeck, 13; first reads early books of Steinbeck, 11-12; growing relation with Steinbeck, 23; joins The Viking Press, 16-17; moves to New York, 14; promotes *Tortilla Flat,* possible prejudices of, 88; reaction of *The Grapes of Wrath,* 18; risks joining The Viking Press, 18; suggests Steinbeck will win the Nobel Prize, 56
Covici, Pascal, Inc., 11
Covici-Friede Co., 12, nearly loses *In Dubious Battle,...* 12-13; publishing philosophy of, 14; 15, collapse of 15-17, 222
Cowley, Malcolm, 57
Cozzens, James Gould, 224
Cream Hill, 119, 124
Crime and Punishment, 229
"Critics, Critics Burning Bright," 140
Cronin, Dr. A. J., 42
Crown Publishers, 5
Cup of Gold, 9, 30, 92(n), 203
cummings, e.e., 14-15

Dante, 211
Death in the Afternoon, 32
Death of a Salesman, 107-108, 124
Decline of American Capitalism, The, 15
Dickens, Charles, 3, 201

Doctor Adams, 15
Don Quixote, 5, 172, 206, 208-209
Dreiser, Theodore, 126

East of Eden, 9, 48, 61-62, 65, 99, 101-102, 127, Steinbeck-Covici writing-editing methods for, 145-146, 148-150; presentation box for, 160-161; 168-169; dedication to Pascal Covici, 168-169; 171-173, 175, first printing of, 176-177; 179-183, 186-187, 190-191, 193-195, 206
Everyman (Burning Bright), 127, 130

F.B.I., 21
Fadiman, Clifton, 27
Farrar, Straus and Giroux, 197
Farrell, James T., 126
Faulkner, William, 16, 126
Faust, 224
Fineman, Irving, 15, 17
Fitzgerald, F. Scott, 4-5
Forgotten Village, The, 10, 22, 32, 55-56
Fowler, Gene, 95, 107-108, 125
"Fra Lippo Lippi," 34
France, Anatole, 224
French, Warren, 10-11
Friede, Donald, 11, 14, sells shares in Covici-Friede and moves to California, 15; 16-17, 61
"Frog Hunt, The," 53
Front Page, The, 14

Gannett, Lewis, 9, 53-54, 117-120, 191
Garland, Robert, 140
Gibey, Louis, 187, 190
Ginsburg, Dr. H. L., 154-155
Goddard, Paulette, 116
Godden, Rumer, 210
Goethe, 224
Gone With the Wind, 5
Grapes of Wrath, The, 13, 15, reaction to, at The Viking Press, 18; 39, 46, 53, 99, 116, 121, 124, 126-127, 166, 176, 195, 197, 206, 223
Graves, Robert, 16
Great Gatsby, The, 4
Green Hills of Africa, 32
Grosset and Dunlap, 123
Guinzburg, Harold, 16-18, 34, 40, 70, 119-120, 124, 130, 134, 136, 141, 156, 189, 217-218, death of, 219; 231
Guinzburg, Thomas, 91, 102, 132, 197, edits America and Americans, 202 (n); 220-221

Haas, Robert, 16
Hamlet, 35
Hammarskjöld, Dag, 217
Hammerstein, Oscar, 134
Harper and Brothers, 4
Hart, Moss, 199
"Harvest Gypsies, The," 13
Haydn, Hiram, 5
Hecht, Ben, 14-15
Heggen, Thomas, 7
Heinemann Publishers, 183
Hellman, Lillian, 185

Hemingway, Ernest, 4, 32, 126, suicide of, 216
"Heritage of a Generation of Novelists, The," 126
Hodin, J. P., 118
Holiday, 221
Hollywood, 31, 40
Holmes, Oliver Wendell, 197
Horton, Chase, 21
Houghton Mifflin, 6-7, 13
Huebsch, Ben, 16, 124, death of, 231
Humanities Research Center (The University of Texas), 17
Hurst, Fannie, 42

Ibsen, Henrik, 210
Irving to Irving, 11, 94
In Dubious Battle, 10, 12-13, 14(n), 223
In the Forests of the Night (Burning Bright), 130(n), 131-132, 134-136

Jackson, Joseph Henry, 13, 14(n)
Jackson, Shirley, 205
James, Henry, 218
Jaws, 62(n)
Jewish Theological Seminary, 154
John Steinbeck, 10
Johnson, Lyndon, 226, 231
Jones, James, 228
Journal of a Novel: The East of Eden Letters, 48, 72(n), 99, 101-102, 145, 151-152, 156, dedication in, 182; 189
Joyce, James, 16

Kazan, Elia, 132-134, 174-175, 181-186
Kazin, Alfred, 230
Kennedy, John F., death of, 231; family, 226
Kent, Rockwell, 15
Kirkus, Virginia, 35
Knights of the Round Table, The, 197
Knopf, Alfred Jr., 5
Korean War, 135(n)

L'Affair Lettuceburg, 15, withdrawn from publication, 18
Lang, Andrew, 96
Latham, Harold S., 4-5
Lawrence, D. H., 16, 195
Leiberman, Josh, 173
Lesbianism, 14
Lewisohn, Ludwig, 15
Life, 37
"Lifeboat," 22, 34
Lindsay, Vachel, 5
Literary Guild, 55
Little, Col. Arthur W., 15-17
Little and Ives, Co., 15, 17
Lisca, Peter, 11-12, 32-33, 37, 58-59, 150-151, 193, 196-197
Llewellyn, Richard, 5
Lockridge, Ross, Jr., 6-7
Lockridge, Vernice, 7
Loesser, Frank, 129
Log from the Sea of Cortez, The, 10, 37, 65, 74, 124, 164-165
Logan, Joshua, 7
Long Valley, The, 9, 15, 18

Lovejoy, Natalia, 74, 78
Lovejoy, Ritchie, 74, 78
Lyman, Mildred, 38, 90

M.G.M. studios, 55, 67
MacArthur, Charles, 14
Macmillan Co., 5
Madison, Charles A., 11, 61, 81, 94, 144, 173-174
Malory, Thomas, 198, 200, 206-207
Malraux, Andre, 16
Maupassant, Guy de, 18-20
McBride, Robert M. and Co., 9
McGee, Billy, 14
McIntosh, Mavis, 13, 24
McIntosh and Otis, 12, 24(n), 38, literary agency policies, 40(n); 90(n), 119(n)
McNally, Terrence, 219
Mechanical Angel, The, 11, 17
"Medal for Benny, A," 22
Memories, 15
Mielziner, Jo, 135, 137
Miller, Arthur, 53, 75(n), 79-80, 107-108, 175-176, 208
Millay, Edna St. Vincent, 4
Mister Roberts, 7
Mitchell, Margaret, 5
Mizener, Arthur, 229-230
Moby Dick, 230
Moon is Down, The, first printing of, 32; 36, sales figures for, 41
Morgan, Henry, 9
Morrow, Honore W., 136-137
Morris, Lloyd, 126
Mullen, Jack, 186, 189
My Valley (East of Eden), 147-148

Norton, Elliot, 139(n)
Negrin, Dr. Juan, 149, 160
Nevius, Blake, 125
Newbegin, John, 35
New York Herald Tribune, The, 34, 59, 125-127
New York Times, The, 229
New York World Telegram, The, 140
New Yorker, The, 172

Of Mice and Men, 13-15, 114, 136, 139, 223
O'Hara, John, 226
Once There Was a War, 10, 34, 146, 202-203
Otis, Elizabeth, 10, 12, 20-21, 25-26, 48, 60-61, 73, 75, 132, 176, 181, 194, 217, 220

Pach, Walter, 15
Pacific Biological Labs, 24, 26, 29, 37
Pacific Spectator, The, 125
Paramount Studios, 12
Paris Herald Tribune, The, 174
Pastures of Heaven, The, 9-11, 223, 231
Pearl, The, 10, 35-37, 39, 42, 45, 46-49, 70
"Pearl, The" (film), 55
"Pearl of the World, The," 46
Perkins, Maxwell, 4-5, 102
Phoenix, 195

Pinckney, Josephine, 55
"Pipe Dream," 133
Poor, Henry Varnum, 50, 132-133
Portable Steinbeck, The, 52-53, 117
Publishers' Weekly, 227
Pyle, Ernie, 133

R.K.O. studios, 40, 55
Raintree County, 6-7
Random House, 5, 13
Reader's Digest, The, 7
Red Pony, The, 9, 15, 48-50, 99, 223
Red Pony Illustrated, The, 44
Revolt Among the Sharecroppers, 15
Revolt on the Campus, 15
Ricketts, Edward F., 10, 21-26, 30, 37, 44-45, 72, death of, 73; 74, 83-84, 130-135, 137-138
Ricketts, Toni, 70
Rivera, Diego, 13, 14(n)
Robinson, Edward Arlington, 5
Roderick Random, 230
Rodgers, Richard, 134
"Rose of Sharon," (*The Grapes of Wrath*), 18-20
Russian Journal, A, 10, 59, 68-70, 146, 203

"St. Katy the Virgin," 197
Salinas Valley (East of Eden), 62, 67, 73, 94, 114-116, 120, 140-141, 147, 163
Salinas Californian, The, 67
San Francisco News, The, 13
Sandburg, Carl, 22, 133
Saroyan, William, 22
Saturday Review, 140, 216
Scott, Waverly, 144, 173, 198(n)
Scott, Zachary, 123
Scribners, Charles Co., 4
Sea of Cortez: A Leisurely Journal of Travel and Research, 10, 23, 25-26, 29-30, 32, 35, 46, 124, 130, 133-135, 137
"Season in the Sun," 139
Seltzer, Thomas, 16
Shakespeare, William, 210
Shaw, George Bernard, 210
Sheffield, Carlton, 35, 39, 93
Ship of Fools, The, 228
Short Reign of Pippin IV, The, 10, 195-198
Smollet, Tobias, 230
"Snake, The," 10, 37
Solow, Eugene, 13
Sophocles, 224
Spillane, Mickey, 229
Steinbeck: A Life in Letters, 17
Steinbeck and Ricketts: The Shaping of a Novelist, 10
Steinbeck, Beth, 77, 80, 119, 176
Steinbeck, Carol Henning, 9, 20-24, 26, divorce from John Steinbeck, 33-34; 62, 76, 93, 100-101, as fictional character in *East of Eden,* 101-102, 106, 107, 115, 124, 165-166
Steinbeck, Elaine Scott, 18, 48, 62, 121-123, 127-129, 132, 135, 136, 141, marriage to John Steinbeck and honeymoon, 143-144; 149, 153-154,

157, 161-163, 166-167, 171, 173, 179-180, 184-188, 192, 195, 204, 222-223, 227, 230-231
Steinbeck, Gwyndolyn Conger, 22-23, 25, 31(n), marries John Steinbeck, 34; birth of first son, Thomas, 35; 36-37, 40, 48, 50, 55-56, second son, John IV, born, 58; 60-62, 64, 74, divorce from John, 75; 86-87, 90, 97-98, 100, as fictional character in *East of Eden*, 101-102, 104, 109-110, 112, 117-118, 120, 121, 129, 133-134, 136, 165-166, 173
Steinbeck, John, acknowledges Pascal Covici's initial interest, 12; begins work on *East of Eden*, 68; begins *The Pearl*, 37; birth of first son Thomas, 35; birth of second son John IV, 58; collapsing marriage to Carol, 25; collapsing marriage to Gwyn, 75; comments on winning the Pulitzer Prize for *The Grapes of Wrath*, 22; concerned with the problems of migrant laborers, 13; death of, 231; dedicates *East of Eden* to Pascal Covici, 168-169; defends end of *The Grapes of Wrath*, 18; defines the novel, 209; demands on, after publication of *The Grapes of Wrath*, 20; denies ever writing solely for money, 146; describes his own creative processes, 150; discusses the manuscript of *East of Eden*, 160, 162; discusses *Sea of Cortez*, 27; disenchanted with California, 44; divorce from Carol Henning Steinbeck, 33-34; divorce from Gwyndolyn Conger Steinbeck, 75; early homes in California, 9; early letters to Pascal Covici lost, 16-17; financial behavior of, 95-96; first financial success, 13; first marriage, 9; first printing of *Bombs Away*, 33; first printing of *East of Eden*, 176-177; first printing of *The Moon is Down*, 32; first published books, success of, 9; first trip to Europe, 13; growing relationship with Pascal Covici, Sr., 23; *L'Affair Lettuceburg*, 15; withdrawn from publication, 18; levels of meaning in Sea of Cortez, 31; loyalty to Elizabeth Otis and Pascal Covici, Sr., 12; marries Carol Henning, 9; marries Elaine Scott, 141, 143-144; marries Gwyn Conger, 34; meets Ed Ricketts, 10; moves to east coast with Gwyn, 32; musical motif in works of, 153; newspaper journalism of, 13; non-teleological thinking of, 10; personal guilt as seen in *East of Eden*, 107; plans *Sea of Cortez*, 21-22; plans to be accredited as a war correspondent, 24(n); philosophy in works of, 32; problems of collaboration with Pascal Covici, Sr., 147; problems of sustained creativity, 41; sees own name in clouds, 50; serious illnesses of, 220; shares creation of *East of Eden* with Pascal Covici, Sr., 156-157; reaction to death of Ed Ricketts, 73-74; requests Covici keep

him supplied with paper and pencils, 149; turns down honorary Ph.D., 214-215; wins Nobel Prize, 224-225; wins Presidential Medal of Freedom, 231; wins Pulitzer Prize for *The Grapes of Wrath*, 22; works on *The Pearl*, 35; writing/editing of *East of Eden*, 162-164
Steinbeck, John IV, born, 58; 60-62, 96, 182, 185
"Steinbeck: One Aspect," 125
Steinbeck, Thomas, born, 35; 59-62, 96, 167, 173, 182, 192
Stevenson, Adlai, 199, 226
Street, Webster F., 67
Sweet Thursday, 10, 74, 133, 194
Swift, Jonathan, 27

Tales of the South Pacific, 7
Targ, William, 43
Three O'Clock Dinner, 55
Time, 172, 193, 216
Time of Your Life, The, 22
"Timshel," 151-152, 154-155, 158
To A God Unknown, 9, 72
Tom Jones, 51
Tortilla Flat, 9, 11-12, 15, 49-50, 52-54, 88, 197, 223
Travels with Charley in Search of America, 10, 206, 212-213, 217, libelous references in, 218, 219, 220, 221-225
Trilling, Lionel, 108
Tristram Shandy, 51
Truman, Harry S, 199
Twain, Mark, 201
Tyger, Tyger (Burning Bright), 136-137

Ulysses, 210
Uncle Tom's Cabin, 126
Up and Down and Around, 16

Veblen, Thorstein, 16
Viking Press, The, 16-21, 36, 55, 83 (n), rejects publication of *The Acts of King Arthur and His Noble Knights*, 197; 202, 203(n), 220
Viva Zapata!, 10, 22, 94, 107-108, 114-115, 119, 121, 123, 128, 130-132, 134
Voltaire, 196

Wagner, Jack, 50, 58, 140
Wagner, Max, 140
Walker, Jimmy, 95
Wallsten, Robert F., 18
Watson, Graham, 199
War and Peace, 210
Wayward Bus, The, 48-51, 54, 58-59, 119, 123, 197
Well of Loneliness, The, 14
Wells, H. G., 5
White, C. A., 137
Wide World of John Steinbeck, The, 12, 196-197
Williams, Annie Laurie, 119
Winchell, Walter, 139(n)
Winter of Our Discontent, The, 10, 147, 206, 209-214
Wolfe, Thomas, 4-5

Zapata, Emiliano, 74, 89